Long Words
Bother Me

For Jill, Bec, and Sarah,
who have made my life a joy

Long Words Bother Me

Tom Burton

Illustrations by Michael Atchison

SUTTON PUBLISHING

This book was first published under the titles:
Words, Words, Words, first published in 1995 by University Radio 5UV
Words in Your Ear, first published in 1999 by Wakefield Press

This edition first published in 2004 by
Sutton Publishing Limited · Phoenix Mill
Thrupp · Stroud · Gloucestershire · GL5 2BU

British Library Cataloguing in Publication Data
A catalogue record for this book is available from the British Library.

ISBN 0 7509 3973 7

Typeset in 10/13pt GillSans.
Typesetting and origination by
Sutton Publishing Limited.
Printed and bound in Great Britain by
J.H. Haynes & Co. Ltd, Sparkford.

'Well,' said Owl, 'the customary procedure in such cases is as follows.'

'What does Crustimoney Proseedcake mean?' said Pooh. 'For I am a Bear of Very Little Brain, and long words Bother me.'

'It means the Thing to Do.'

'As long as it means that, I don't mind,' said Pooh humbly.

CONTENTS

ABBREVIATIONS

Bibliographical details will be found under "Works Cited Frequently" (pp. 237–9). Unless otherwise stated, the latest edition has been used. When it is necessary to distinguish between editions a numeral is added after an acronym to indicate the edition quoted.

ACOD	*The Australian Concise Oxford Dictionary*
AND	*The Australian National Dictionary*
CT	*The Canterbury Tales*
DAC	*A Dictionary of Australian Colloquialisms*
EDD	*The English Dialect Dictionary*
EETS	The Early English Text Society
LGW	*The Legend of Good Women*
ME	Middle English
MED	*Middle English Dictionary*
MnE	Modern English
NODE	*The New Oxford Dictionary of English*
OE	Old English
OED	*The Oxford English Dictionary*
OF	Old French
ON	Old Norse
PL	*Paradise Lost*
TC	*Troilus and Criseyde*

TYPOGRAPHICAL CONVENTIONS

Italics are used throughout for foreign words and to isolate forms that are the subject of discussion.

Single quotation marks enclose definitions and translations. Double quotation marks enclose quotations (other than definitions).

Vowel length is marked only in etymologies.

Old and Middle English characters are modernized along the lines normally used in editions of Chaucer: thorn and eth are replaced by *th*, and yogh by *g*, *gh*, or *y*, as appropriate; *u/v* and *i/j* are standardized in accordance with modern practice.

NOTE
We have tried to contact all copyright owners, but if we have overlooked anyone, we would be pleased to hear from them so that matters can be cleared up.

ACKNOWLEDGEMENTS

This book is an accident. I had been invited by Radio Adelaide (in its earlier incarnation as University Radio 5UV) to give a series of five-minute talks on language. With the arrogance of one who lectures for a living, I thought five minutes would be a doddle: just note down a few key points, speak more or less off the cuff, and there you are. No worries – or, as the T-shirts say, "No wuckin furries". Ha! That's when I got my come-uppance. (Now there's an odd phrase, *come-uppance*. Why isn't it *come-downance*? I've never seen it fully explained. Can it really be a hangover from that archaic expression, "Marry, come up!", much favoured by Fielding and other eighteenth-century writers, 'expressing indignant or amused surprise or contempt' as the *OED* neatly defines it? And "Marry" in such phrases has nothing to do with weddings, by the way: it's an oath by the Virgin *Mary*. – But I digress, like the ill-disciplined hound that followed the false trail of the red herring instead of the true scent of the fox.) When I went into the studio to record the first three talks, I weighed about as much as your average jumps jockey; when I came out about an hour later I could have ridden as the lightest of apprentices. The stress of trying to fit everything that had to be said into the tiny space of five minutes, in a coherent order, was way beyond anything I'd ever felt in the usual fifty-minute slot. That's when I began to have some respect for newsreaders and weather forecasters and others who have to fit a wealth of material into a short, fixed space.

"I don't think I can cope with this," I said to the producer (my former student, Richard Margetson). "I'm going to have write these things down and read them out."

"Not bloody likely!" he said (or something along those lines).

"Whyever not?"

"Because you'll sound like an article in an academic journal, and people will go to sleep or change stations in thirty seconds flat."

Well, that stung me. "I think I know how to write conversationally," I said, nursing my injured dignity.

"All right," he said, "we'll give it a go – but I'm warning you: any time you start sounding like a treatise, I'm going to interrupt and make you speak to me instead of reading, right?"

So that's how we proceeded – with occasional interruptions from Richard to begin with, it must be confessed. By the end of the series I'd accumulated about forty-odd scripts. It seemed a pity to throw them out or light the fire with them; and so they became a little book, *Words, Words, Words*. A second series of talks followed, and became a second book, *Words in your ear*. The two books are now brought together, revised and re-ordered, and with new material added. The subject matter is the quirkiness of the English language – especially (but not exclusively) the ways in which words and phrases change their meanings over time and in different parts of the world. Other linguistic matters have elbowed their way in, as they will (pronunciation, problems in usage, regional dialects, and so forth). My approach is word-centred rather than process-centred: each piece is intended to be more or less complete in itself, so that some of the terms that occur fairly frequently are explained more than once. I do not attempt to describe all possible types of semantic change, but deal only with those occurring in the words chosen. Similarly, I have not supplied an introduction detailing the different processes of linguistic change, but have instead supplied a glossary of technical terms.

Anyone who sets out to write on English vocabulary must depend heavily on the great historical dictionaries of English, the *Oxford English Dictionary* (and its various shorter versions), the *Middle English Dictionary*, and the specialized glossaries devoted to individual authors, like those for Chaucer and Shakespeare. Similarly, anyone attempting to write on Australian English will want to consult the books by Baker and Turner, the *Macquarie* dictionary, the various Australian Collins and Oxford dictionaries, Wilkes's *Dictionary of Australian Colloquialisms*, and, of course, the *Australian National Dictionary*. But whereas one depends almost totally on the dictionaries for definitions, I have, as far as possible, supplied illustrative quotations from my own experience, whether from reading or from listening to conversation. I make no attempt to offer a complete history of each word, such as may be found in the *OED*: my aim is merely to comment on the most striking developments in the word's history, and to illustrate these with quotations that I find memorable.

Semantic change has long been a popular topic amongst historians of the language; there are complete books devoted to it, and most histories of the language have a section on the subject. Folk etymology is one of its more amusing manifestations. From many works on these subjects I have derived profit and pleasure. I have endeavoured to keep track of my debts to them, but am not confident that I have always succeeded. Where I am conscious of having taken a particular example from a particular source (as in the case of *head*, from Simeon Potter), I have said so; but where the same examples are used by several writers, I have taken them as being of general currency, and have not acknowledged a particular debt.

It is inevitable that my own interests and biases will show through. Most of my medieval quotations are from Chaucer, and a good many are from *Sidrak and Bokkus* (the Middle English book of knowledge I spent more years editing than I care to admit). Most of the early modern ones are from Shakespeare, and many of these are from *King Lear*, which I once had the pleasure of directing for the University of Adelaide Theatre Guild. Anyone who has the patience to read the whole book will see that cricket interests me more than soccer or footy, and that I don't know the first thing about sailing. But it seemed to me more honest (as well as safer) to stick to what I was familiar with than to bend over backwards in a false attempt to get even coverage.

My interest in words has been fostered over many years by the encouragement of teachers and colleagues to whom I here offer thanks long overdue. Arnold Parker and Brian Wilson got me hooked, as a schoolboy, on whether the flesh that Hamlet wished would melt was too *solid* or too *sullied*. As a student at the University of Bristol I heard lectures on the history of English from Susie Tucker, whose book on the single word *enthusiasm* is a classic of its kind; and when I started editing Middle English texts at Bristol, Basil Cottle and John Scattergood introduced me to the pleasures (as well as the pains) of compiling a glossary.

At the University of Adelaide I had the good fortune to begin my tertiary teaching career in one of the few English departments in Australian universities in which an interest in language was explicitly announced in the title "Department of English Language and Literature". (Latterly, however, in common with most other departments of English in the Western world, it has succumbed to the insidious creep of "cultural studies" and has dropped the words "Language and Literature" from its title.) In this department I have had the rare good fortune to have had as colleagues one of the foremost of Australian lexicographers, George Turner, besides several editors of early texts with strong lexicographical interests – Tim Mares, Alan Brissenden, and John and Dorothy Colmer (Shakespeare), Michael Tolley (Blake), and Vida Russell (*The Golden Legend*), who will assuredly recognize some of her own favourite examples here, and whose lectures on language I am still trying vainly to emulate.

It is also my good fortune to be teaching in a university that has its own radio station – not just another station, at that, but, in Radio Adelaide, Australia's first community radio station, which continues to set the standard for community radio throughout the country. I am particularly grateful to Jeff Langdon and Laine Langridge, the station and programme managers at the time my talks were delivered, for their interest in "Words, Words, Words", and to Richard Margetson for his tact and skill in having kept me (usually) below four minutes. I am grateful also to other radio hosts who have given me time and airspace for talks on words: in Adelaide Carole Whitelock, Philip Satchell, Jim Grifsas, and Simon Royal (ABC), Leon Byner (5AA), and Christopher Cordeaux (5DN); and in the UK a number of BBC regional stations (Radios Bristol, Gloucestershire, Shropshire, and London Live).

Individuals representing a variety of clubs and associations have, at various times, invited me to speak to their members on matters connected with the history of the language or with problems of usage: Wendy Abbott-Young, Gladys Hogg, Carys Portus, Diane Kinnaird, Kate Twidale, and Helen Carey (the Lyceum Club), Dorothy Colmer, Haydn Williams, and Zofia Krzemionka (the English Association), Colin Horne (Friends of the State Library of South Australia), Helen Baker (the Fellowship of Australian Writers), Heather Britton (the Society of Women Writers), Barbara Wiesner (the South Australian Writers' Centre), Susan Freeman and Cheryl Appelkamp (the Independent Arts Foundation), Claudia Quinn-Young, Colin Lawton, Marcia Nicholl, and Madge Mitton (the University of the Third Age, Adelaide), Margaret White and Beryl Murphy (the Over Sixties Education Association), Margaret Collings (the Richard III Society), Kathie Stove (the South Australian Society of Editors), Jacqueline and Tamra Cookes (Mostly Books, Mitcham), the Organizing

Committee for the English Language and Literacy Services 1999 Conference at Port Adelaide, Cath Simmons (Kingswood Ladies' Probus Club), Joan Oehme (West Lakes Ladies' Probus Club), Lyn Nykiel and Janet Hayes (Queen Adelaide Club), Joyce Fitzpatrick (Sand Writers, Goolwa), Margie Killick (Friends of the Stirling Library), Anne Both (the Delta Foundation), Betty White and Howard Cuffe (the University of the Third Age, Tea Tree Gully), Terry Tooth (the University of the Third Age, South Coast), Terry Boes and Shirley Hamilton-Smith (Southern Writers), and Julie Gameau (the Penguin Club of Australia). Their enthusiasm, and that of the members of the organizations they represent, has been a source of great encouragement in the preparation of this book.

Michael Atchison is one of the very few cartoonists whose drawings make me laugh out loud. His own interest in words is well known from his "Word for Word" strip syndicated in newspapers in many countries. I am delighted and flattered by his willingness to supply illustrations for this text. I am very grateful to the several kind people who pointed out errors in earlier versions of this book, particularly Bill Scammell, formerly Chancellor of the University of Adelaide, and Bill Mellor, of Sand Writers, Goolwa. I owe a special debt to Christopher Bright, whose peerless editing has saved me from a number of embarrassing infelicities, and who has suggested more improvements in content than I've been able to keep track of. Throughout the preparation of the book I have had constant encouragement from Sarah Flight, the Paperback Editor at Sutton Publishing.

I am lucky also to have a family that puts up with my word mania without undue complaint, perhaps because they're pretty interested in words themselves. My wife, Jill Burton, is Associate Professor of Applied Linguistics at the University of South Australia and Series Editor of *Case Studies in TESOL Practice* and *Making Sense of Language*. Our older daughter, Rebecca Burton, herself a writer, has just had her first book published – a novel of Young Adult Fiction entitled *Leaving Jetty Road*. Our younger daughter, Sarah Burton, writes legal analyses (in both English and French) in the Division for the Execution of Judgements of the European Court of Human Rights at the Council of Europe in Strasbourg. In such articulate company a bloke struggles to get a word in edgeways. I hope they will not be insulted by the dedication to them of this book.

PREFACE

There was an old man of Boulogne
Who sang a cacophonous song:
It wasn't the words
That frightened the birds
But the horrible double-entendre.

They're funny things, words. They can make you laugh or they can make you wince or they can make you do both at the same time (like the rhymes in this anonymous limerick). They can start out meaning one thing (*obnoxious*, 'open to hurt, vulnerable') and end up meaning the opposite ('hateful, offensive'). They can mean different things at the same time (was that *funny* 'ha-ha' or *funny* 'peculiar'?). They can mean different things in different countries (*luxury*, English, 'extreme comfort'; *luxure*, French, 'lechery'). They can be pronounced differently in different regions and at different times (the Black Prince would have rhymed *cut* with *put* – as they still do in the North of England; a *wife* to us was a *weef* to King Alfred). Words can have spellings that conceal their origins (like *jaunty*), and they can have new spellings imposed on them to reveal their origins (*dette* and *doute* to Chaucer, but *debt* and *doubt* to us). They can change their meanings in the most unpredictable ways (how on earth did *silly*, 'happy or blessed', come to mean 'stupid'?). Synonyms can become antonyms (*knight* and *knave*); words that sound different can turn into homonyms (*need* and *knead*, *wrought* and *rort*).

Words can betray our prejudices (*barbarian* 'someone who doesn't speak my language'). They can die for no apparent reason (whatever happened to *sotship*?). They can be the same, in form and sound, as words that are completely unrelated (how many kinds of *spell* are there, or of *gin*, for that matter?). They can change their spelling to differentiate between senses (*flour* and *flower*, *deft* and *daft*). They can acquire good senses (*admire*) or bad ones (*lust*). They can't be controlled: *le weekend* is a fixture in France, in spite of the fulminations of the French Academy; and if most people think *empathy* is the smart way to say *sympathy*, we might as well kiss *sympathy* goodbye. Today's error is tomorrow's accepted form. Democracy rules, OK?

"Long words Bother me," said Winnie the Pooh; and they bother me, too – especially in the mouths of politicians and postmodernist bull artists. But for most of us words are *fun*; and here are a few of my favourites.

ADMIRATION

Admiration was a word not known to Geoffrey Chaucer; it didn't come into English until a hundred years or so after his death. And when it did come in, as *admirers* of Shakespeare and Milton (in the current sense) don't need to be told, it came without the approving overtones that it has for us today: in the sixteenth and seventeenth centuries the usual sense of the verb *to admire* was merely 'to wonder at or be surprised by' something; that of the noun *admiration* was 'wonder or amazement'; that of the adjective *admirable* was 'surprising'; and so on.

When Rosencrantz tells Hamlet that his odd behaviour at the play within the play has struck his mother into "amazement and admiration" (3.2.314), he is not at all implying that she approves of this behaviour: quite the reverse. When Sir Andrew Aguecheek sends his challenge to Viola (in her disguise as a man), calling her "a scurvy fellow", and adding "Wonder not nor admire not in thy mind why I do call thee so" (*Twelfth Night* 3.4.146–50), he's not asking her to praise his terminology: he's merely saying that she shouldn't be surprised at being addressed in such terms. And when, in response to Goneril's haughty behaviour towards him, Lear pretends not to know who she is, asking her, "Your name, fair gentlewoman?", her acid reply, "This admiration, sir, is much o'th' savour/ Of other your new pranks" (*King Lear* 1.4.214–16), self-evidently indicates not that he has been applauding her behaviour, but that he is (or is pretending to be) astonished by it.

In just the same way, when Milton describes Satan's reaction on his first setting eyes on his own hideous son, Death, "Th' undaunted Fiend what this might be admir'd,/ Admir'd, not fear'd", it's quite clear from the context that Satan is filled not with praise for the beauty of his boy but with amazement and disgust at the "execrable shape" that has appeared before him (*PL* 2.677–81). In all these instances *admire* and its derivatives retain the neutral etymological sense that goes back to Latin *(ad)mirari* 'to wonder (at)', without implication of either approval or disapproval. The current sense, with its connotations of approval, is a nice example of amelioration.

One of the complications for readers of Shakespeare and Milton is that the approving senses developed very quickly after *admiration* and its derivatives were adopted into English, so that there are times when one can't be sure in which sense the word is being used, the older (neutral) one or the newer (approving) one. When Ferdinand addresses Miranda (whose name, of course, means 'fit to be wondered at') as "Admired Miranda!/ Indeed the top of admiration, worth/ What's dearest to the world" (*The Tempest* 3.1.37–9), it's clear enough that he admires her in our sense of the word. But what does Hamlet mean by his reply to Rosencrantz about his mother's amazement at his behaviour, "O wonderful son, that can so astonish a mother! But is there no sequel at the heels of this mother's admiration?" (3.2.315–17)? Does *admiration* here just mean 'astonishment', or is Hamlet suggesting sarcastically that his mother is pleased with his behaviour? It's impossible to say; but given Shakespeare's fondness for wordplay, the latter must at least be a possibility.

What can one say about such vagaries of language except (as Hippolyta said of the mix-ups in *A Midsummer Night's Dream*) that they are "strange and" (in its early sense) "admirable" (5.1.27)?

APRIL SHOWERS

One of the best-known passages in the whole of medieval English literature is the opening paragraph of the General Prologue to Chaucer's *Canterbury Tales*:

> Whan that Aprill with his shoures soote
> The droghte of March hath perced to the roote,
> And bathed every veyne in swich licour
> Of which vertu engendred is the flour;
> Whan Zephirus eek with his sweete breeth
> Inspired hath in every holt and heeth
> The tendre croppes, and the yonge sonne
> Hath in the Ram his half cours yronne,
> And smale foweles maken melodye
> That slepen al the nyght with open ye
> (So priketh hem nature in hir corages),
> Thanne longen folk to goon on pilgrimages,
> And palmeres for to seken straunge strondes,
> To ferne halwes, kowthe in sondry londes;
> And specially from every shires ende
> Of Engelond to Caunterbury they wende,
> The hooly blisful martir for to seke,
> That hem hath holpen whan that they were seeke.

Not only is this passage well known in its own right; it also demonstrates to a nicety some of the chief effects of the changes in pronunciation and meaning that have occurred in the five hundred years since it was written. If one reads out the first ten lines of the passage in modern English pronunciation, they sound like this:

> When that April with his showers sweet
> The drought of March hath pierced to the root,

And bathed every vein in such liquor
Of which virtue engendered is the flower;
When Zephirus eek with his sweet breath
Inspired hath in every holt and heath
The tender crops, and the young sun
Hath in the ram his half course run,
And small fowls make melody
That sleep all the night with open eye....

The meaning seems reasonably clear; but the modern pronunciation makes it sound as if Chaucer couldn't scan and couldn't rhyme: the lines contain anything from seven syllables upwards (only the fourth line, "Of which virtue engendered is the flower", is a more or less regular pentameter); and only one of the five couplets has an exact rhyme (*run/sun*) – the other supposed rhymes are *sweet/root*, *liquor/flower*, *breath/heath*, and *melody/eye*. In modern pronunciation this doesn't look like very skilful poetry.

The meaning, moreover, is not quite as transparent as it at first appears. What is this *liquor* that the plants have been bathing in? It sounds like rum or brandy. How can crops be *inspired* by the wind? They must be pretty poetical plants to respond in such an arty-farty fashion: one doesn't think of wheat or barley in this way. And what are these small *fowls* that sleep with their eyes open? – bantams? pullets? They don't sound very romantic whatever they are.

The truth is, of course, that these words have changed their meanings in the centuries since Chaucer wrote: *fowl* (OE *fugol*) was in his day the general term for a bird of any kind, wild or tame; *liquor* (OF *licour*) meant simply 'liquid'; and *crops* were the tips or shoots of any plant, not necessarily plants grown for money: the plant-shoots have been bathing in the moisture of rain or dew; and all the birds, not just those in the farmyard, have been having sleepless nights. It was not until after the medieval period that these words developed their current specialized senses 'domesticated birds, poultry', 'alcoholic liquid', and 'plants cultivated agriculturally'. As for *inspired*, the current sense is figurative; but Chaucer was using it in its earlier, etymological sense of breathing (Latin *in* + *spīrāre* 'to breathe into' – cf. *respiration* and *perspiration*): the west wind has brought the shoots to life by breathing into them.

And if one reads the passage in what the experts tell us is something approaching Chaucer's own pronunciation, it will sound a little foreign at first (like a cross between Scottish and French), but the rhyme and rhythm are restored, and one is less likely (I believe) to be tricked by a word like *liquor* if it's pronounced (as Chaucer would have pronounced it) *likoor* (with the stress on the second syllable, rhyming with *lure*).

ASHTRAYS, MOTORBIKES, AND AUSTRALIAN TERMS OF ABUSE

Amongst the most delightful things about living in Australia (apart from the space, the sunshine, and the superb wine) are the vivacity and colour of the spoken language. Australian terms of abuse are some of the wittiest and most memorable that I've encountered amongst English speakers anywhere in the world. Gerry Wilkes's *Dictionary of Australian Colloquialisms* is a veritable goldmine of laconic insults.

There are, for example, a fistful of unforgettable similes for uselessness, mainly in the form "as useless as ..." or "about as useful as ..." this or that useless thing: "as useful as an ashtray on a motorbike" or "as a glass door on a dunny" or even "as a sore arse to a boundary rider". A *boundary rider* (one needs to know) is a person "employed to ride round the fences etc. of a cattle or sheep station and keep them in good order" (*Australian Oxford Dictionary*); and when one remembers the size of some of the outback stations in Australia – we're not talking about little properties of a few thousand acres here: we're talking in terms of hundreds of square miles – one appreciates that the last thing someone patrolling the perimeter on horseback would need is to be saddle-sore.

These similes are complemented by a set of expressions for incompetence beginning "he (or she, or you, or whoever it may be) couldn't ..." do such-and-such, the second half of the saying naming the simple task that the person who is the object of derision (supposedly) can't perform. One political leader claimed that certain members of the opposition "couldn't blow the froth off a glass of beer", another that his opposite number "couldn't lead a flock of homing pigeons". Someone complained that his local policeman "couldn't find a grand piano in a one-roomed house"; someone else that a dodgy pilot "couldn't knock the skin off a rice puddin'". The selectors of a rugby team that lost heavily after they'd omitted a star player "couldn't pick a seat at the pictures"; and, in similar vein, the coach of a losing football team "couldn't train a choko vine over a country dunny", a bad player "couldn't get a kick in a stampede", and a hopeless boxer "couldn't fight his way out of a paper bag" or "couldn't go two rounds with a revolving door". Perhaps most memorably of all, "Ninety per cent of cockies couldn't knock the dags off a sick canary". To understand this jibe one needs to know that a *cocky* is a small farmer, named disparagingly after the *cockatoo*, and so called, as Wilkes explains, 'from the sometimes wretched existence led by the cocky, from his reputation for exploiting hired help, [and/or] from the contempt of the grazier or the stockman for those who scratch the earth'; also that *dags* (a term originally from British dialect and subsequently given wide currency by the sheep industry in Australia and New Zealand) are the locks of 'wool clotted with dung' (as Bruce Moore puts it in the *Australian Oxford Dictionary*) that tend to festoon the rear end of a sheep.

People who seem to lack common sense come in for their share of ribbing, in a formula that expresses that lack as their being one thing (or a few things) short of a full set (a formula now used widely in other countries, but thought to have originated in Australia). Thus a person may be "a chop short of a barbecue", "a few sandwiches short of a picnic", "a few beans short of a bag", "a paling short of a fence", or "a few flagstones short of a patio". It's even been suggested rather unkindly that "for every man a few bricks short of a load there are two women off with the fairies". It's clear enough from these examples that it's the formula that's fixed, not the items that fill it: these expressions are constantly being renewed by the ingenuity of speakers who think up fresh variations.

Tight-fistedness comes in for some particularly caustic treatment, in a formula that says someone is "so mean (that) he wouldn't ..." and leaves it to the speaker to complete the sentence. Banjo Paterson supplies the two earliest examples, "They reckon he's that mean he wouldn't give you a light for your pipe at a bushfire" and "He's that mean he wouldn't give a dog a drink at his mirage". More recent variations include "If he owned the ocean, he wouldn't give you a wave" and "He'd be too mean to give you a fright if he was a ghost". A neatly foreshortened example claims that "Albert wouldn't shout if a shark bit him": this seems at first blush to suggest heroic stoicism – until one remembers that *shouting* in Australia means paying for a round of drinks.

All these examples are from Wilkes's dictionary – and surely he should get a gong for collecting them (if he hasn't already). But one of the paradoxes of a dictionary of colloquialisms is that colloquialisms (as their name implies) belong to the *spoken* language (Latin *loquor* 'I speak'), whereas dictionaries generally collect only forms recorded in *writing*. I can't resist this opportunity to record here some of the pithiest examples that have been given to me by callers on talkback radio. There are some wonderful variations on the tight-fistedness theme: (he's so mean that) "he'd skin a louse for its wax", but "he wouldn't give you the steam off his piss"; "he's as tight as a fish's backside, and that's watertight" – so tight, indeed, that "he looks under his bed each morning to see if he's lost any sleep". So-and-so isn't very bright: "if his brains were dynamite, there wouldn't be enough to blow his hat off" – he must be *more* than "one shingle short of a roof" or "a few cans short of a sixpack". He's about as much use "as a chocolate kettle" or "as a flyscreen door in a submarine" or "as a one-legged man in an arse-kicking competition"; he's so damned useless, in fact, that he "couldn't organize intercourse in a brothel". But no one can say he doesn't try: he's "busier than a cat with diarrhoea trying to dig holes in concrete".

No wonder logophiles love Australia! And no wonder Aussie sports teams (whether they're winning or losing) are recognized as undisputed world champions at *sledging*!

AUGHT AND NAUGHT

Middle English has two nouns *aught*, not related etymologically, yet not far apart in meaning. The first, descended from Old English *ǣht* (with a vowel similar to that in the first syllable of American *daddy*), is related to the past tense of the verb *āgan* 'to own' and means literally 'that which is owned', i.e., one's property, possessions, or wealth. But it's the other kind of *aught* that I'm considering here.

This second noun (with initial *a* or *o*) is a combination of the Old English adverb *ā* 'ever' and the noun *wiht* 'a creature, being or thing', meaning literally 'ever a whit, anything at all'. Arveragus, in his famous response to the confession of his wife, Dorigen (in Chaucer's Merchant's tale), that she has promised to sleep with another man, uses the word in just this sense: "Is ther oght elles, Dorigen, but this?" (*CT* V 1469) – which is more or less equivalent to current English 'Is that all?'

The word could also function as an adjective or an adverb. The adjective meant 'worth something', hence 'worthy or valiant', as when the owl in the thirteenth-century poem *The Owl and the Nightingale* claims she is a worthier bird than the nightingale because she follows "aghte" men to war (389), whereas the nightingale merely sings ditties to lovers. As an adverb it had the sense 'at all', and could be used with the same looseness as the current equivalent. A bank teller asked me recently, when some form of identification was needed, "Did you bring your driving licence with you at all?", to which, if I'd had the wit, I might have replied, "No, not even the top left-hand corner of it." But she was in good company: Chaucer does the same thing with *aught* in the Man of Law's tale, when King Alla, seeing a boy whose looks remind him strongly of those of his lost wife, Custance, wonders if the child can indeed be hers:

> This Alla hath the face in remembrance
> Of dame Custance, and ther on mused he
> If that the childes mooder were aught she
> That is his wyf.... (*CT* II 1032–5)

Well, either she was the child's mother or she wasn't: there's no interim possibility. But who ever said that language was governed by logic?

Naught (likewise spelled with *a* or *o*), is simply a negative form of *aught* (*nā wiht*), meaning 'never a whit', 'not at all', 'nothing at all', likewise used as a noun, an adjective, or an adverb. The positive and the negative uses, in the senses 'worth something' and 'worthless', occur together in a medieval comment on the power of wealth: when a man is rich, we are told, he is highly regarded and influential; if he loses his money, he loses his power and his reputation with it, "And the catel [i.e. 'chattels, property'] maketh al, ywis/ That he was oght and now noght is" (*Sidrak and Bokkus*, L4467–8). In time there is a development from the idea of being worth nothing to that of being worth less than nothing, i.e., of being evil. This sense is common in Shakespeare, as in Lear's comment on Goneril: "Beloved Regan,/ Thy sister's naught" (2.2.305–6). If one were to put this in mathematical terms, one would be saying that *nought* (which is neither negative nor positive) develops a negative sense indicating a quantity lower than zero.

I believe, however, that the origin of this sense is theological rather than mathematical. The reasoning is something like this: God made everything; everything that God made is good; anything that is not good cannot have been made by God; therefore anything that is not good has no true existence; therefore it is nothing; thus *nothing* or *naught* = 'not made by God' = 'evil'. This is more or less the answer given in *Sidrak* to the question, "What is sin?"

> Synne, forsothe, is right noght
> For that God it nevere wroght.
> God of hevene made al thing
> And al was of Goddis making
> And for hise werkes good wore,
> Synne is noon of hem therfore;
> And for he made it not, sothely
> It is noght in substaunce truly.   (L11791–8)

As for *naughty*, it is a combination of the noun *naught* and the adjectival suffix -*y* (as in *crafty* from *craft*), and its early senses were similar to those of the adjective *naught*: in financial terms it could mean

'possessing nought', i.e., 'poor, worth nothing'; in moral terms it could mean 'worthless' or, worse, 'evil'. One of the most difficult lines for actors in *King Lear* is that with which Gloucester begins his furious response to Regan when she plucks a tuft of hair from his beard shortly before his blinding: "Naughty lady", he storms, "These hairs which thou dost ravish from my chin/ Will quicken and accuse thee" (3.7.36–8). "Naughty lady" is usually cut in modern productions, because it almost invariably causes a laugh; and it does so because *naughty* has lost its original intensity and has become restricted chiefly to the behaviour of children and animals, in senses such as 'mischievous' or 'wayward' or 'disobedient'. We don't use the word of adults now except playfully, implying forbidden sexuality, as in "a naughty film". But these associations are quite inappropriate to the action in *King Lear*: Regan's *naughtiness* is not that of a wayward child or a loose woman; it is that of moral evil, and 'evil woman' is precisely what Gloucester means when he calls her "Naughty lady".

In Australia functional shift has gone full circle and turned *naughty* back into a noun as a euphemism for the sexual act: "I get a lot of knock backs," says the narrator in Frank Hardy's *Legends from Benson's Valley* (quoted in *DAC*), "but I get a lot of naughties". He sounds pretty pleased with himself; but he perhaps has less to crow about than the person who supplied the *Macquarie* dictionary with the phrase "a nightly naughty".

Awful, Pompous, and Artificial

One of my students, Rolland Boylen, asked me recently (when we'd been discussing some words that don't have the same meaning in current English as they had in the Middle English text we were translating) if I knew what King Charles II had said when he first set eyes on the model for the new St Paul's Cathedral. I had to confess I didn't. So Rolland told me: "King Charles described it as 'awful, pompous, and artificial' – and he was intending to be complimentary."

These three words are lovely examples of what is technically called degeneration or pejoration, that is, acquiring less favourable senses than they originally had. *Awful* has, besides, suffered a loss of intensity, such that its force is far weaker than it used to be.

Evidently, as King Charles used it, *awful* meant, literally, 'filled or filling with awe, awe-inspiring', just as *dreadful* and *frightful* meant 'filling one with dread or with fear'. What has happened with all three of these *-ful* words is that they've lost both their literal senses and their force and have become virtually synonymous adjectives meaning 'very bad': "What did you think of the film?" "Dreadful!" – That doesn't have to mean it was a horror movie; it more probably means that it bored you to tears. And as adverbs these words don't even have to mean 'very *bad*': they just mean 'very *very* or *extremely* whatever-it-is': you might well describe Shirley Hazzard as an "*awfully* good writer" without being scared of her; and if you belong to the chardonnay set and you have to turn down an invitation to a cocktail party, you will doubtless tell your would-be hostess that you're *frightfully* sorry you can't come (pronounced, of course, "fraffly") when all you're doing is trying rather hard to be polite.

In its original sense, 'awe-inspiring', *awful* has long since been replaced by *awesome*. But even this, now, through overuse as an exaggerated intensifier, is losing its intensity in the same way as *awful*, as I was memorably reminded recently when my friend Emerson Brown (who used to teach at Vanderbilt University in Tennessee) told me that one of his students had described a plate of spaghetti as "totally awesome" (pronounced, of course, "todally ahsum").

As for *pompous* (ultimately from Latin *pompa*, 'a solemn procession'), King Charles of course used it to mean 'magnificent or splendid'; whereas now, sadly, it has degenerated to the point where it suggests only an exterior *show* of magnificence over a hollow shell. In this sense it seems to be used particularly of old men, in such derogatory combinations as "a pompous old fart".

Similarly, *artificial* is now used almost exclusively in derogatory senses: 'contrived, false, not natural', hence (by implication) perhaps even '*un*natural'; whereas King Charles evidently meant that St Paul's had been designed and built with great *art*, skill, and ingenuity (which is, etymologically, what the word means: 'made with art').

One could say, I suppose, that these degenerations in meaning are a rather sad comment on human nature. Be that as it may, we now know what to say to the politicians when they ask what we think of the notorious new barbecue facilities at Parliament House in Canberra: we just say that we find them, in the modern sense, "awful, pompous, and artificial", yes?

BARBARIANS, BULLIES, THUGS, AND RUFFIANS

I suppose it's a reflection on the chauvinistic tendencies of the human race that so many of our terms for people we disapprove of are words for foreigners. The Greek word *barbaros*, for example (from which, via Latin and French, come the English derivatives *barbaric*, *barbarian*, and *barbarous*), meant, etymologically, someone who couldn't speak Greek, hence 'foreigner'; but since most of us think that foreigners don't know how to behave, it's only a series of short steps from 'foreign' to 'uncivilized' to 'heathen' and so eventually to 'savage' (see the etymological comment under the adjective *barbarous* in *OED*). I can't believe any amount of legislation will prevent linguistic development of this kind, though it may very well prevent the derogatory use of specific racial names like *Turk* to indicate someone who (in the words of the *New Shorter Oxford*) is 'ferocious, wild, or unmanageable'.

The altercation a while ago between a member of the South Australian Legislative Council and the editor of Adelaide's daily newspaper, *The Advertiser*, in which the editor was accused of being a *thug* and the MLC of using *bully-boy* tactics, is a nice example of the similar way in which many of our terms of abuse, especially terms indicating violence, are borrowed from foreign languages. Given the ferocious reputation of the Vikings, one might be forgiven for thinking that *thug* was a Norse word. In fact it isn't; but it's foreign nonetheless: it's from the Hindustani word *thag*, of which the etymological sense is 'cheat, swindler', but which was used (with an upper case *T*) of members of 'a religious organization of professional robbers and assassins in India, who strangled their victims' (*New Shorter Oxford*). Now, through generalization, we've lost the specific connotations of the religious organization and the strangling, but we've retained the sense (to quote the definition in the *New Shorter Oxford*) of 'a brutal or vicious ruffian'.

Ruffian itself is (via French) from Italian *ruffiano* 'a pander', which is thought to be connected with *rofia*, a dialect word for scab or scurf: so if you think a ruffian is a scurvy fellow, you're etymologically correct. But I think the *New Shorter Oxford* is behind the times in giving the current sense of *ruffian* as 'a violent, lawless person': surely this is a word that has lost its intensity, and is used now mainly of children, as an approximate equivalent of affectionate, semi-approving terms like *larrikin* or *scallywag* (the origin of both of which is obscure)?

As for *bully*, it's thought to be from Middle Dutch *boele* 'lover' and was used in English originally as a term of endearment equivalent to 'darling or sweetheart' or (between men) 'good friend or mate', as when Flute refers to Bottom in *A Midsummer Night's Dream* as 'sweet bully Bottom' (4.2.18) or when Pistol proclaims his affection for the young king in *Henry V* with the words "I love the lovely bully" (4.1.49). From there we get 'fine fellow'; hence a bloke who behaves as if he's it and those beneath him are, um, unmentionable; hence the current sense, someone who uses brute force to terrorize the weaker.

So there you have it: *thugs* are Indian; *bullies* are Dutch; *ruffians* are Italian; *hooligans* (some say) are Irish; ferocious people are *Turks*; and anyone who can't speak our language is a *barbarian*. What a friendly lot we English speakers are! Our language has its own built-in equivalent of the old White Australia policy.

BARRACKING

Not long after my family and I had arrived in Australia in the early 1970s, a new friend, who thought we needed to be initiated into some of the local customs, took us to watch a footy game. We were somewhat taken aback when he asked us which side we were going to barrack for. I said, "Barrack *for?*" He said, "Yes, who are you going to support? Who do you want to win?"

This usage came as a great surprise to us, because in England to *barrack* means exactly the opposite: it means 'to shout rude things at, to hurl abuse at, to jeer at' (to *sledge*, as we'd now say) and, besides, it's a transitive verb, followed immediately by the object, not by a preposition: you don't barrack *at* or *for* or *against* people, you just *barrack* them – and you're not being very kind to them when you do. I began to wonder whether these two usages were the same word used differently, or whether they in fact came from two different sources. I found a variety of answers in the dictionaries I consulted.

The *Macquarie* is the only dictionary that treats them as two different words: it derives the transitive sense 'to jeer at' from Aboriginal *barak* (a word used as a negative – the sense being, I suppose, 'to hurl negatives at'). If this is right, it's a nice example of an Aboriginal word being taken into standard (British) English. The intransitive use followed by *for*, in the sense, 'to support or to shout encouragement', is derived by *Macquarie* from a dialect word from Northern Ireland, meaning 'to brag or to boast of one's fighting powers' – see the *English Dialect Dictionary*.

My former colleague, George Turner, in the *Australian Concise Oxford Dictionary*, Gerry Wilkes, in his *Dictionary of Australian Colloquialisms*, Wilkes and Bill Krebs, in their *Collins* dictionaries, and Bruce Moore, in the *Australian Oxford Dictionary*, all treat both words as coming from this Northern Irish dialect word *barrack* meaning 'to boast or brag'; but this doesn't explain how the word has reversed its sense in the standard British use.

Grahame Johnston, in the first edition of the *Australian Pocket Oxford Dictionary* in 1976 (revised by George Turner in 1984), had suggested that both words might be derived either from this same Northern Irish *barrack* 'to boast' or from the Aboriginal word, *borak* or *borax*: it's not clear to me whether this is merely a variant spelling of the negative *barak*, mentioned in the *Macquarie*, or whether it's a different word; but it's used in the phrase 'to poke borax at' meaning 'to ridicule'. This would nicely explain the standard British sense, 'to jeer at', but not the Australian usage, to barrack *for* (unless, of course, shouting encouragement *for* a team is taken to be the same thing as shouting abuse at their opponents).

Bill Ramson, in the *Australian National Dictionary*, sides with those who derive both words from the Irish term: he claims that "It is unlikely that there is any connection with *borak*." And George Turner, in *The English Language in Australia and New Zealand*, goes further than he does in *ACOD*, suggesting that "*borak* is possibly a pidgin variant of *barrack*" (p. 106), i.e., that *borak* is derived from *barrack*, not vice versa. As for the Oxford dictionaries produced in England, confusion reigns. The word doesn't appear at all in the first edition of *OED* (in which the only *barracks* are the military ones, which are from an entirely different source); the second edition prefers the derivation from *borak*, though it also mentions the Irish possibility; the *New Shorter Oxford* thinks it's "probably" from the Northern Irish dialect word, and makes no mention of *borak*; none of the three makes any mention of the Australian use, "to barrack *for*"; but this sense appears at last in the *New Oxford Dictionary of English*, designated as "Austral./NZ".

So where do *barracking* and *barracking for* come from: Aboriginal or Northern Irish? You pays your money and you takes your pick: as for myself, though heavily outnumbered, I'm barracking for the separate origins proposed in *Macquarie*.

BASTARDS

In standard English the word *bastard* has from the first been used as a term of abuse, a usage exposed and attacked by Gloucester's illegitimate son Edmund in *King Lear* in the soliloquy that ends with his famous prayer, "Now, gods, stand up for bastards!" (1.2.6–22). Edmund asks why he should be called

> 'bastard'? Wherefore 'base',
> When my dimensions are as well compact,
> My mind as generous, and my shape as true
> As honest madam's issue? Why brand they us
> With 'base'? with 'baseness, bastardy – base, base'?

He seems here to be suggesting that there's some etymological connection between the word *base* in *base-born* 'low-born, born out of wedlock' and the word *bastard*, as if the *bas-* at the beginning of each word comes from the same origin. But I think that's just coincidence: *base* is of course from French *bas* 'low'; *bastard* is derived from OF *bast* 'pack-saddle', plus the pejorative suffix *-ard*, as in *coward*, *drunkard*, *sluggard*, etc.

What have pack-saddles to do with illegitimate children? Well, it is said that muleteers on their travels used their pack-saddles as beds (just as an Aussie swagman uses his swag – his Matilda – as a bed). So: a child begotten in a pack-saddle bed as opposed to the marital bed would be illegitimate.

But whereas the technical sense of the noun (an illegitimate child) is not much in use nowadays (except of historical characters like William the Conqueror or fictional characters like Edmund) – because we're no longer bothered about whether or not people who have children together are married – we've retained the colloquial and quite unjust sense of *bastard*, that is, an odious or hateful person, anyone whom one dislikes intensely: "Who's your tutor?" "So-and-so." "He's a right *bastard*."

What's confusing for English people who come to Australia is that alongside this abusive use of the word there is simultaneously its exact opposite, the affectionate use, which shows not that you're despised but that you're accepted: when an Aussie asks you "How are you going, you old bastard?" you know you're in, because *bastard* is here equivalent to *mate*.

The coexistence of these two opposite uses in Australia, as well as the survival of the original sense, was memorably illustrated a few years ago on the television series about the bodyline cricket tour of 1932–3. The English captain, Douglas Jardine, went to the Australian dressing room at the end of a day's play, when he'd been batting, to complain that the Australian fielders had been calling him rude names throughout his innings (*sledging*, as it's now called, whatever Ian Chappell may say to the contrary). He demanded an apology because, as he put it, the Australians had "impugned [his] mother's integrity" (or words to that effect). Vic Richardson, to whom Jardine had been speaking, turned to the other Australian players in the dressing room and called out, over the hubbub, "Oi! Which of you bastards called this bastard a bastard?"

BEAVERS AND CASTOR OIL

It has become a truism of modern linguistics, following the work of Ferdinand de Saussure in the early twentieth century, that language is a purely arbitrary phenomenon: that there is no necessary connection between a word and the thing it names, between the signifier and the signified. But in the Middle Ages the linguistic creed was otherwise: it was thought that the names of things, especially in the classical languages of Latin and Greek, had some specific appropriateness to the things they named.

The medieval bestiaries provide some lovely examples of this belief. The Latin name for a beaver, for example, is *castor*, which is explained (following Isidore's *Etymologiae* 12.2.21) as follows: *Est animal quod a castrando castor dicitur*, that is, 'There is an animal which, because of castration, is called *castor*'. The full entry, in T.H. White's delightful *Book of Beasts* (a translation of a twelfth-century Latin bestiary) reads as follows:

This is an animal called CASTOR the Beaver, none more gentle, and his testicles make a capital medicine. For this reason, so Physiologus says, when he notices that he is being pursued by the hunter, he removes his own testicles with a bite, and casts them before the sportsman, and thus escapes by flight. What is more, if he should again happen to be chased by a second hunter, he lifts himself up and shows his members to him. And the latter, when he perceives the testicles to be missing, leaves the beaver alone.   (pp. 28–9)

On this White comments, in one of his irresistible footnotes:

The medicine was called 'castoreum'. It was situated not in the testicles, but in a different gland. The testicles of a beaver are internal and cannot be bitten off. 'The originall of the conceit,' says Sir Thomas Browne, 'was probably Hieroglyphicall, which after became Mythologicall unto the Greeks, and so set down by Aesop, and by process of tradition stole into a totall verity'.   (p. 29)

In short, the supposed connection with castration is spurious; and the etymology is as nice a piece of academic folk etymology as one could hope to find.

But what about *castor oil*? Is that the same stuff as the *castoreum*? Well, no; or rather, no and yes. Castoreum (which, by the way, may also be called simply *castor*), is defined in the *OED* as 'a reddish-brown unctuous substance, having a strong smell and nauseous bitter taste, obtained from two sacs in the inguinal region of the beaver; used in medicine and perfumery'. Evidently, then, the medicine *castor(eum)* gets its name from the Latin name of the animal even if the animal does not get its name from castration.

But castor oil is from a plant, not an animal: it is (to quote *OED* again) 'a pale yellow oil obtained from the seeds of *Ricinus communis* or Palma Christi' ('Palm of Christ', so called because the leaves are shaped like a hand). So how does it get the name *castor*? Nobody knows; but *OED* suggests that 'this oil actually took the place of the drug castor . . . in use in midwifery, etc., and thus popularly assumed its name'.

As for *sugar castors* and the *castors* that furniture rolls about on, these have nothing to do either with beavers or with Palms of Christ: these words are both from the verb *to cast*, meaning, in the first instance, 'to throw', and in the second, 'to turn or veer'. Sometimes with etymologies you feel you might do just as well to *cast lots*.

BLUE

One of the great delights of talking about language is the input you get from time to time from others who share a fascination with it. Here is one such contribution, kindly sent to me by Alan Cleggett (with whom I was put in touch by my younger daughter, Sarah):

> Blue was at work the other day when he made a blue. There was a helluva blue about it, so they called in the blues. A while later they slapped a bluey on him; and now he's in the jug and he's blue.

This lovely story illustrates many of the ingenious ways in which words can acquire new meanings in colloquial usage, especially, in this instance, in Australian usage.

"Blue was at work": one may assume from this that he had red hair, which is why he was nicknamed *blue* or *bluey*. I don't know whether I'd go so far as to agree with the quotation for this sense in the *Australian National Dictionary* (R.H. Conquest, 1978 quotation for *Bluey*, sense 6) claiming that this is "typical Australian logic"; I'd say rather that it's not unusual for nicknames to be ironic. Alan Cleggett justly compares it with the nicknames *Shorty* for tall people and *Lofty* for those whom the thought-police would have us call the "vertically challenged".

". . . when he made a blue", that's to say, 'a blunder'. The likeliest explanation I've seen for this use is found in a letter quoted by Sidney J. Baker in *The Australian Language*. His correspondent suggests that it originated in the shearing sheds in the days when hand shears had frequently to be sharpened by an expert against a fast-spinning whetstone. "If a cutter was held against the wheel too long it would turn blue and lose its temper. Nothing enraged a fast shearer ... more than if the expert made a blue of one of his cutters. If you made a blue you most likely had a fight on your hands" (p. 126).

"There was a helluva blue about it", that is, of course, 'a fight'. This perhaps is a logical extension of the previous use: if you annoy people by *making a blue*, the ensuing punch-up may well be called a *blue*. (Or, if you cause steel to lose its temper literally, you may expect the people who need it in good shape to lose their tempers metaphorically.) The *Australian National Dictionary* suggests that it may derive from the swearing that's likely to accompany a furious stoush, which may be so colourful as to make the air blue. But I must confess that I rather like Alan's alternative suggestion that it may allude to "the bruises one has after being engaged in a bout of fisticuffs". He points out in support of this that the French for a bruise is *un bleu*.

"So they called in the blues", that is, 'the police', so called (mainly in Victoria?) because of their blue uniforms. But here's a use that I haven't found applied specifically to the police in any dictionary, though Australian dictionaries record it as a nickname (also derived from the colour of the uniform) for the Carlton VFL team in Victoria, the Newtown Rugby League team in New South Wales, or any team representing New South Wales in state competition. We go one better in South Australia by calling the Sturt football team (my local club) the Double Blues. I've heard it said that this nickname derives from the location of their home ground, at the junction of Oxford and Cambridge terraces – and indeed the colours of their uniform (or *strip* as it's usually called nowadays) are light blue (Cambridge) and dark blue (Oxford); but, be that as it may, the name Double Blues became suddenly, at the moment of their threatened extinction a few years ago, altogether too close for comfort.

"A while later they slapped a bluey on him", that is, 'a summons', so called because it's written on blue paper; "and now he's in the jug and he's blue", that is, 'miserable', a very old figurative use, going right back to the middle of the sixteenth century and doubtless derived from the pallor of the skin when one is cold, frightened, or depressed.

And these are only some of the Australian uses! When one thinks of blue movies and bluestockings (an unlikely pairing, I suppose); of blue blood and blue-eyed boys; of blue cheese and blueberries; of blue-chip stocks, blue moons and the blue-rinse brigade; of blue murder, blue pencils, blue-collar workers, and blue-stone houses . . . well, perhaps enough is enough.

BOARS, BOERS, BOORS, BORES, AND BOWERS

A *boor* has nothing to do etymologically with a *boar* or with a *bore*: though a *boor* may behave like a pig, and though such behaviour may *bore* you to tears, there is no etymological connection: the overlap in senses is – or was – sheer coincidence, although if one considers how nearly synonymous are the adjectives *boorish* and *boarish*, it does seem probable that the ill-mannered overtones of *boor* have been influenced by the swinish connotations of *boar*.

Boar is from OE *bār* (not to be confused with a pronunciation of the word *bear* that can still sometimes be heard in parts of America, as in the old song about Davy Crockett, who 'killed him a bar when he was only three': I spent months of my childhood wondering who *Himmabar* was before it struck me that what the boy had killed was *a bear*, and that the *him* was redundant or reflexive). In *boar* the long *a* from OE has followed the normal development to a long *o* in MnE (as in *oar* and *lore* from OE *ār* and *lār*); there's no mystery there.

The *bore* in a *water-bore* and a *12-bore* shotgun is a hollow cylindrical tube made by the action of *boring* (from the OE verb *borian*); it has no connection with the kind of *bore* who talks till the cows come home or *bores the pants off you*. We don't know where that kind of *bore* comes from, though the *New Shorter Oxford* says, without further elaboration, that 'early sources suggest Fr[ench] derivation'. But a *boer* is indeed connected with a *boor*; in fact they're different reflexes of the same Germanic word, which appears in Dutch as *boer* and in Low German as *būr* (either of which may be the immediate origin of our *boor*). There are two related words in OE: (1) *būr*, the ancestor of MnE *bower* (of which the general sense was 'a dwelling', before it developed such specialized senses as 'an arbour' or 'a lady's boudoir'); (2) *gebūr* 'someone living in a dwelling, a dweller'. If *gebūr* had survived in its own right into MnE, it would have given us *ybour* or *ybower* – the normal development from a long *u* in OE is to the diphthong heard in *out* (from OE *ūt*) and *shower* (from OE *scūr*); and the OE prefix *ge-*, when it survives, becomes *y-*, as in archaic forms of the past participle like *yclad* 'clothed' and *yclept* 'called'. Well, *gebūr* has not survived in MnE as an independent word, but it does survive as the second element in *neighbour* (OE *nēahgebūr*, literally 'nigh-dweller, person who lives close by').

The verb from which all these nouns derive is a common Germanic verb (*būan* in OE) of which the root meaning is 'to live or to dwell' – and that remains the sense in *neighbour*, as we've just seen. But since in an agrarian society to live in a place necessitated cultivating it, *būan* developed also the sense 'to cultivate or to farm', and a *bū-er* came to mean not just 'a dweller' but 'a farmer or peasant'. And that is the earliest recorded sense of both *boor* and *boer*: the early Dutch settlers in South Africa, the *Boers*, were farmers; and in its earliest recorded use in English a *boor* means 'a husbandman, peasant, or countryman'. The current connotations of uncouthness have developed, of course, as a result of middle and upper class metropolitan snobbery: as with other terms denoting lowness in rank or occupation (like *lout* or *villain*) and/or life at subsistence level beyond the Black Stump (like *peasant* or *country bumpkin*), *boor* has become a term denoting rudeness, insensitivity, lack of education, and lack of manners.

We don't expect boorish behaviour in a lady's bower, do we? Who would have thought that these words both derive from the same Germanic verb with the innocent meaning 'to dwell'?

BOOT AND BOOTLESS

When, in disgrace with fortune and men's eyes,
I all alone beweep my outcast state,
And trouble deaf heaven with my bootless cries,
And look upon myself and curse my fate,
Wishing me like to one more rich in hope,
Featured like him, like him with friends possessed,
Desiring this man's art and that man's scope,
With what I most enjoy contented least:
Yet in these thoughts almost myself despising,
Haply I think on thee, and then my state,
Like to the lark at break of day arising
From sullen earth, sings hymns at heaven's gate;
      For thy sweet love remembered such wealth brings
      That then I scorn to change my state with kings'.

Shakespeare's 29th sonnet is so well known and loved that it hardly needs comment; yet I wonder how many, even of its greatest admirers, think that the reason for heaven's deafness to the speaker's "bootless cries" in the third line is that his prayers were in such a hurry to get to their destination that they didn't stop (as it were) to put any boots on, and have thus presented themselves in a lamentable state of undress, like Falstaff, standing "stained with travel and sweating with desire to see [the king], thinking of nothing else, putting all affairs in oblivion, as if there were nothing else to be done but to see him" (2 Henry IV 5.5.24–7).

How many of us, similarly, when we first encounter Caesar's refusal to recall the banished Publius Cimber, with the question to the Roman senators, "Doth not Brutus bootless kneel?" (Julius Caesar 3.1.75), take it to mean that Brutus has removed his shoes as a show of respect before kneeling to make his plea? And how many of us, hearing that Puck "bootless make[s] the breathless housewife churn" (A Midsummer Night's Dream 2.1.37) have visions of a barefoot housewife churning for all she's worth?

But *bootless* in these contexts has nothing to do with footwear. The boots we wear are derived from Old Norse *bøti* or Old French *bote* (modern French *botte*); the boot in *bootless* is from Old English *bōt* 'a remedy or cure'. This word often appears in Old and Middle English in alliterative collocation with its antonym *bale* 'evil-doing, danger, torment, or misery' as in the proverb, "When bale is highest boot is nighest" (Whiting B22), of which there's a nice example in *The Owl and the Nightingale*, "Wone the bale is alre hecst/ Thonne is the bote alre necst" (687–8), that is, 'When misery is at its worst [literally 'highest of all'] the remedy is at hand [literally 'nearest of all']'. Another memorable example of this collocation is found in Criseyde's prayer, when she hears that she must leave Troy and be separated from her beloved Troilus, that God should take pity on her "And with the deth to doon boote on hire bale" (*TC* 4.739), i.e., 'grant her death as a cure for her misery'; still another in this surprisingly modern-sounding cry from *William of Palerne*, "But ich haue bote of mi bale . . . I am ded as dore-nail" (627, quoted in *MED*, s.v. *bale* n.(1), 3), i.e., 'If I don't get a cure for my misery I'm as dead as a door-nail'.

In theological terms *bōt* could mean 'salvation or redemption', hence 'redeemer': in many a Middle English lyric Jesus is thanked for being, or besought to be, our *bote*. It could also mean 'penance', especially in the phrase *don bote* 'do penance, repent, make amends'. And in the phrase *to bote*, which survives in the same idiom as Modern English *to boot*, it meant 'as an added benefit', i.e., 'in addition, besides'.

If we return, then, to the quotations with which we began, we can see that the literal sense of *bootless* in all three examples is 'without a remedy', i.e., 'to no avail, useless(ly)', a sense that may still sometimes be heard today, though not often. The closest synonym I can think of (though the similarity in sound is sheer coincidence) is 'fruitless(ly)': the poet's cries in Sonnet 29 are fruitless because heaven is deaf to them; Brutus kneels fruitlessly because Caesar's mind is made up; and the housewife churns the cream fruitlessly because mischievous Puck is preventing it from turning into butter.

As for the noun *boot* (Old English *bōt*) from which the adjective is derived, it had, as I have said, the primary sense 'a good, benefit, or profit', a sense that survives in the phrase *to boot* 'as an added benefit, besides'. Somewhat to my surprise, I find in the *Australian National Dictionary* that the noun is said to be still in use in Australia in the sense 'something added in from one side to ensure the equality of an exchange'. The most recent quotation for this sense is from Furphy's *Such is Life*: when the Irishman, M'Nab, wants to swap his black horse with the cross-gendered name, Cleopatra, for the narrator's gray mare, Fancy, the narrator asks "And how much boot are you going to give me?" – i.e., 'my mare's worth more than your horse: how much extra will you give me to make up the difference?' Well, I've lived in Australia for many years, and I've never heard this use, so either I move in the wrong circles, or else it's obsolete; but it's interesting that it survived here much longer than it did in England: the latest quotation for this sense in *OED* is dated 1726.

What about related words with a different spelling? It's not unusual for words with a long *o* in Old English (*oo* in Modern English) to have forms, or to have cognates, with long *e* (*ee* in MnE). The plural of book (OE *bōc*), for example, used to be *beech* (OE *bēc*), just as the plural of *goose* (OE *gōs*) is still geese (OE *gēs*). The verb to *deem* (OE *dēman* 'to judge'), though we mightn't notice the connection, is cognate with the noun *doom* (OE *dōm* 'judgement', as in *Doomsday*, 'the Day of Judgement'). In the same way, our noun *boot* has a cognate verb *to beet* or *to bete* meaning 'to make good, mend or repair'. It's not much heard today except perhaps in the old-fashioned phrase *to beet the fire*, which means not to hit it (beat it) with a stick, but to put sticks on it to stoke it (as we'd now be more likely to say). And the relationship is not limited to that between a noun and a verb: the noun is also cognate with the comparative and superlative adjectives, *better* and *best*: all these words go back to the same Germanic root, with a different vowel according to the different function of the word. Beat that!

BOXES

It's generally believed by lexicographers that a *box*, in the sense 'a container' (usually rectangular and usually with a lid), was originally a container made specifically from the wood of the box-tree, which takes its name from the Latin word for the genus, *buxus*. One particular species of this tree is popular in formal gardens in the northern hemisphere in hedges, mazes, and ornamental bushes because it's easily clipped into the desired shape. It is presumably a shaped box-tree of this type in which Sir Toby Belch and his cronies hide in *Twelfth Night* to eavesdrop on Malvolio when he finds the famous letter forged by Maria. This is the letter purporting to come from Olivia, tantalizing Malvolio with the observation that whereas "some are born great" and "some achieve greatness", others "have greatness thrust upon 'em" (2.5.140–1), that is, if he plays his cards right, Olivia will raise him to her rank by marrying him. The various Australian trees called *box* don't in fact belong to the same genus as the European *box*, but, as the *Australian National Dictionary* explains, they have similarly close-grained timber.

What happens when *box* comes to mean 'container or receptacle of any kind' is that the focus of attention has shifted from the material of which it's made (boxwood) to the function that it serves (containing things) so that one can talk without contradiction about, for example, a *cardboard box*, which is self-evidently made not of boxwood but of cardboard (just as a *cake-tin* is nowadays more likely to be made of plastic than of tin). Once it has lost the specifying sense 'made of boxwood', *box* behaves rather like the word *head*; that is, a number of different specialized senses develop independently from the main sense, 'container', each linked directly to the centre rather than evolving out of some other non-original sense.

Boxing Day is named after the boxes of presents that used to be given to employees by their employers on the day after Christmas: it may have been from this sort of context that *box* came to be used to indicate the contents rather than the container (as in "she ate the whole box of chocolates in one go"). From the idea of a smallish receptacle for things we get such combinations as *letterbox*, *mailbox*, and *moneybox*, and such independent uses as that of the *box* beneath the driver's seat on a horse-drawn carriage, after which the seat itself is named (hence to be *in the box seat* is to be the one holding the reins, to be in control). From the idea of a larger receptacle for people or animals we get combinations such as *sentry box*, *telephone box*, *witness box*, *horsebox* (which in Australia and New Zealand is more usually called a *float*), and *loosebox* (which is big enough for animals to move around in). From this source also come independent uses such as that of the *box* one sits in at the theatre. From the rectangular shape we get the *box* enclosing a given portion of print on a page, the (*penalty*) *box* in soccer, the *boxes* for the batter and the pitcher in baseball, and, indeed, *the box* (as it's come to be called) that enables couch potatoes to become armchair experts in such sports without ever playing them.

And if we go back to the main sense 'container or receptacle' without reference either to the shape of the thing or to the material it's made of, we find informal senses such as that of the *box* (now usually made of aluminium) into which a batsman puts his genitals to protect them from fast bowlers, and the *box* belonging to a woman into which men who use this kind of slang would *like* you to think they put their genitals whenever they get half a chance.

BUXOM

If you asked people today to name the *buxomest* person they could think of, what would be the likeliest response? Dolly Parton? Diana Dors? Sabrina? Sophia Loren? Marilyn Monroe? There might be any number of responses, depending, no doubt, on the speaker's age, taste, and nationality; but it's a safe bet that the person named would be a woman, and that she'd have a voluptuous figure. Indeed, there is an airman's pneumatic life-jacket named after Mae West because, as David Crystal puts it in *The Cambridge Encyclopedia*, "when inflated, [it] was considered to give the wearer the generous bosom for which she was herself noted".

But if you had asked the same question in the Middle Ages, the likeliest answers – shocking though this may seem to us today – would have been Jesus or Abraham or the Virgin Mary. The respondents would not have been perving at Mary's figure or implying that Abraham and Jesus were hermaphrodites: the word *buxom* had nothing to do with one's sex or one's physique: it was applied to one's behaviour.

It is derived from the Old English verb *būgan*, the ancestor of our verb 'to bow': *buhsum* meant 'bowable or bendable', hence, in behavioural terms, '(com)pliant or obliging', hence 'obedient or submissive'. As we have seen, it was not originally gender-specific, and it had no sexual connotations: it was used of men and of children, as well as of women. Abraham was described as being *buxom* to God because he obeyed the command to sacrifice his beloved son Isaac (or would have done if the angel hadn't stopped him); Jesus was *buxom* to his father in accepting death upon the Cross; Chaucer's Shipman tells us that a wife wants six things in a husband, that he be "Hardy, and wise, and riche, and therto free [i.e., 'generous']/ And buxom unto his wyf and fressh abedde" (*CT* VII 176–7); in the Sarum marriage service a wife had to swear to be "bonair and buxom" to her husband "in bed and at board"; a medieval proverb about disobedient children says, "Better is the child unborn than unbuxom" (Whiting C200); and the Virgin Mary is described by Wyclif as being "buxumer to [God's] bidding than ony hond-mayde" (*OED*, sense 1a), which, as the context indicates, is a comment on her obedience, not her figure.

How do we get from 'obedient' (of anyone) to 'big-busted' (of women)? (I take it that this is indeed the usual sense in current English, although, amazingly, it's not recorded in the 1986 revision of the *OED*, or in the 1993 *New Shorter Oxford*, or even in the online *OED3*, all of which give as the current sense 'Chiefly of a woman [as if it might still sometimes be used of a man]: full of health, vigour and good temper; plump and comely'. Not until 1998, when Judy Pearsall defined it forthrightly in *NODE* as '(of a woman) plump, with a full figure and large breasts', was this sense to be found in a British dictionary (and even here the idea of plumpness is retained); before that one would have had to look in an American dictionary such as *Webster's* or the *New Heritage*, or in an Australian one such as the *Macquarie* or the Australian *Collins*, to find the plain sense 'full-bosomed'.) Is the suggestion that women with big breasts are more submissive, compliant, or obliging than others? Well, some men like to think so; but I'm inclined to think that's just a male fantasy: the change in meaning in this case appears to arise through the influence of sound (the 'clang association' as it's called – perhaps unfortunately in the present instance – from the German *Klang* 'sound'): since *buxom* sounds like a combination of *bust* and *bosom*, it has developed senses to match.

CHIVALRY AND CAVALRY

Is chivalry dead? That's a question we often hear today; and one has to admit that if some of the extremer feminists had their way it would be. This was brought home to me recently by a young male student who said that he would never forget having his fingers burned on his first day at university, when he held a door open for a female fellow student who said, as she went through it, "Thanks, sexist pig!" But, as the young man said to me, "I would have held the door open for another *bloke* if I'd reached it before him: it had nothing to do with her sex." Fortunately this kind of ill-mannered response to an act of common courtesy is confined to the fanatical fringes; but it's sad that it's this kind of behaviour that gets feminism a bad name. No wonder men think twice these days before daring to be chivalrous!

But how did *chivalry* come to have its current sense, with its connotations of courtesy, especially that of men towards women? This is not what it meant in the Middle Ages. The word is in fact derived from Old French *chevalerie*, from *cheval* 'a horse'. A *chevalier* was a horseman, especially a knight on horseback (as it still is, figuratively, in Hopkins's celebrated poem, "The Windhover"); and *chevalerie* or *chivalry* was the collective term for a group of 'knights or horsemen equipped for battle' (*OED*). It was more or less synonymous, in other words, with what we would now call *cavalry* – a word from the same ultimate root, Latin *caballus* 'a pack-horse', which likewise came into English from French, but which French had earlier taken from Italian (hence the two different forms, *chivalry* and *cavalry*).

Well, *chivalry* at first denoted the people mounted on horseback; but in time it became transferred to their actions. Thus it could mean 'knightly prowess' or 'a feat of knightly valour' or 'knightly pursuits' in general; and it's probably in this last sense that it's used of Chaucer's Knight in the General Prologue to the *Canterbury Tales*, "That fro the tyme that he first bigan/ To riden out, he loved chivalrie,/ Trouthe and honour, fredom and curteisie" (I 44–6), who, that is, 'from the time when he first began to go campaigning, loved knightly deeds, fidelity, honour, generosity, and courtly conduct'. But because one of the chief ways in which knights were expected to demonstrate their knightliness was in defending people who were unable to defend themselves, it came in time to denote not only 'courage, honour, and courtesy', but also, and particularly, an 'inclination to defend or help a weaker party' (*New Shorter Oxford*). I suppose it's precisely the implication of condescension towards a weaker party that makes some women react violently against it, like the student who was so furious at having the door opened for her.

As for *cavalry*, its development in English has been more or less the reverse: it began as the abstract quality, 'horsemanship'; from there it acquired the more elevated sense 'knighthood'; and it has come at last to a concrete sense as the collective term for horse soldiers, irrespective of their behaviour. But who can predict which way language will go (from concrete to abstract, as with *chivalry*, or from abstract to concrete, as with *cavalry*), or why?

Clerks, Clerics, and Clergy

We are accustomed to think of the *clergy* as a group of people, ordained ministers of the Church; and this concrete sense has been continuously in use in English since the thirteenth century. But there was also, in the Middle Ages, an abstract sense that we have since lost: the word was used not only of the people but of what they knew; and since the clergy were the only educated people, *clergie* became synonymous with 'knowledge or learning' of any kind, not necessarily theological. When, for example, King Bokkus asks whether leprosy can be healed "with kunnyng of clergie" (*Sidrak* L4977), he's not asking whether there are any priests clever enough to cure it: he wants to know whether there's any scientific knowledge (see *cunning*), any knowledge accessible through study, that can do so.

As for the related word *clerks*, we no longer think of them as belonging to the clergy, for whom (except in the phrase "clerk in holy orders") we reserve the term *clerics*. But in Old English *clerc* and *cleric* were not two different words: they were alternative spellings of the same word, adapted from Latin *clericus* 'a clergyman or priest'. In time, through the influence of the French form *clerc* (which is itself, of course, descended from the same word in Latin), the disyllabic form *cleric* disappeared from English from the fourteenth to the sixteenth century and *clerk* became the standard form.

But how did *clerk* come to mean 'office-worker' as it does today? *OED* has one of its eloquent mini-essays on the subject, under the word *clerk*, which I shall quote in full: "The original sense was 'man in a religious order, cleric, clergyman'. As the scholarship of the Middle Ages was practically limited to the clergy, and these performed all the writing, notarial, and secretarial work of the time, the name 'clerk' came to be equivalent to 'scholar', and specially applicable to a notary, secretary, recorder, accountant, or penman. The last has now come to be the ordinary sense, all the others being either archaic, historical, formal, or contextual". And since *clerk* had come to have this sense 'pen-pusher' or 'office-worker', the form *cleric* was revived in the seventeenth century, as a separate word, with the original sense, 'member of the clergy'. But whereas the noun has now two distinct forms, with the senses differentiated, there remains still only the one adjective, *clerical*, which can mean either 'pertaining to the clergy' (as in a *clerical collar*) or 'relating to office work' (as in the *clerical duties* in advertisements for secretarial jobs). Language wasn't meant to be easy!

The *clerks* in Chaucer's *Canterbury Tales* are almost all scholars, with the exception of Absalon in the Miller's tale, who was a mere *parish clerk*, i.e., a lay person who undertakes various duties for the Church: in Absalon's case these included taking the collection – except from the women of the parish, from whom he thought it would be discourteous to take money (I 3348–51). The book-loving Clerk in the General Prologue is a student at Oxford, as is Nicholas in the Miller's tale; Aleyn and John in the Reeve's tale are Cambridge students; and the Wife of Bath's fifth husband, "Jankyn clerk" (III 548), is a scholar who appears to have made a special study of the anti-feminist writings of Valerius and Theofrastus (669–72). These clerks have the academic tendency to be rather proud of their superior intellectual abilities. This is apparent in Nicholas's scornful comment that "A clerk hadde litherly biset his whyle,/ But if he koude a carpenter bigyle" (I 3299–300), i.e., 'a scholar would have wasted his time if he couldn't pull the wool over a carpenter's eyes'; it's equally apparent in Aleyn and John's confidence that Symkyn the miller won't steal any of *their* corn (I 4009–12). The lesson they all have to learn is nicely expressed in the proverb of which Symkyn sets out to teach Aleyn and John the truth (and which must be as true today as it was then), namely "The gretteste clerkes been noght wisest men" (I 4054), i.e., 'The most highly educated scholars are not necessarily the cleverest people'. As my old friend Tony Slade has occasionally been heard to mutter after a particularly tedious committee meeting, "Academics may be quite smart in their own fields, but some of them couldn't add up two and two or find their own way to the bus stop".

CLODS, CLOTS, AND CLOUDS

There is a well-known Middle English lyric, spoken by a love-sick male who goes out riding one springtime and overhears the song of a young woman vowing to get revenge on her faithless lover. It begins:

> Now springes the spray
> All for love I am so seek
> That slepen I ne may.
> Als I me rode this endre day
> O' my pleyinge,
> Seih I whar a litel may
> Bigan to singe,
> 'The clot him clinge!
> Way es him i' love-longinge
> Shall libben ay!'

'Now (that) the twigs come into leaf I am so sick for love that I cannot sleep. As I went riding the other day to amuse myself, I saw a little maiden who sang "The clot him clinge! Miserable is the one who must live always in (the throes of) love-longing!" '

When present-day readers come upon the first line of her song "The clot him clinge!", they are almost bound to think that the *clot* in question is the maiden's ex-lover, and that she's wishing something dreadful will happen to the silly idiot to pay him back for his unfaithfulness (such as that he may have no one to hug or cling to but himself) – indeed, that's just how the poem ends, with the young woman declaring: "Yiif I may, it shall him rewe/ By this day!" ('If I can, I'll make him sorry about today!' or 'By this day [I swear] I'll make him sorry!').

Well, that's a graphic and a plausible interpretation of "The clot him clinge", but it's not quite as gruesome as the true one. The word *clot* does not here mean 'fool': it is in fact the same word as *clod* 'lump of earth'. And *cling* without *to* does not mean 'stick to': it means 'shrivel' or 'cause to shrivel' – as in Macbeth's threat to the hapless messenger who brings him the news that Birnam wood has started to move: "If thou speak'st false,/ Upon the next tree shall thou hang alive,/ Till famine cling thee" (5.5.36–8), i.e., 'till you shrivel up from hunger'. What the young woman in the lyric is actually saying is 'May the earth shrivel him' or 'May he rot in earth (for making me so miserable!)'.

It turns out not only that *clot* and *clod* are variants of the same word, but that *cloud* is closely related. The ultimate Germanic root is a word meaning 'a lump or mass', especially one caused by the sticking together of small particles to form a larger mass. *OED* tells us that in early use *clod* and *clot* were synonymous, and that it was only later that *clod* became restricted to solids like earth and *clot* to liquids, as in a *blood-clot*. The sense 'fool' may be a shortening of *clodpoll* or *clotpoll* 'thickhead or blockhead' or a direct figurative use (cf. *lump* as in "he's a useless lump", which is perhaps more likely to be heard today than the equivalent phrase that I heard frequently when I was a child, "he's a clumsy clot").

As for a *cloud*, it began life in Old English as a lump of earth, a rock, or even a hill; thus when the Norwegian sailor, Ohthere, told King Alfred that his homeland was very "cludig" (the ancestor of MnE *cloudy*), he wasn't talking about the sky, but about the earth – which was very rocky, and therefore difficult to plough. And what is a cloud now but a lump of condensed vapour in the sky? How convenient, and how unusual, that each of these different lumps should have acquired its own pronunciation and spelling!

COCKS AND ROOSTERS

As loyal South Australian footy fans will know, the North Adelaide football team is traditionally nicknamed the Roosters; but it came as something of a surprise to me, a relatively new chum who has long admired the colourfulness of Australian idiom, that *rooster* is the standard term in Australia for a male chook, in preference to *cock*, which is the more usual term in Britain. (Chris Bright points out to me the anomaly that "no one would ever dream of saying other than 'cock' in discussing St Peter's three denials, so sermons are preached about the 'cock' crowing; then you go outside and hear a 'rooster' do the same".) *Rooster* has always struck me as a mealy-mouthed term; Hugh Rawson, in his *devious derivations*, is surely right in suggesting that its introduction in the early nineteenth century, along with the alteration of *apricock* to *apricot*, *haycock* to *haystack*, and *cock-horse* to *rocking horse*, is the result of a pre-Victorian prudish desire to avoid the suggestive word *cock*.

But how did *cock*, an innocent enough word in Old English, merely the male equivalent of 'hen', come to acquire the sense 'penis', a sense not recorded in *OED* until 1618, and there stigmatized as 'not admissible in polite speech or literature' (sense 20)? *OED* itself suggests that the connection is by way of *cock* in the sense of 'a spout or short pipe serving as a channel for passing liquids through, and having an appliance for regulating or stopping the flow', or, in other words, 'a tap' (sense 12). In response to this one can only ask, "How many penises have you ever encountered that are equipped with an appliance for turning them off in mid-flow?" But *OED* has anticipated this objection, and points out that in some of the earlier quotations under the sense 'spout' "the power of closing the 'cock' was no essential feature", i.e. that a *cock* was not necessarily a *stop-cock*, but that the word simply meant 'a short spout for the emission of fluid', and that in other quotations it was equivalent to 'nozzle or mouthpiece'.

This all sounds perfectly reasonable; yet I am at something of a loss to know why the sense 'penis' has not been traced directly to the original sense 'male bird'. There is a well-known Middle English lyric in which this connection is made. It begins:

> I have a gentil cok,
> Croweth me day;
> He doth me risen erly,
> My matins for to say.

That is: 'I have a noble cock; he crows me day (i.e., wakes me up by crowing to me at break of day); he causes me to get up (or 'rise') early to say my morning prayers.'

There follows a description of a fine farmyard cock, with a red comb, a black tail, white spurs, and so forth; but then the poem ends as punningly as it began, with the claim that "every night he percheth him/ In min ladyes chaumber" ('every night he perches in my lady's chamber'). It hardly needs pointing out that *chamber* can mean 'physical cavity' as well as 'bedroom', or that it's a funny kind of woman who keeps a chicken (albeit a male one) in her bedroom.

And who could miss the satire on male phallic pride in Chaucer's famous description of the cock Chauntecleer in the Nun's Priest's tale, strutting round the yard amidst his harem of hens, barely deigning to put his feet down in the muck, and screwing his favourite wife, Pertelote, twenty times before breakfast?

> He fethered Pertelote twenty tyme,
> And trad hire eke as ofte, er it was pryme.
> He looketh as it were a grym leoun,
> And on his toos he rometh up and doun;
> Hym deigned nat to sette his foot to grounde.
> He chukketh whan he hath a corn yfounde,
> And to hym rennen thanne his wyves alle. (*CT* VII 3177–83)

Chaucer didn't need Beatrice Faust to tell him that, when it comes to sex, most women are "process-orientated" whereas most men are "performance-orientated". Small wonder that a man who carries on like Chauntecleer is nowadays called a *prick*.

COMFORTABLE

When King Lear describes his second daughter, Regan, somewhat over-optimistically, as "kind and comfortable" (1.4.285–6), he doesn't mean that she has a nice lap to sit in, or that she's soft and cuddly; he's saying that he's sure she will be more supportive or *comforting* to him than her older sister, Goneril, who has just required him "a little to disquantity [his] train" (227), i.e., to get rid of some of his followers. (He has yet to discover the truth of the Fool's words that though Regan may appear as like Goneril "as a crab's like an apple. . . . She will taste as like [her] as a crab does to a crab", 1.5.16–19.) Similarly, when Kent is imprisoned in the stocks a little later and asks the sun to approach so that he may read Cordelia's letter by its "comfortable beams" (2.2.155), he's obviously not sitting *comfortably* in the modern sense, enjoying the warm sunshine; he nevertheless finds the sun's beams *comforting*, i.e., 'helpful', because they give him the light by which to read the letter.

These uses of *comfortable* in *King Lear* are different in sense from the current meaning; but what they have in common with it is that the suffix *-(a)ble* has an active rather than a passive sense: a *comfortable* chair (in the current sense) isn't one that is able to be comforted but one that gives comfort to the person using it, like the *comforter* on American beds. (For similar examples see *visible*.)

Comfortable has always had an active as opposed to a passive sense, but the sort of *comfort* that's implied, as with other adjectives derived from the noun, is of course dependent on the meaning of the noun itself, and that has varied somewhat over time, developing from the root sense, 'strengthening or encouragement', to embrace such senses as 'refreshment or sustenance', 'pleasure or enjoyment', 'help or relief (from physical pain or sickness)', 'consolation or support (in spiritual or mental distress)', and 'a state of wellbeing free from physical or mental pain' (*OED*, senses 1–6). The "comfortable doctrine" that Olivia received from Orsino (through Viola) was designed to give her pleasure by flattering her (*Twelfth Night* 1.5.213). The Queen's plea to the Duke of York,

"Uncle, for God's sake, speak comfortable words" (*Richard II* 2.2.76), was for words that would bring her relief from anxiety in the face of Bolingbroke's unforeseen return from exile during Richard's absence in Ireland. Bertram's instructions to Helena, when he had to leave home shortly after the death of his father, "Be comfortable to my mother" (*All's Well* 1.1.74), meant roughly 'Comfort my mother by giving her consolation and support'. And when Hezekiah "spake comfortably" to his people in the face of Sennacherib's threatened attack on Jerusalem, what he was doing was giving them a pep talk: "Be strong and courageous, be not afraid nor dismayed for the king of Assyria, nor for all the multitude that is with him" (2 Chronicles 32: 6–7). The ensuing overthrow of the Assyrians through divine intervention, reported in 2 Kings 19: 35–7, was the inspiration for what must surely be the most famous anapaestic poem in the language, Byron's 'The Destruction of Sennacherib':

> The Assyrian came down like the wolf on the fold,
> And his cohorts were gleaming in purple and gold;
> And the sheen of their spears was like stars on the sea,
> When the blue wave rolls nightly on deep Galilee....

The last examples are all connected with words and speaking, and in every instance we would today say *comforting* or *comfortingly* rather than *comfortable* or *comfortably*: it would seem that *comfortable* has now lost its active sense when it comes to speaking, though it retains it in other contexts – where, however, its moral and spiritual overtones have mainly given way to material ones. When Gloucester's eyes are torn out (to return to *King Lear*), he cries out that their lustre has become "All dark and comfortless" (3.7.83), that is, 'giving no comfort or help, cheerless'. Though their meanings are opposite, it's not difficult to see the connection between Gloucester's chilling use of *comfortless* and the common current senses of *comfortable*, i.e., of houses, furniture, and things in general, 'giving comfort or promoting contentment', and, of people, 'at ease, free from pain, reasonably well-off financially', or 'having a clear conscience' – perhaps with some suggestion of complacency?

CUNNING

If anyone today were to call me "a cunning clerk", I'd be inclined – if I weren't such a mild-tempered bloke – to make a rather rude reply. But in the Middle Ages, I should have been highly flattered by such a compliment on my erudition.

We are accustomed to thinking of *cunning* as a derogatory word: the noun suggests to us (as the *New Shorter Oxford* puts it) 'skill in deceit or evasion'; the adjective is used of people who have or of things that demonstrate this underhand skill. But it was quite otherwise in the Middle Ages: the Old English verb *cunnan* (the ancestor of modern English *can*), from which both the adjective and the noun are derived, meant simply 'to know'; the noun *cunning* meant 'knowledge' or 'skill'; the adjective meant 'knowledgeable' or 'skilful' or even (as in "a cunning clerk") 'learned' (see *clerks*).

It must be the innocent sense of the noun that Chaucer's Prioress is using when she says, in the prayer to the Virgin Mary that precedes her tale, "My konnyng is so wayk, O blisful Queene,/ For to declare thy grete worthynesse/ That I ne may the weighte nat susteene" (*CT* VII 481–3), that is, roughly, 'My knowledge (or skill) isn't sufficient to undertake the responsibility of praising your worthiness'. And it's evidently the innocent sense that's intended in the several Middle English proverbs in which *cunning* is praised, such as "Cunning has no foe", "Cunning is no burden", and "Cunning surmounts all earthly treasure" (Whiting C611, C614–15).

The same still holds true for the adjective two hundred years later: when Capulet tells his servant to hire "twenty cunning cooks" to prepare the feast for Juliet's wedding (*Romeo and Juliet* 4.2.2), there's no suggestion that corners are being cut: Capulet just wants the best cooks he can get hold of, ones who know their trade and are good at it. The trouble is, human nature being what it is, just about any kind of skill or knowledge, taken to a high level, tends to be thought of as illicit or unnatural. One remembers, for example, that Paganini was so good at playing the violin (so *cunning* as they'd have called him in the Middle Ages) that it was rumoured he'd made a pact with the devil. The result is that most words implying skill or knowledge acquire unfavourable senses beside their first neutral or favourable ones; and once started on the slope of degeneration, they usually find their way to the bottom.

Thus *craft* and *crafty*, *sly* and *sleight* have histories very similar to that of *cunning*; and *knowing*, though it perhaps doesn't (yet) imply anything as deceitful as *cunning* itself, nevertheless implies greater knowledge than is appropriate. How strange that *skill* and *skilful* appear (so far) to have escaped this general decline!

CURIOUS

Many of the words discussed in this book have what one might call "a very curious history", that is, an 'odd, strange, unusual, or interesting' history. But if we describe people, as opposed to things, as *curious*, we mean that they're inquisitive, either in a good sense ('eager to learn') or in a bad sense ('over-inquisitive, prying').

These meanings are both some way from the original senses derived ultimately from the Latin noun *cura*, meaning 'care', a word with many derivatives still in use in English. The *curator* of a museum or art gallery, for example, is the person entrusted with the care of the objects housed in it; the *curate* of a parish has the souls of the parishioners in his or her *cure*, that is, care or spiritual charge. When medics *cure* our diseases they do so by taking care of us, and so the remedy itself comes to be called *a cure*; when meat is *cured* the care in question is that involved in preparing it for the preserving process; and to *procure* something for someone is to get it with care or effort.

As for *curious* itself, what has care to do with it? Well, as far as things are concerned the word originally meant 'made with care', hence often 'elaborately or delicately wrought', like the "curious" pin with "a love-knotte in the gretter ende" with which the Monk in the General Prologue to the *Canterbury Tales* fastened his hood (I 195–7), or the "curiouse portreytures" in the temple of glass in Chaucer's *House of Fame* (125). And the current sense with which I began, 'odd, strange, or interesting', is not so far from this sense after all, since it suggests that the object in question excites interest by virtue of its being *carefully made*, or novel, or different in some way from run-of-the mill stuff.

As for the sense 'inquisitive', used of people, this is perhaps somewhat further removed from the original. When the merchant in Chaucer's Shipman's tale sets out on a journey to Flanders and urges his wife to be "buxom and meke" to everyone and to be "curious" to keep their "good" (*CT* VII 242–3), he is asking her to be obliging to other people (see *buxom*) and to take good care of their own goods. From this sense of 'bestowing care' on things or 'taking pains' with them (*OED*, sense 1) it's a logical step to taking great pains with them or being fastidious about them (sense 2); from there it's only a small step to being careful or minutely accurate in observing things (sense 3) – the sense that Hamlet was overdoing when he imagined "the noble dust of Alexander . . . stopping a bung-hole": as Horatio admonishes him in reply, "'Twere to consider too curiously to consider so" (5.1.199–201); and it's just one further step from there to the current sense simply of being inquisitive (sense 5), or of behaving like a stickybeak.

THE DADDY OF THEM ALL

When Saddam Hussein said, during the Gulf War of the nineties, that the allies were facing "the Mother of all Battles" I take it (since I can't find it in *OED*, though it's clear enough what was meant) that he was translating an Arabic saying into English.

The closest expression recorded in *OED* — and it's evidently a fairly recent idiom, since the earliest quotation is from Kipling in 1892, little more than 100 years ago — is *the father and mother of* a something or other "used colloquially to indicate extreme severity, exceptionally large size, etc." *OED* adds that the phrase sometimes occurs with the words *and mother* omitted, especially in Australia and New Zealand. I can't say I had ever heard the expression *the father and mother of a* before I found it in *OED*, though I was certainly familiar with *the father of a hiding* before I came to Australia, perhaps because I was once given one when I was at school — for using indecent language, as it happens.

The related expression, *the daddy of them all*, can, I think, confidently be claimed as an Australianism, since, though it's also used elsewhere, it is, as the *Australian National Dictionary* tells us, "recorded earliest in Australia", and appears to have been popularized here. It means, of course, the best or biggest or most impressive example, the 'supreme instance' (*Dictionary of Australian Colloquialisms*) of whatever one's talking about: "Though shaky in the shoulders, he's the daddy of them all;/ He's the gamest bit of horseflesh from the Snowy to the Bree" (1898, W.H. Ogilvie, *Fair Girls and Gray Horses*, the first quotation in both *AND* and *DAC*).

As for myself, I'm delighted to be able to say that I first encountered this expression not in a book but, as it were, in the flesh. I had gone down to that most beautiful of cricket grounds, the Adelaide Oval, not long after settling in Adelaide — to do some research in linguistics and semiotics. (That there was a match on at the time was, of course, sheer coincidence.) It was a Sheffield Shield game between South Australia and New South Wales. Trevor Chappell at that stage in his career was playing for New South Wales. When he came in to bat, two old blokes in the row in front of me at the bottom of the John Cresswell Stand (as it then was) started talking about him.

"I 'eard Victor Richardson say, before 'e died . . ." one of them began. A pause, while he took a swig from his stubbie (they still allowed bottles into the ground in those days); then he started again, with an improvement: "Victor Richardson said to me, before he died, 'I've got three grandsons,' 'e said, 'and each of them's a champion. But that Trevor,' 'e said, ''e's gunna be the daddy of 'em all!'"

Well, Victor Richardson may have got it wrong about the pecking order amongst his grandsons, but I shall be for ever grateful to him and to those two old blokes for teaching me, in such unforgettable fashion, the Australianism that has become, for me, *the daddy of them all.*

DAFT AND DEFT

The discovery that *daft* is etymologically the same word as *deft* came as a great surprise to me, since the two words have opposite meanings in current English to go with their different spellings, the one meaning 'stupid', the other 'skilful'. In Old and early Middle English, in contrast, both forms meant 'mild, gentle, meek', and were applied, as terms of approbation, to the Virgin Mary. In the *Middle English Physiologus*, for example, we are told that when God wished to be born as Man he "dennede" (that is, 'made a den for himself') "in that defte meiden" (p. 1/18); and the Lincolnshire priest Orm (quoted in *MED*) describes Mary as "Shammfasst, & daffte, & sedefull" (that is, 'modest, and humble, and chaste'). (See also *shamefaced*.)

There is no difficulty about the two different spellings of the word, since they derive from an Old English vowel (æ, pronounced like the short *a* in Modern English *hat*) that can yield either *a* or *e* in Modern English; nor is there any mystery about the development of the sense of *deft* from 'gentle' to 'apt' and so eventually to 'skilful': the problem is how, for *daft*, 'gentle' could come to mean 'stupid'.

This is one of the very few instances I know of where both our major historical dictionaries, *OED* and *MED*, appear to get it wrong. *OED* has a remarkably detailed introductory essay under *daft*, arguing that the earliest sense was 'becoming' (of persons), and that the development must have been via 'meek, mild, innocent' to 'irrational' (of animals), and thence to 'silly, foolish, deficient in sense' (of persons). The argument makes excellent sense, but it's not borne out in the ensuing definitions, which proceed in one leap from 'mild, gentle' to 'silly, foolish, stupid', without demonstrating any of the supposed intermediate senses.

But if one studies the quotations in *OED*, one finds that the intermediate senses are in fact there, under the wrong definitions. In one of the quotations under the sense 'stupid', taken from a poem involving a debate between the body and the soul as to the cause of their damnation in the afterlife, the soul blames the body because, with its fleshly lusts, it had led them both astray. The body replies, in self defence, that it's the soul's fault they've been damned, because the soul was endowed with reason, and should have known better, whereas it, the body, was "as a beest doumbe and daft"; that is to say, not that it was stupid, but that, like an animal, it lacked the faculties of speech and reason. Here, then, is the postulated intermediate sense 'irrational', i.e., 'lacking in reason'.

A second quotation under the sense 'stupid' is from a poem about St Cuthbert, in which the boy Cuthbert takes a toy bell he has broken to a smith to get it repaired. The smith says he would like to help, "Bot to make it I am daft,/ For I can noght of potter craft" (441–4). He's not saying he's too stupid to mend it, but that, since he knows nothing about making pots or bells, he lacks the necessary expertise. *Daft* doesn't mean 'stupid' here; it means 'inexpert, untaught, or ignorant' (in the neutral sense 'lacking knowledge'). I have come across another example of this sense in *Sidrak and Bokkus*, in which we are told that craftsmen are very valuable people because they teach "other that ben dafte/ Konnyng here lyvelode to wynne" (B6540–1): the *daft* people they teach are not fools; they're just people who have not yet been taught a skill with which to earn their livelihood; like the smith in *The Life of St Cuthbert*, they are ignorant in the sense 'untaught' – and here, too, is an instance of *cunning* in the innocent sense 'knowledge'.

The point of all this is not to prove that the editors of *OED* and *MED* are *daft* in the current sense, but to demonstrate how difficult is the art of lexicography, no matter how *deft* one may be with words.

DANGEROUS

In one of the best-known passages in what Chaucer's Friar calls the "long preamble" to her tale (*CT* III 831) the Wife of Bath describes her violent relationship with her fifth husband, whom she claims nevertheless to have loved better than any of the others:

> Now of my fifthe housbonde wol I telle.
> God lete his soule nevere come in helle!
> And yet was he to me the mooste shrewe;
> That feele I on my ribbes al by rewe,
> And evere shal unto myn endyng day.
> But in oure bed he was so fressh and gay,
> And therwithal so wel koude he me glose,
> Whan that he wolde han my *bele chose*;
> That thogh he hadde me bete on every bon,
> He koude wynne agayn my love anon.
> I trowe I loved hym best, for that he
> Was of his love daungerous to me. (503–14)

That's to say, roughly, he was the beastliest to her of all her husbands; she can still feel his beatings on all her ribs, and will do till she dies; but he was so good in bed, and so good at chatting her up when he wanted what she here (with uncharacteristic coyness) calls her 'beautiful thing', that he could win her round to loving him at once, even if he'd just given her a thrashing. Indeed, she reckoned she loved him best because he was "daungerous" in his love to her.

But what does this word "daungerous" mean? Of course it's our word *dangerous*, but does it have the same meaning? My students tend to think so, and I'm inclined to have some sympathy with their view, even though the current sense of *dangerous*, i.e., 'causing danger, putting at risk', isn't recorded in the standard dictionaries until shortly after Chaucer's death (*MED*, sense 4). But these beatings Jankyn is administering are not just a bit of friendly bum-slapping: she feels them *on her ribs*; he has beaten her *on every bone*. It doesn't seem at all unreasonable to me to call such beatings *dangerous* in the current sense.

Yet scholars almost always take "daungerous" here to mean 'stand-offish, niggardly, hard to get, or hard to please', relating it to *Daunger*, the personification of disdain, that power that separates a would-be lover from his lady: they argue that what attracts the Wife so strongly to Jankyn is that, good though he may be at love-making, he keeps her in a state of constant desire by making love to her only infrequently. In support of this interpretation they can point with some justice to the lines immediately following the passage just quoted:

> We wommen han, if that I shal nat lye,
> In this matere a queynte fantasye:
> Wayte what thyng we may nat lightly have,
> Therafter wol we crie al day and crave.
> Forbede us thyng, and that desiren we;
> Preesse on us faste, and thanne wol we fle.
> With daunger oute we al oure chaffare;
> Greet prees at market maketh deere ware,
> And to greet cheep is holde at litel prys;
> This knoweth every womman that is wys. (515–24)

That is, 'We women have an odd caprice in this matter, to tell you the truth: whatever we can't easily have we long for and beg for the whole time. Forbid us something, and that's just what we want; press (something) on us, and we'll run away. We put out our goods with "daunger" [that word again!]; a great crowd at market makes things expensive, and too good a bargain is valued little; every sensible woman knows that.'

What is this "daunger" that the Wife claims women offer their wares with? It's normally translated as 'caution, niggardliness, or reserve': to put out what one has to offer *with daunger* or *daungerously* is, in short, to play hard to get, to pretend that it's not on offer but must be sought; the Wife says that's what women usually do; critics argue that it's what Jankyn does to her. Well, I go along with that; it's a perfectly reasonable argument. But I don't think it's the whole story.

The noun *da(u)nger* is derived ultimately from Latin *dominarium* '(a person connected with) lordship', from *dominus* 'lord'. In its earliest uses in English it meant 'domination, power, or control' (*MED* sense 1); the corresponding sense of the adjective was 'domineering, overbearing'. It's not hard to see how that sense gave rise to the sense 'standoffish, hard to please': domineering people usually *are* hard to please, aren't they? They can be pretty tight-fisted, too, which gives rise to 'niggardly'; and they aren't always easy to deal with: on the contrary, they can be pretty risky to deal with, which gives us the current sense, 'dangerous'.

So which of these senses did Chaucer have in mind when he had the Wife of Bath say that she loved Jankyn best because he was "daungerous" to her? I'd say all three. There's no need for us to try to restrict the word to one meaning when it could have several simultaneously: that Jankyn was domineering towards her we know, because she tells us plainly, "He nolde suffre nothyng of my list" (633), that is, 'He wouldn't let me do anything I wanted to'; that he was sparing in his love-making we have already seen; and that his beatings were dangerous to life and limb her battered ribs are testimony. Lexicographers and editors may feel pressured to choose one meaning in preference to the others; but Chaucer, like all good poets, has it all ways.

DEAL AND DOLE

Advertisers who claim that such-and-such a company will give you "a great deal" or "a good deal" are punning on two senses of the noun *deal* (OE *dǽl*): the root sense is 'a part or portion', hence "a great deal" or "a good deal" is a large portion (if you buy from us you'll get a lot for your money); a derived sense is 'a transaction or business arrangement', hence "a great or good deal" is 'a bargain' (if you buy from us the arrangement will be to your advantage).

But how does the sense 'bargain' derive from the sense 'portion'? Well, indirectly. Beside the noun *deal* 'a portion' there is the verb *to deal* (OE *dǽlan*) meaning (as one would suppose) 'to divide into portions, to share out, to distribute'. The most taxing problem in Chaucer's Summoner's tale is how the sick Thomas's fart (which was his contemptuous gift to the visiting friar) can be "evene deled" (i.e. 'equally divided') amongst his fellow friars (*CT* III 2249). If you *deal* someone a blow you 'deliver' it to them. The dealer in card games is the person who *deals* (i.e. 'distributes') the cards to all the players. The people involved in all these *dealings* have shared in an activity in which some are distributors and some recipients: thus *dealings* comes to mean 'interactions'; *to deal* acquires the sense 'to have an interaction with'; and *a deal* comes to mean 'an interaction'.

Such interactions may be entirely unspecific, as when one of Chaucer's other friars, the friar in the General Prologue to the *Canterbury Tales*, maintains that it is beneath him to associate with lepers and the poor: "It is nat honest; it may nat avaunce,/ For to deelen with no swich poraille" (I 246–7), i.e., 'It's neither honourable nor advantageous to have anything to do with such scum'. But given the human preoccupation with sex and money, it will cause no surprise that the dealings in question are very often of a financial or a sexual nature. Thus Dido in Chaucer's *Legend of Good Women* fancies Aeneas so much that she starts to pine away, losing both her colour and her health: "Dido hath now swich desyr/ With Eneas, hire newe gest, to dele,/ That she hath lost hire hewe and ek hire hele" (1157–9). And thus our advertisers can offer us *a great deal* financially, implying simultaneously that we're getting a lot for our money. They might equally claim that they were giving us *a fair deal* or *a square deal* ('equitable treatment') rather than *a raw deal* or *a rough deal* ('unfair treatment').

But what's the connection between *deal* and *dole*? They are, in fact, variant spellings of what is ultimately the same word, and their root meanings are the same: *a dole* is a portion that has been dealt out; *the dole* is money that is distributed to the unemployed; and *to dole out* is to distribute in portions (usually small – as those *on the dole* would doubtless agree). There is no connection between *dole* meaning 'grief' (which is very common in Middle English in the phrase *maken dole* 'to lament') and *dole* meaning 'portion': the latter is a native English word (OE *dāl*, cognate with OE *dǣl*); the former is from French. Nor is there any connection between the *deals* we have been considering and a *deal* table, even though such tables were made originally from portions of timber of a given size: this latter word *deal* came into English in the fourteenth century from Middle Low German or Middle Dutch *dele* (modern Dutch *deel*) 'a plank', and it has acquired the specialized sense of a particular kind of wood, the fir or pine wood of which such planks were usually made. That it has come to be spelled the same way as the native English word meaning 'a portion', and that a plank is a portion of timber, are sheer coincidences.

Big deal!

DEER AND WORMS

When Edgar assumes the disguise of Poor Tom in *King Lear* he talks a great deal about the cold and other hardships he has endured as a bedlam beggar, including the lack of food, which forces him to eat things that would normally be considered disgusting: "mice and rats and such small deer/ Have been Tom's food for seven long year" (3.4.130–1). It's quite clear from the context that he doesn't mean he's been killing what we would call *deer* in the forest and feasting on venison; on the contrary, as he tells us himself a few lines earlier, he's been eating "the swimming frog, the toad, the tadpole, [and] the wall-newt" and he's been drinking "the green mantle of the standing pool" (no *sandwiches* or *pavlovas* or *hamburgers* for poor old Tom). All of those creatures that Edgar mentions – mice, rats, frogs, tadpoles, and the rest – would have been called *deer* in Old English: the word was a general term for animals as opposed to plants.

The *Middle English Physiologus* was formerly called the *Bestiary*; as its earlier name implies, it is about *beasts* (a French word that replaced the English word *deer* in the general sense 'animal', before it in turn became more or less replaced by the Latin word *animals*). This poem has a section on the ant, describing how diligently it collects food in summer and stores it up for the winter, and going on to draw from this the moral that humans ought to imitate the ant's behaviour by storing up sustenance for the afterlife through good works on earth. In the moral the ant is referred to as a *deer*, which strikes us as unintentionally comic: "Do we forthi so doth this der", the moral urges us (p. 8/176), i.e., 'Let us do, therefore, as does this deer' (i.e., this animal, or this creature).

A little later in the same poem the ant is referred to as a *wirm*, i.e. 'worm' (p. 8/179), which in Middle English is a generic term for any creepy-crawly creature, be it snake, worm, lizard, cockroach, or earwig: the word covered reptiles and insects of all kinds, including even maggots, which were confused with earthworms as devourers of dead bodies in the grave. It's this sense that gives rise, in Marvell's 'To his Coy

Mistress', to the speaker's gruesome comment to the woman he's pursuing about the fate in store for her in the grave:

> then Worms shall try
> That long preserv'd Virginity:
> And your quaint Honour turn to dust;
> And into ashes all my Lust.   (27–30)

But the original sense of *worm* was specifically 'a snake or a dragon' – the dragon in *Beowulf* is called a worm, and fans of Tolkien will be familiar with that use of the word.

What these two words demonstrate are the common processes of generalization and specialization: *deer* begins as a word of very general meaning ('animal'), develops a highly specialized one ('animal of the kind that has antlers'), and loses the original generalized sense; *worm* begins with a specialized sense ('snake or dragon'), then develops first a more general one ('any creature that creeps or crawls'), and afterwards another specialized one ('earthworm, bodyworm, etc.') that is somewhat different from the first.

DELVING AND SPINNING

"When Adam dolf and Eve span,/ Who was then the gentleman?" This archaic version of John Ball's well-known couplet used to puzzle me horribly when I was a schoolboy learning about the Peasants' Revolt of 1381. I had no idea what *dolf* meant; I couldn't see why Eve would have been spinning round in circles if she hadn't been drinking; and, since the *man* of *gentleman* has to be stressed to rhyme with *span*, I supposed it was something to do with what we'd now call gender roles. Wrong on all counts!

I wasn't all that far out with *span*, though: at least I had the right verb. It is indeed an old form of the past tense of *spin*: like *ring*, *sing*, *swim*, and *swing*, *spin* belonged to that class of Old English strong verbs with a vowel sequence *i – a – u* for the infinitive, past tense, and past participle (I *spin*, I *span*, I have *spun*). But what usually happens is that differences like these get whittled away in time by the process called analogy, so that the *a* of the past tense has been lost with *spin* and *swing*; and it's perhaps in the process of being lost with *ring* and *sing*. This gives us "I *spun*" and "I *swung*" instead of "I *span*" and "I *swang*", and (for some speakers) "I *rung*" and "I *sung*" instead of "I *rang*" and "I *sang*" (see *ring*, *rang*, *rung*). There's no problem there; my difficulty was that I'd got the wrong kind of spinning. Eve wasn't tottering around in a drunken stupour; she was spinning cloth to make clothes, because fig leaves have their limitations.

As for *dolf*, it is (as I afterwards discovered) the past tense singular of another originally strong verb, but one that has changed (one might justly say "weakened") in both form and meaning. The infinitive is *to delve*, meaning 'to dig'; and the past tense is now *delved*. The process of analogy was already under way with *dolf*. In Old English the vowel sequence for *delve* would have been e (present) – ea (past singular) – u (past plural) – o (past participle): *delfe*, *dealf*, *dulfon*, *dolfen*. Already, in the (sixteenth-century) version of the couplet I began with, the o of the past participle (*dolfen*) has displaced the ea of the past tense singular (giving us *dolf* instead of the earlier forms *dealf* or *dalf*) in the same way as the u of the past participle *spun* has now displaced the a of the past tense *span*. But analogy has since gone further with *delve* than it has with *spin*: whereas with *spin* the number of vowel changes has been reduced, with *delve* the vowel changes were first reduced and then dispensed with altogether; and *delve* has now joined the ranks of the weak verbs, forming the past tense by adding a *-d* instead of changing the vowel.

As for the meaning of *dolf* or *delved*, we use the verb today only in figurative contexts: one might *delve* into the wardrobe to find something presentable to wear, for example, or into a mystery to try to solve it; but in neither of those cases would one actually be wielding a spade, whereas Adam, of course, was doing exactly that when he was expelled from Paradise and had to grow his own crops instead of just plucking the fruit provided.

In *dolf* and *span* in the first line of the couplet, then, we have past tense forms of two originally strong verbs, both of which have changed in form since the fourteenth century, and one of which has changed in meaning, too. But as for the *gentleman* in the second line, he will have to be the subject of a separate article (see *gentle*).

DRENCH

We use the word *drench* nowadays chiefly in passive constructions such as "I'm absolutely drenched", meaning 'I'm soaked to the skin' or 'I'm wet through'.

But this is not how the word was used originally. *Drench* is in fact cognate with *drink*, of which it's a causative form: *to drench* means, literally, 'to cause to drink, to make (someone) drink (something)'. It's still used in this original sense by vets and farmers: if one of your cows gets sick and has to be given medicine orally (as opposed to having an injection, say), you'll probably end up holding the cow's mouth open while the vet shoves a bottle in and pours the medicine straight down its throat. What the two of you are doing to the animal is *drenching* it, and the drink that it's forced to swallow in this rather undignified manner is called *a drench* (noun).

From this original meaning of the verb, 'to cause to drink', there developed a slightly different sense, 'to drown', which seems to have come about through a sort of black humour: what happens when you drown is that you are forced to drink more than you can take, not only into your stomach, of course, but into your lungs. A drowned person, then, has been well and truly *drenched* in the original sense of being 'forced to drink' something; that sense then fades into the background, leaving only the new sense 'drowned'. Fans of Chaucer's Miller's tale will recognize this latter sense from the passage in which Nicholas, the Oxford student, as part of his devious plan to get together with his landlord's sexy young wife, persuades old John, the carpenter–landlord, that there's going to be a second flood to outdo Noah's flood. On hearing this devastating news, "The carpenter answerde, 'Allas, my wyf!/ And shal she drenche? Allas, myn Alisoun!'" (*CT* I 3522–3). That is, not "Oh, poor Alison! She's going to get soaked!", but "Oh, my poor wife! Must she be drowned?" What troubles the poor old boy is the fear that his beloved wife is actually going to *die* in the threatened flood.

How does the word subsequently lose the sense of death by water and come to indicate merely a thorough wetting? The obvious answer, I suppose, is that hyperbole is a fact of human nature: people who have got soaked will say, for the sake of emphasis, that they are dead from water (*drenched* or *drowned*), when it's perfectly clear that they're alive and well. However, language doesn't always work in obvious ways, and it's just as possible that the modern sense of *drenched*, that is, 'wet through', developed through a figurative use of the word. When people weep copiously, one can say, figuratively, that they're drowning in tears. That's exactly what Chaucer says about Troilus when he first falls in love with Criseyde. Like a true courtly lover, he bewails the fact that he loves this godlike creature whose little toe he isn't worthy to see, never mind to kiss, and who will never know how he feels, since he daren't tell her, except in his imagination. In his imagination he implores her to take pity on him, and to give him a friendly look to save him from the death that he will otherwise certainly die. Thus, in imagination

> He spak, and called evere in his compleynte
> Hir name, for to tellen hire his wo,
> Til neigh that he in salte teres dreynte   (*TC* 1.541–3)

   – he called on her name continually until he nearly "dreynte", that is, 'drenched', that is 'drowned', in salt tears.

Well, of course, one doesn't literally *drown* in tears; but one can get pretty wet. And it may be that tears are the roundabout route by which *drench* has lost the sense of drowning and has come to its current, weakened, sense simply of getting extremely wet.

ELEPHANTS

> Oh, my name is Tiger Lily:
> I'm a pro in Piccadilly;
> My mother is another in the Strand –
>   in the Strand;
> Oh, my father sells his arse'le
> At the Elephant and Castle:
> We're the finest fuckin' family in the land –
>   in the land.

This snatch from a low-life version of "A policeman's lot is not a happy one" from Gilbert and Sullivan's *Pirates of Penzance* came into my mind unbidden the other day as I was reading Bill Bryson's delightful book on English, *Mother Tongue*. Bryson suggests, in his chapter on names, that the common pub name *Elephant and Castle* (from which the district in London takes its name) may be a corruption of the *Infanta de Castille*. He doesn't say where he got this idea; but I don't think it's right.

Elephants are a popular subject in the medieval bestiaries, where we are told (in T.H. White's translation): "The Persians and the Indians, collected into wooden towers on them, sometimes fight each other with javelins as if from a castle" (p. 25) – and, indeed, the technical term for one of those wooden towers in which the soldiers rode on the elephant's back is a *castle*. It is this detail that the artists generally use for their illustration for the elephant in the manuscripts; and sometimes the castle is depicted as if it were built, literally, on the model of a miniature castle. I don't think there can be much doubt that this is the origin of the name *Elephant and Castle*: the pairing would have seemed as natural in the Middle Ages as horse and cart or ox and plough.

But this isn't the only interesting piece of information the bestiaries give us about elephants. They also (following Isidore's *Etymologiae* 12.2.14) offer an etymology for the word *elephant* itself, which reads (in White's translation again):

> People say that it is called an Elephant by the Greeks on account of
> its size, for it approaches the form of a mountain: you see, a mountain
> is called 'eliphio' in Greek. In the Indies, however, it is known by
> the name of 'barrus' because of its voice – whence both the voice
> is called 'baritone' and the tusks are called 'ivory' (ebur).   (p. 25)

What can one say about such etymologies, except that if they're not
right, they jolly well ought to be, because they're so ingenious?

The bestiary gives us one other detail about elephants that will bear
repeating, though it has nothing to do with words. After telling us that
they "possess vast intelligence and memory" and that they "march about
in herds", it adds that they "copulate back-to back". On this White
comments, in the loveliest footnote I have ever come across in a
scholarly work:

> The copulation of elephants was a matter for speculation in the
> dark ages, and still is, as it is rarely witnessed. Solinus quotes Pliny
> to the effect that their genitals, like those mentioned by Sir
> Thomas Browne in his note on hares, were put on backward. It
> was supposed that, being modest, they preferred to look the
> other way while they were about it. Albertus Magnus held that
> they copulated like other quadrupeds, but that, owing to the great
> weight of the husband, he either had to dig a pit for his wife to
> stand in or else he had to float himself over her in a lake, where
> his gravity would naturally be less. In fact, they copulate in the
> ordinary way and, according to Lieut.-Colonel C.H. Williams,
> more gracefully than most.   (p. 25, n. 2)

FART

Possibly the best known of all surviving Middle English lyrics is the popular cuckoo song:

> Sumer is icumen in –
> Lhude sing, cuccu!
> Groweth sed and bloweth med
> And springth the wde nu.
> Sing, cuccu!
>
> Awe bleteth after lomb,
> Lhouth after calve cu,
> Bulluc sterteth, bucke verteth.
> Murie sing, cuccu!
> Cuccu, cuccu,
> Wel singes thu, cuccu!
> Ne swik thu naver nu!
>
> Sing, cuccu, nu! Sing, cuccu!
> Sing, cuccu! Sing, cuccu, nu!

This means not (as one might suppose) 'Summer is a-coming in', but 'Spring has come': *icumen* is the past participle, not the present participle; and *sumer* in Middle English (as is clear from what follows in the poem) is used of spring, when the earth comes to life again after winter, rather than of the later, hotter, period we now call summer, when everything is already in full bloom. The poem continues: 'Seed grows and the meadow blooms and the wood shoots now. Sing, cuckoo! The ewe bleats for her lamb; the cow lows for her calf; the bullock starts (i.e., jumps or moves suddenly); the buck "verteth" (whatever that may mean); sing merrily, cuckoo! Cuckoo, cuckoo, you sing well, cuckoo! Don't ever stop now! Sing now, cuckoo! etc.'

What are we to make of the problematic word *verteth* in the line "Bulluc sterteth, bucke verteth"? Four solutions have been proposed: (1) It means 'harbours in the green', presumably from the French adjective *vert* 'green'. (2) It is from the Latin verb *vertere* 'to turn' (as in *convert, divert, revert*, etc.); the sense is parallel to that of *sterteth*; both mean 'capers, gambols, frisks, cavorts,' etc. (3) It is from the same Latin source, but the sense is 'moves to and fro'. (4) It is the native English word *farts* with the voiced initial *f-* still heard in some southern and western areas of England.

Common sense, combined with the absence of other non-native words in the poem (unless *cuccu* is taken from French rather than directly from the bird's call), has led most commentators to accept this last explanation, although Rosemary Greentree has recently made the ingenious suggestion that the poet was using the word in all of these senses simultaneously (cf. *dangerous* and *forlorn*); but that 'fart' was a possible sense was not accepted initially without a furious debate in the scholarly journals. The following extract is a fair sample of the heat generated:

> Mr Hoepfner objects that to take 'verteth' to mean 'farteth' would contradict the sense parallelism which is a distinctive feature of the lyric. Has he never seen an ass or a colt in a pasture kick up his heels and heard him at the same time discharge a resounding salute from the fundamental orifice? Is it improbable that a stag in a deer park should manifest his well-being in the same fashion? The explosion of energy in the combination of kick and crepitation is common enough among the larger four-footed beasts both in life and in literature. . . .

I suspect that my long-suffering family might well add that it's common enough among male two-footed beasts, besides, especially those of a certain age. What this example shows, however, is not how words change their meanings but what a deal of academic hot air can be generated by words that are (as the *OED* puts it) "not in decent use".

As for the noun *fart*, its earliest recorded use in the literal sense occurs in the famous answer that Nicholas provides to Absolon's request to Alison ("Spek, sweete bryd, I noot nat where thou art") in Chaucer's Miller's tale:

This Nicholas anon leet fle a fart
As greet as it had been a thonder-dent,
That with the strook he was almoost yblent.   (*CT* I 3806–7)

(That is, 'Nicholas let fly a fart as powerful as a thunderclap, so that Absalon was nearly blinded by the blow.') Somewhat to my surprise, however, I find that the figurative sense, 'a type of something worthless', is marked as obsolete in *OED*, with no quotations later than 1685, although my impression is that the phrase "I don't give a fart" is still in common use. As for its application to people, in such phrases as "He's a pompous old fart" (first recorded as recently as 1937), I'm inclined to think that this usage is not entirely figurative, since it is in the nature of people so characterized that they are given to expelling hot air from both ends.

FAST

The history of *fast* (adjective and adverb) is not unlike that of *speed* (noun and verb).

The word originally meant 'firm' or 'firmly', and is still used in that sense, especially as an adverb qualifying verbs that have to do with holding, sticking, or gripping. I well remember riding on the haycart in days long past when we had an old Fordson tractor powered by what I would call *paraffin*, which is generally in Australia called *kerosene* (or, of course, just *kero*), but which, in its specifically agricultural application, used then to be called *TVO* or *Tractor Vaporizing Oil*. This tractor was an extremely noisy beast, and when the driver was going to move it from one pile of bales (where it had been stationary) to the next, he used to turn around and shout at the top of his voice to the cluster of children riding on the cart behind it, "Owd faaaast!", that is, 'Hold fast', i.e., hold on tightly or firmly.

This is much the same sense as in Shylock's proverb, "Fast bind, fast find" (*The Merchant of Venice*, 2.5.53), that is, if you lock something up securely, you'll find it safely where you left it (or so he hoped). It's also, of course, the sense in which it's used in the phrase *fast asleep*, meaning firmly or deeply asleep. As all cricket-loving South Australians know (and a good many Lancastrians besides), the former Australian leg-spinner, Peter Sleep, is nicknamed *Sounda* (short for *sound asleep*): he might equally have been nicknamed *Fasta* (short for *fast asleep*), which would have been a nice pun, because, of course, he's a slow bowler, not a fast one. Dylan Thomas makes the same pun at the opening of *Under Milk Wood*, when First Voice says to the audience, "all the people of the lulled and dumbfound town are sleeping now. . . . Only your eyes are unclosed, to see the black and folded town fast, and slow, asleep" (p. 1).

How did an adverb that was used in contexts implying *lack of motion* come to be used in contexts implying *swiftness of motion*? – Because the root meaning, 'firmly', tends to be used as a mere intensifier of whatever verb it accompanies. The merchant in Chaucer's Shipman's tale, for example, shuts his door "faste" ('securely') when he wants to count his money (*CT* VII 85); the guests at the wedding feast of January and May in the Merchant's tale drink "faste", that is, 'copiously' (*CT* IV 1769) – but one can see how this sort of context may also imply 'swiftly' (if you drink a lot, the chances are you drink it quickly – and, besides, January was in a hurry to get to bed); the combatants in the Knight's tale are urged to "ley on faste", that is, to 'attack furiously' (*CT* I 2558) – but again, one can see how swiftness comes to be assumed; the murderer of the young King Kenelm "bigan to delve faste", that is, 'dug vigorously' to make a grave, and buried the boy's body there "faste inou", 'very safely', or so he hoped (*Saint Kenelm* lines 117–19) – but one can bet he was in a hurry, too; and when the verb qualified is the verb *to run*, the qualifying adverb, *fast* or 'firmly', obviously has to mean 'quickly'.

When *fast* is used as an adverb there's never much of a problem because, as these examples show, the governing sense is that of the verb, and *fast* merely intensifies that sense, whatever it may be. But when it's used as an adjective, one can never quite predict which of the two surviving senses it's going to have ('firmly fixed' or 'swiftly moving'): *fast friends* are loyal friends, and *fast colours* don't run; if you're *bedfast* you're stuck in bed yourself, but if you're a *fast worker* you specialize in getting other people into bed; and it's probably fair to say that the society we live in encourages us all to pull the odd *fast one* to make a *fast buck*.

FORLORN

We tend to think of *forlorn* as a sympathetic word: we imply, when we use it, that we are affected by the suffering of the person we're describing, who is miserable or lonely or in a hopeless situation (or all three). Yet only a few hundred years ago it was (or could be) more or less a term of abuse: when the annal for the year 1137 in the *Peterborough Chronicle* says that the robber barons of King Stephen's reign were "al forcursede and forsuoren and forloren", the chronicler wasn't expressing any sympathy for them; he was saying that they were 'accursed' (in the technical sense that they had been excommunicated), and 'perjured' (because they had broken their oaths of allegiance to the king), and 'disgraced' or 'damned'. The prefix *for-* in the case of "forsuoren" has a negative or reversing effect: *to forswear* is 'to swear falsely'; *to be forsworn* is 'to have sworn falsely', hence 'to have perjured oneself'. In the other two cases *for-* has an intensifying effect: *to be forcursed* is 'to be cursed in the strongest possible terms', hence 'to be excommunicated'; *to be forloren* (since *loren* is the past participle of *lesen*, from OE *lēosan*, the ancestor of MnE *lose*) is 'to be utterly lost', hence, in a deeply religious society, 'to be eternally lost from God', that is, 'damned'.

But 'damned' was a specialized sense, more or less restricted to the passive; in the active voice the verb retained the general sense 'to lose completely'. This could be a positive when the thing that was lost was undesirable, as when the eagle in the *Middle English Physiologus* wants to straighten its twisted beak: it strikes its beak against a stone "til his bec biforn/ Haveth the wrengthe forloren" (58–9), that is, 'until its beak, in front, has completely lost its "wrengthe" ' (i.e., its 'wrongness', its 'crookedness'). More often, however, what is lost is desirable, and the loss is negative. Thus, when Criseyde has deserted him, Chaucer's Troilus is like a "man that hath his joies ek forlore" (*TC* 5.23); when Hypermnestra's father (in the *Legend of Good Women*) orders her to kill her husband on their wedding night, she "hath nygh hire wit forloren" (2663); and when Aurelius (in the Franklin's tale) spends all his money in his fruitless pursuit of Dorigen, we are told that he "his cost hath al forlorn" (*CT* V 1557).

Sadness would be a likely concomitant of losses such as these – of one's joys, or one's sanity, or one's money. When one considers, besides, that another common meaning of ME *forlesen* was 'to desert or abandon', it's not hard to see how the participial adjective *forlorn* has acquired its current complex of senses, neatly summed up in *A Shakespeare Glossary* as 'abandoned, forsaken, desolate, (hence) unhappy, wretched'.

But we may well wonder what Keats meant by "forlorn" when, in his 'Ode to a Nightingale', he wrote that the bird's song that held him entranced was

> Perhaps the self-same song that found a path
> Through the sad heart of Ruth, when, sick for home,
> She stood in tears amid the alien corn;
> The same that oft-times hath
> Charm'd magic casements, opening on the foam
> Of perilous seas, in faery lands forlorn.
>
> Forlorn! the very word is like a bell
> To toll me back from thee to my sole self!   (65–72)

It looks as if in the second of these two instances (the first word of the final stanza) the word has its usual sense 'unhappy'. Keats's own comment here bears out Pope's well-known dictum that "The sound must seem an echo to the sense": it's surely the long vowel sound of the second syllable, "-lorn", that tolls like a bell, bringing Keats back from his dream or vision to the realization that the imagination is not as powerful as people have claimed, since it cannot in reality make him one with the nightingale; and it's this realization that makes him sad, or, indeed, *forlorn*.

And yet I don't think that's what the word means in the first of the two instances in the poem: those "faery lands" may be charmed, but they're hardly miserable. What they are is cut off from the rest of the world, or lost to it. What Keats is doing, in the manner of all the best poets, is getting the maximum semantic mileage out of the word by calling to mind its etymological sense side by side with its current one.

FUN AND GLEE

The word *glee* has two senses surviving in current English: the general sense of happiness or delight, and the special musical sense in which it is used of a particular kind of song. Neither of these is original; but neither is far removed from the original.

The earliest sense recorded in *OED* is 'entertainment, play, sport'; and the word is much used in Middle English literature in phrases such as *maken glee* 'to enjoy oneself' and the somewhat tautologous *game and glee* 'pleasure and entertainment'. When Sir Thopas commands his merry men "To make hym bothe game and glee" (*CT* VII 840), he's asking them to entertain him so as to take his mind off the battle he has to fight the next day against the three-headed giant (and Chaucer is perhaps taking the mickey out of the alliterative poets who were so fond of this stock phrase, *game and glee*).

The nearest modern equivalent in this sense is probably the word *fun*; and *glee* was used in Middle English in idioms similar to those in which *fun* is used today. To *make glee* and to *have fun* are to enjoy oneself; but to *make fun of* or to *make glee of* others is to have fun at their expense. (This mocking sense is the earliest one in which *fun* is used: lexicographers think the noun comes from the verb *fon* 'to make a fool of', of which *fond* is the past participle: to be *fond* of something is, originally, to be foolish about it. And perhaps there's an element of this mocking sense lurking in the current use of *glee*: it's defined in *Collins*, for example, as 'great merriment or delight, often caused by someone else's misfortune'.) And just as we say today that an unpleasant experience is *no fun*, in Middle English they said it was *no glee*: that is precisely what the poet of *Arthour and Merlin* says at a moment when Arthur is under heavy attack: "Thai . . . With four launces smiten Arthour/ Al at ones, that was no glewe" (3291, quoted in *MED*).

Curiously this general sense of *glee* very nearly died out after the Middle Ages: Johnson records it in his dictionary in 1755, defining it as 'joy; merriment; gayety', but he remarks that "It is not now used except in ludicrous writing or with some mixture of irony and contempt"; but it has certainly made a come-back, perhaps assisted by its compounds *gleeful* and *gleesome*.

As for the current musical sense, what we have here is a double specialization. The first step is the use of *glee* to mean not just entertainment in general but specifically musical entertainment; and that sense is recorded in *OED* even before the Norman Conquest. To *make glee* in this sense is simply to play music, and an entertainer who did so was called a *gleeman*. But then we get a second specialization, in which the word comes to denote not any old music but music of one particular kind, specifically (as the *OED* defines it with great precision) music 'for three or more voices (one voice to each part), set to words of any character, grave or gay, often consisting of two or more contrasting movements, and (in strict use) without accompaniment'.

But the musical sense is not the only specialized sense of this word. It can also be used euphemistically (like *mirth*), in compounds such as *chamber glee*, to mean sexual intercourse (literally 'bedroom pleasure'), as in Henryson's Fable of the Cock and the Fox, when one of the hens, seeing the cock carried off by the fox, says (roughly speaking): Good riddance! He wasn't up to much anyway –

> Off chalmerglew . . . full well ye knaw
> Waistit he wes, off nature cauld and dry.

He may have been hot stuff once (both literally and figuratively), but now he's dried up and cold.

GENTLE, GENTILE, GENTEEL, AND JAUNTY

"When Adam dolf and Eve span", I asked in an earlier piece (see *delve*), "Who was then the gentleman?" The meaning of this couplet would be clearer to us today if the later forms of the verbs I discussed were used: this would give us "When Adam delved and Eve spun/ Who was then the gentlemun?" We'd probably recognize that *delved* is used here of digging with a spade as opposed to digging figuratively; and if *gentleman* is to rhyme with *spun*, the stress will be put on the first element, *gentle*, with the *a* of *man* reduced to the neutral vowel, schwa – the vowel heard as the first sound in *abroad* and *about* (represented in phonetic script by an upside down *e*, but which I've spelled here, for convenience, with a *u*). Faced with this evidence, we'd probably realize that the question is not about which of the pair wore the trousers, because in this context the *man* in *gentleman* means 'person', not 'male': the interest is not in *gender*, but in *gentility*: the sense is, 'When the whole of the world's population had to work to survive, where were those people whose inherited wealth freed them from having to earn their living?' The implied answer, of course, is "There weren't any." This is why the rhyme was such a powerful slogan in the Peasants' Revolt of 1381: it's a reminder that all humans are born equal, that no one has an inborn right to a higher position than others.

Gentility was a hot topic in the Middle Ages. Etymologically it was a matter of birth: the earliest meaning of *gentle* in English is 'high-born, of noble birth', from Old French *gentil*, which is itself from Latin *gentīlis*, literally 'belonging to the [same] family' (from *gens*, *gentis*, 'race or family'). But, as the old hag in the Wife of Bath's tale argues, in the famous pillow lecture to the young knight she's sharing a bed with, and who is too unchivalrous to make love to her (because of her age, her ugliness, and her low birth),

> ... for ye speken of swich gentillesse
> As is descended out of old richesse,
> That therfore sholden ye be gentil men,

> Swich arrogance is nat worth an hen.
> Looke who that is moost vertuous alway,
> Pryvee and apert, and most entendeth ay
> To do the gentil dedes that he kan;
> Taak hym for the grettest gentil man.   (*CT* III 1109–16)

That is, roughly speaking (and to summarize a bit), 'Stuff your noble ancestry: we're judged by our actions, not our birth. Whoever behaves most nobly (or gently) is considered the noblest (most gentle) person.'

Thus *gentle* came to be applied to noble conduct, irrespective of the social standing of the person whose conduct was so characterized; and in time, by a logical progression, it acquired the current sense, 'mild, benign, unaggressive'. *Gentile*, in contrast, though also from OF *gentil*, has stayed closer to the original sense of Latin *gentīlis* 'belonging to the [same] family'; but it's used, curiously, of those who do not belong to the family in question, hence its biblical use for people who are not Jewish and its use by Mormons to designate non-Mormons.

Two other words derived from OF *gentil*, in both of which the French origin is still apparent in the pronunciation (though not, in the second instance, in the spelling), are *genteel* and *jaunty*. These were originally synonymous, both of them suggesting the kind of style expected of people of high birth or high social station. But whereas *jaunty* has become something of a purr-word, progressing from 'stylish' to 'sprightly' or 'carefree', *genteel* has come to suggest behaviour that attempts to be stylish and succeeds only in being affected. Unpredictable? That's language!

GIN AND ENGINES

When I was a small boy I used to be very puzzled as to why the ferocious iron-toothed traps (known as *gin-traps*) that were in common use in those days for catching foxes and other vermin had the same name as the *gin* my parents occasionally drank (they preferred rum – especially Barbados rum – when they could get it, but that's another story). Did foxes like gin, I wondered, and how were the traps baited with it? Needless to say, I was barking up the wrong tree. The *gin* we drink is named ultimately (via Old French *genevre*, of which it's an abbreviated form) after the *juniper* berries with which it's flavoured; it is not related to the *gin* in *gin-trap*, which is the same as the second syllable of *engine*: this *gin* and *engine* are both from Old French *engin*, and *gin* is what is called an aphetic form, that is, a form that has come about through the loss of an initial unstressed syllable. (None of these words has any connection with the Australian Aboriginal kind of *gin*, which is an anglicized pronunciation of *diyin*, the word for 'a woman' in the Dharuk language from the Port Jackson area of Sydney.)

Well, what has an *engine* to do with a *gin-trap*? The connecting link is the *ingenuity* with which they're made: the ultimate origin of these three words, as indeed of the adjectives *ingenuous* and *ingenious*, is the Latin noun *ingenium* 'that which is inborn', hence 'native wit, skill, or ability', hence also 'that which requires skill in the making', hence 'a device or contraption', hence, eventually, 'a trap'.

In the Middle English poem *The Fox and the Wolf*, the word *gin* is used – most confusingly for beginners – in almost all of these senses in different lines. Early in the poem the fox raids the hen-house and devours several hens. Then, overcome with thirst, he goes in search of water. He comes upon a well in the farmyard, with two buckets on a rope attached to a pulley: when the empty bucket is lowered down the well to be filled, the full bucket is pulled up. The fox, we are told, "ne hounderstod nout of the ginne" (line 77); that's to say, he 'understood nothing of the contraption'. (I know just how he felt: that's exactly how I feel when I open the bonnet of a car to look at – yes – the *engine*, or when I take the lid off a cistern in a vain attempt to make the ball-cock behave.) Well, the fox jumps into the empty bucket, which descends to the bottom of the well. The poet comments:

> To late the vox wes bithout
> Tho he wes in the ginne ibrout
> ....
> Adoun he moste, he wes therinne –
> Ikaut he wes mid swikele ginne;   (lines 82–6)

that is, 'Too late the fox took thought after he had fallen into the trap. . . . he had to go down, he was in it – he was caught with a treacherous contrivance'. But his *ingenuity* did not desert him: when his cousin, the wolf, came to the well some time later, the fox "thoute mid somne ginne/ Himself houpbringe, thene wolf therinne" (lines 125–6), i.e., he 'thought how, with some stratagem [some *ingenious* idea], to bring himself up, and to bring the wolf in there [into the well in his place]'.

We've more or less lost the word *gin* now, except in specialized senses such as that of the *gin-trap* I began with, and a *cotton gin*, which is an *ingenious* device for separating the cotton from its seeds. We still have *engines*, of course, but we tend to think of them as things powered by a motor, whereas Shakespeare and Milton were still using the word in the various senses in which both it and its aphetic form had been used in Middle English. When Othello bids farewell to

> Pride, pomp, and circumstance of glorious war!
> And O, you mortal engines whose rude throats
> Th'immortal Jove's dread clamours counterfeit,   (3.3.359–63)

the contrivances he's talking about are pretty clearly cannons. When Lear upbraids himself for casting off Cordelia –

> O most small fault,
> How ugly didst thou in Cordelia show,
> Which, like an engine, wrenched my frame of nature
> From the fixed place, drew from my heart all love,
> And added to the gall!   (1.4.245–9)

– the engine in question is evidently some instrument of torture. And when Milton tells us in *Paradise Lost* that though Satan had hoped

> To have built in Heav'n high Towr's; [he did not] scape
> By all his Engines, but was headlong sent
> With his industrious crew to build in hell,   (1.750)

he must be using *engines* to mean 'wiles'. (And, yes, that's an aphetic form of *escape* in the first line of the quotation.)

As for the famous "two-handed engine" that stands ready to smite the corrupt clergy in Milton's *Lycidas* (line 130), no one knows what it is, though more than forty guesses have been made. Here's one case, perhaps, where the poet was too *ingenious* for his readers.

GLOTTAL STOPS

This item, for a change, is about phonetics rather than semantics. To explain what's meant by a *glottal stop*, I must first explain what a *stop* is.

Spoken language is produced by expelling air from the lungs and modifying or shaping that air in a variety of possible ways as it escapes from the body. One thing we can do is to stop the air momentarily before letting it out. Take the word *bun*, for example. When you pronounce the initial /b/ you put your lips together and, for a split second, you completely block off the passage of air – you stop it – so that, when you open your lips and release the air it comes out with a mini-explosion: /b/. This is what is called a *stop*, or, by some writers, because of that little explosion, a *plosive*. If you want to classify it further, you call it a *bilabial* stop, because the stoppage is caused by the two lips.

But if you say *fun* instead of *bun*, there's no complete stoppage before the air escapes on the sound of the initial /f/: you partially block the passage of air by putting your top teeth on your bottom lip and making the air escape around the teeth, but you don't at any point completely stop the air escaping. The /f/ sound is called a *spirant* or a *fricative* as opposed to a stop, and if you want to classify it further you call it a *labio-dental* spirant, because the impediment is caused by the lips and the teeth.

But let's get back to stops. The stoppage can be made at a variety of different points in the vocal apparatus. In *bun* the /b/ is made, as we've seen, with the two lips. In *but* the final /t/ sound is another stop, made this time by putting the tongue against the hard ridge behind the upper teeth called the alveolar ridge: this, then, is an *alveolar* stop. In *cut* the initial /k/ is made by putting part of the tongue up against the soft part of the mouth behind the palate called the velum: this is a *velar* stop. Now if you go still further back in the mouth, you get to a part called the glottis: this is the opening at the top of the windpipe, between the vocal cords, which is covered when we swallow by that flappy piece of cartilage at the back of the throat called the epiglottis.

Some languages produce a consonantal sound by stopping the flow of air momentarily back there, at the glottis: the sound produced is called a *glottal* stop. (It's normally represented in phonetic script by a symbol like a question mark without the dot; but I use the symbol # to represent it here.) This sound doesn't exist in RP (the 'Received Pronunciation' of standard British English), but it is there in certain other dialects of English, most notably cockney, whence it's been imported into the speech of some Australians. A pot of tea is, to a cockney, a "po# of tea": the glottal stop is the sound you get instead of the /t/ of tea. As George Turner used to say, in his lectures on phonetics: "What does a cockney take to bed on a cold night?" Answer: "An o# wa#er bo#l", thus demonstrating three glottal stops in a row: the "uh" sound you get instead of the /t/ in all three of those words is a glottal stop.

I can add a couple of nice examples from my own experience. Years ago, when I was doing a Dip. Ed. in teaching English as a Second Language, the phonetics lecturer announced rashly: "There is no glottal stop in English." (He meant, of course, "in RP"; but that's not what he said.) The bloke I was sitting next to was a cockney: he leapt to his feet and shouted out in high dudgeon: "Wha# abou# bu#er?" On the other occasion I was on study leave in England and had gone to watch my elder daughter playing in a hockey match. Early in the game someone in the home team missed a sitting goal, which drew from one of the other girls in the team the furious comment, "Wha# a fuck-up!" One of the other spectators (undoubtedly a member of the chardonnay set) was moved to exclaim, "Oh, really: what *frightful* language!" To which, had I had the courage, I would have replied, "Rubbish! What lovely language! That's one of the clearest glo#l stops I've ever heard."

But I'm not sure that these experiences compare with this delightful story passed on to me by my friend Malcolm Mitchell (a version of which I've since found also in Tom McArthur's *Living Words* – it's evidently a popular story amongst the Scots).

A schoolteacher in Glasgow was trying to cure one his pupils of glottal stops.

"The worrd is *butter*, Willie."

"Bu#er, Sir?"

"No, Willie: bu-TT-er."

"Bu-#-er, Sir?"

"No, Willie: T-T-T: bu-TT-er."

"Bu-TT-er, Sir?"

Great smile. "Ay, Willie: tha#'s be#er!"

GOSSIP

When we use the word *gossip* nowadays, we mean 'idle talk' (often, but not exclusively, of a scandal-mongering kind), or 'a person given to idle talk', generally (but not necessarily) a woman: the kind of person and the kind of talk Dylan Thomas satirizes with such glee in *Under Milk Wood*:

> Can't hear what the women are gabbing round the pump. Same as ever. Who's having a baby, who blacked whose eye, seen Polly Garter giving her belly an airing, there should be a law, seen Mrs Beynon's new mauve jumper it's her old grey jumper dyed, who's dead, who's dying, there's a lovely day, oh the cost of soapflakes! (p. 31)

These modern uses show a sad descent from the word's original meaning. Etymologically *gossip* consists of *God* + *sibb* 'blood relative' (a word that's probably better known now in its diminutive form *sibling* 'brother or sister'): your *God-sib* or 'God-relative' was your godparent. This sense is found in Anglo-Saxon times in the famous *Sermo Lupi ad Anglos*, a sermon preached by Wulfstan, Archbishop of York, during the Viking invasions in the time of King Ethelred the Unready or the Redeless (see *read and rede*), in which Wulfstan laments that "godsibbas and godbearn" ('godparents and godbairns', i.e., 'godchildren') are being "forspilde" (i.e., 'utterly destroyed' or 'killed left, right and centre' – see *spill*) by the invading heathens as God's punishment for the moral degeneracy of the English. (The loss of the final *d* of *God* before the *s* of *sibb* is paralleled in *gospel*, originally *gōd-spell*, 'good news'.)

In time, through generalization, *gossip* came to denote also the godparent of one of your children, or your fellow godparent. But since the people you choose to be the godparents of your children are usually your closest friends or your own siblings, the word came, by a natural enough extension, to mean a favourite relative or close friend. When the wolf in the Middle English poem *The Fox and the Wolf* wants to ingratiate himself with the fox, he addresses him as "gossip", i.e., 'dear friend' (lines

209, 220, 243): the tone is almost that of a child saying "pretty please". What's happened here is that the *God* part of the relationship has been pushed into the background and the friendship has come to the fore. Thus *gossip* came to denote your closest friend, your bosom pal, your confidant – the person to whom you told your most intimate secrets; and by extension it came to include the secrets themselves: the juicy things you told your *gossip* constituted the *gossip* that passed between you.

These ideas are both memorably illustrated by Chaucer's garrulous Wife of Bath, in a passage describing how she met her fifth-husband-to-be when he was a student at Oxford lodging with her best friend, Alison, at a time when she herself was still married to husband number four:

> My fifthe housbonde – God his soule blesse! –
> Which that I took for love, and no richesse,
> He som tyme was a clerk of Oxenford,
> And hadde left scole, and went at hom to bord
> With my gossib, dwellynge in oure toun;
> God have hir soule! Hir name was Alisoun.
> She knew mine herte, and eek my privetee,
> Bet than oure parisshe preest, so moot I thee!
> To hire biwreyed I my conseil al.
> For hadde myn housbonde pissed on a wal,
> Or doon a thyng that sholde han cost his lyf,
> To hire, and to another worthy wyf,
> And to my nece, which that I loved weel,
> I wolde han toold his conseil every deel.
> And so I dide ful often, God it woot,
> That made his face often reed and hoot
> For verray shame, and blamed hymself for he
> Had toold to me so greet a pryvetee.   (*CT* III 525–42)

Here we see how the closeness between the Wife of Bath, her "gossib", Alison, and a couple of other friends is such that she tells them all the most private details of her marital life, including such scandalous titbits as whether (or when) her husband had pissed against the wall. Urinating in public, one must remember is – or was, at any rate (I don't know if it still is) – an offence punishable by law, as readers of Hardy's *The Mayor of*

Casterbridge will well remember. No wonder her husband blushed and kicked himself for having told her such secrets in the first place!

This extract also suggests how naturally (by functional shift) the noun *gossip* came in time to be used also as a verb (as it still is): what the Wife of Bath is doing when she relays *gossip* to her *gossips* is, of course, *gossiping*.

HAPAX LEGOMENA

A *hapax legomenon* or a *hapax* for short (plural *hapax legomena*, like *phenomenon/phenomena*) is a word or form of which only one recorded instance is known – excluding, of course, references to that occurrence in dictionaries or commentaries. The words are a direct transliteration of a Greek phrase, meaning literally 'once said' or 'said only once'. Creative writers tend to be great users of *hapaxes* – some of Dylan Thomas's wonderfully inventive functional shifts in *Under Milk Wood* spring instantly to mind: "Gossamer Beynon *high-heels* out of school" (p. 45); Mrs Organ Morgan "bursts into tears, and, in the middle of her salty howling, nimbly spears a small flat fish and *pelicans* it whole" (p. 48); "Young girls lie bedded soft or glide in their dreams, with rings and trousseaux, *bridesmaided* by glow-worms down the aisles of the *organplaying* wood" (p. 1).

Instances like these are so good that they're not likely to remain hapaxes for long, because other people will pounce on them and use them, and so, like Macbeth's famous use of *incarnadine* as a verb –

> Will all great Neptune's ocean wash this blood
> Clean from my hand? No, this my hand will rather
> The multitudinous seas incarnadine,
> Making the green one red   (2.2.58–61)

– they will pass into general currency; and why not? But most examples found in the works of authors of former ages are likely to remain hapaxes, because, however apt they may be, they've had their chance to pass into common currency, and evidently they've lost it. I've come across quite a few of these in *Sidrak and Bokkus*. Some of them are forgettable, but a small number are sufficiently striking that I wonder why they weren't in general use or why they didn't pass into it.

How about *drearfully*, for example, as an emphatic alternative to *drearily*? Here it is, describing King Bokkus as he sits contemplating the ruins of the tower he is trying to have built, but which collapses every night, no matter what precautions he takes: "The kyng sate full drerefully/ For he ne wyst what to done" (B178–9P). Or *becleave* as a transitive verb with the sense 'cleave to' or 'cling to' (along the lines of *bemoan* 'moan about')? Sidrak gives us a dire warning about the individual soul's responsibility, in the next life, for the sins committed during this one: "What he did, evell or well,/ Shall becleve hymself eche deell" (B6121–2), i.e., 'every single thing one does, good or bad, will stick to one'. Would you like a one-word compound meaning 'grain of earth' or 'grain of sand'? Sidrak gives us *earth-grit* (along the lines of *coffee-grounds*): "Might erthe greete tolde be/ Or water dropes of the see?" (B5237–8), that is, 'Is it possible to count the [individual] grains of sand [on earth] or the drops of water in the sea?' Still on the topic of water and land, there is also *flood-gang* meaning 'movement or path of floodwater' (the second element is *gang* in the old sense of 'road or passage' that survives in *gangway*):

> The course of that flodegange
> In his comynge was so stronge
> That there it neshe grounde fande
> Hit frette awey erthe ande sonde, (B4549–52T)

that is, 'The movement of the floodwater was so violent that wherever it found soft ground it ate away both earth and sand.' And if you don't like coarse terms for sexual intercourse, you could try reviving *gether-coming*, i.e., 'a coming-together', which occurs in a curious passage describing the supposed effect on a child's appearance and character of the parents' mood at the time of its conception: "Yif [they] at here geder comyng/ Be glad and blithe in all thyng,/ Of glad sembelant the childe shall be" (B2473–5). So, be warned: if you don't want ugly, bad-tempered children, don't make love when you're in a bad mood.

It's quite possible that some of these examples are hapaxes by chance – that they were in fact in common use, but don't happen to survive more than once in the written records. But in the last instance I suspect we have a genuine once-off coining, because the scribe of this particular manuscript was a bit coy when it came to sexual matters. Elsewhere, for example, in a passage that gives advice on how to maintain a healthy lifestyle – don't eat too much, don't drink too much, don't sleep too long, and don't have sex more than once a week – where most of the other manuscripts use the coarse word *swive* (which is roughly equivalent to current English *stuff* or *screw*) for this last piece of advice, the scribe of this manuscript writes *chambir mirthe*, that is, 'bedroom pleasure' (B6528; see *mirth*). That, for me, is the daddy of all hapaxes.

HEAD

Most of the words discussed in this book show a logical development in which one can readily see how one sense leads to another, that one to the next, and so on, in a regular series like links in a chain. This kind of development is generally called *concatenation*, i.e., 'chain-linking', and the *OED* makes a point of arranging the different senses of each word as far as possible in such an order as to make the links in the chain self-evident. In doing so it is following the lead of the great lexicographer, Samuel Johnson, who said, in the introduction to his own famous dictionary published in 1755:

> In every word of extensive use, it was requisite to mark the progress of its meaning, and show by what gradations of intermediate sense it has passed from its primitive to its remote and accidental signification; so that every foregoing explanation should tend to that which follows, and the series be regularly concatenated from the first notion to the last.

There is, however, a different kind of sense development, a sort of sideways rather than forwards development (hence the name *lateralization* that some linguistic commentators give it, though *semantic transfer* is probably the more usual term). In this kind of development, many different senses are independently developed from the root meaning: each sense has its own direct link to the original sense rather than an indirect link via some other secondary sense. In pictorial terms one could describe this kind of development as *radiation*, with the word's root meaning positioned like a sun in the centre, with a shower of different senses coming out from it at different angles, like the rays of the sun.

The word *head* (as Simeon Potter points out) is a good example of this kind of development, showing many simultaneous figurative uses of the word in different senses. The head of a hammer or of a nail, for example, is so called because it resembles a head in shape; the head of the page, the table, the bed, and the stairs occupy the same position as the head does on the body; the head of the school, the department, or the state, is head in the sense of 'chief'; similarly a head (or heading) in an argument is one of its chief subdivisions; the head on a coin is a picture of someone's actual head; geographically a head is a promontory that sticks out at the end of a narrow neck of land, as in Beachy Head (UK), Buckle Head (WA), or Indented Head (Victoria); and in phrases like "a hundred head of cattle" or "the cost was $10 a head", we're employing a figure of speech called *synecdoche*, in which a part of a thing (in this case its head) stands for the whole thing.

This all sounds perfectly straightforward, but the last time I used this example in a lecture I discovered to my total confusion that it had hidden dangers. No sooner had I finished my explanation than a voice called out loud and clear from somewhere towards the back of the lecture theatre, "What about *the heads* on a ship?"; to which (before I could confess my ignorance) another voice replied, from the other side of the room, "And what about *giving someone head*?"

The last of these is not to be found in *OED*, but I don't suppose it needs any explanation; as for the first, there's a dispute about it. My informant told me, after the lecture, that it was a jocular usage: *the heads* are the ship's latrines, and he suggested that they were called *heads* as a joke, since the sailors address them with their rear ends, not their front ends (except, of course, when they're seasick). Well, that's a nice idea, but the *OED*'s less colourful explanation (sense 21) is perhaps more likely: it points out that the latrines were originally situated in the bows of the ship, and that the bows, being the front end, are sometimes called the *head*, whence the name of the latrines.

HOONS, LOUTS, YOBS, AND BLUDGERS

When the tyres of our car squealed on the hot road surface as I went round a roundabout one summer, my younger daughter, Sarah, who had recently passed her driving test, cried out from the passenger's seat with censorious glee, "Hoon!" I took this to be a teasing comment to the effect that I was driving like a yobbo; and that's pretty much what the *New Shorter Oxford* said, when I checked it. (As our elder daughter, Bec, always used to say, "It's no good arguing with *him*: if he thinks he's losing, he gets out the *OED* to prove you're using the words wrongly!" Spare a thought for our daughters, gentle reader: they have two English teachers for parents: every time one of *them* opened her mouth to speak when they were growing up, one of *us* would jump down her throat. No wonder they took to speaking in foreign tongues!)

But what the *New Shorter Oxford* did not tell me was the origin of this curious word *hoon*: it said it was a mid 20th-century Australianism; it gave a nice economic definition covering both the verb and the noun, '(Behave like) a lout or idiot', but as for the etymology, it said only that the origin was unknown. That's an opinion shared by every other dictionary I have looked in, not one of which can say where the word comes from. As for the meaning, there is general agreement in the Australian dictionaries that the word is used as an insult and that it implies exhibitionism of a foolish or loutish kind; but there's an added sense in the Australian dictionaries, not found in the *Oxford*: 'a procurer of prostitutes'. What I've been unable to work out from the dictionaries (since the order in which the definitions are listed varies) is which sense came first: the procuring of prostitutes or the loutish behaviour.

If the dated quotations given in the *Australian National Dictionary* and Wilkes's *Dictionary of Australian Colloquialisms* present a true reflection of the semantic development, the sense 'lout' must have preceded the sense 'pimp', since there's no suggestion of prostitution in the earliest quotation (from Xavier Herbert's *Capricornia*, 1938). But if that's so, the development is just the reverse of that in the word *bludger*. There's no mystery about the origin of this word: it's a shortening of *bludgeoner* 'a person who is armed with or uses a bludgeon'; the short form *bludger* came into use in Australia in the late eighteenth century in the specialized sense 'one who lives off the earnings of a prostitute' (the implication being, I suppose, that the workers had to be driven to their work with a *bludgeon*, or were beaten with one if they didn't earn enough); from there, through the normal process of generalization, it came to be applied (as the earliest quotation for sense 2 in the *Australian National Dictionary* puts it) to 'any person who takes profit without risk or disability or without effort or work', or, indeed, to any person or thing the speaker considers worthless. Eventually, (through re-specialization) we come to the modern *dole bludger*, who lives on unemployment benefit and (so those who use the term imply) makes no effort to find a job; and thus (through back formation) to the verb to *bludge*.

As for *louts* and *yobs*, they have no connection with prostitution at all – at least, no etymological connection. *Lout* appears to be derived from either of two related verbs in Old English, *lūtan* 'to bend, bow or stoop' (hence someone of low social station) or *lūtian* 'to lurk, skulk, or sneak' (hence someone not to be trusted); a *yob* is merely a *boy* spelled backwards (back slang, as it's called), and used contemptuously.

KNIGHT AND KNAVE

These alliterating nouns are much loved by historians of the language since they demonstrate so neatly two opposite kinds of specialization. In Old English the words were synonymous: both meant 'male child, boy, or youth'; neither carried approving or disapproving connotations. Each independently developed the specialized sense 'boy or youth employed as a servant', but thereafter they developed in opposite directions: *knight* acquired favourable senses through the process known as *amelioration* (from Latin *melior* 'better'); *knave* acquired unfavourable senses through the process known either as *pejoration* (Latin *peior* 'worse') or as *degeneration*. Thus (to borrow Brook's terms) *knight* has developed into a *purr-word*, *knave* into a *snarl-word*.

Knight appears to have become further specialized early on as a word for someone giving military service. It then lost some of its youthful connotations (which were taken over by the word *squire*) and came to denote a man who was particularly good at military service, as a result of which he was raised by his lord to noble rank, awarded a coat of arms, and entitled to be styled "Sir". At about this time the word began to acquire the chivalric connotations associated with medieval knighthood: the skill in combat on horseback, the championing of women, the loyalty to one's lord and one's fellow-knights, the truth to one's word, the undertaking to fight only in a just cause: all those qualities summed up in the annual Pentecostal oath taken by the knights of the Round Table in Malory's *Morte D'Arthur* –

> never to do outrageousity nor murder, and always to flee treason; also by no mean to be cruel, but to give mercy unto him that asketh mercy, . . . and always to do ladies, damosels, and gentlewomen succour. . . . Also that no man take no battles in a wrongful quarrel for no law, ne for no world's goods.   (3.15)

Thus to this day, figuratively, *a knight in shining armour* is a man who defends the underprivileged, especially women.

But at the same time as the word acquired these specialized chivalric senses, another branch kept the emphasis on the rank awarded as a mark of good service generally, irrespective of what kind of service that might have been. Thus we have our sporting knights (Sir Donald Bradman, Sir Garfield Sobers, Sir Stanley Matthews, Sir Clive Woodward), our knights of the arts (Sir Laurence Olivier, Sir Neville Marriner, Sir Robert Helpmann), our political knights (Sir Winston Churchill, Sir Robert Menzies, Sir Joh Bjelke-Petersen), and even our knights of pop music (Sir Cliff Richard, Sir Paul McCartney, Sir Mick Jagger).

But whereas with *knight* the early emphasis was on the kind of service offered (i.e., military), with *knave* the emphasis fell instead on the status of the servant, which was low: thus the word developed the sense 'a person of low status, a menial'. Human nature being what it is, however, and the upper classes tending to be snobbish, the word soon acquired moral overtones to match its social ones: it is a small step down then from 'a menial' to (in *OED*'s somewhat archaic wording, which nevertheless exactly captures the tone of the judgemental attitude that gives rise to this sense) 'an unprincipled man, given to dishonourable and deceitful practices; a base and crafty rogue'.

My impression is that *knave* is not much in use nowadays, except amongst card-players, as the name for the lowest of the court cards; and even there I'd say it has largely been replaced by *jack* (which, *OED* tells us, was originally specifically the knave of trumps in the game of all-fours, before becoming generalized as a term for any of the knaves).

As for the jocular use of *knave* noted in *OED* ("Good night Roger olde knave"), I can't say I've ever heard it, except as a conscious archaism amongst Shakespeareans in their cups; in Australia we'd be more likely to use our modern equivalent, "How are you going, you old *bastard*?"

LATINISMS

It has become almost impossible in recent years to open a newspaper during a cricket match in which Australia is playing without reading that Shane Warne has *decimated* the opposition. What the writers mean by this is that he's dismissed a fistful of batsmen, probably half or more of the opposing team. They're using the word *decimate* in the loose sense that has now become widespread, that is, 'to destroy a large proportion of' or 'to inflict heavy losses on'. Its original sense was both more specific and weaker: it's from the Latin *decimus* 'tenth' (from which we get *decimal currency* and the *decimal system*) and it meant 'to take away one in every ten', whether by taxing at ten per cent (as Cromwell taxed the Royalists in 1655) or by putting to death one in ten of a group of mutineers (as was done in the Roman army). So if Warne's Latin were as good as his bowling, he might have cause to feel miffed, since what the commentators are saying etymologically is that he's knocked over only one of the ten batsmen to be dismissed – which for him would be a pretty poor day at the office.

I have yet to read that opposing batsmen are *petrified* of him, but I think this would be a doubly apt description: we use it loosely to mean 'terrified' (and he does seem to inspire fear in the opposition); but it means literally 'turned to stone' (from Latin *petra* 'stone', as in Matt. 16: 18: "Thou art Peter and upon this rock I will build my church"); and, as the former captains in the commentary box are fond of pointing out, it is precisely those batsmen who are most rigid in their movements, most firmly anchored to the crease, most like statues, that spin bowlers are likeliest to get out.

One of the most misleading Latinisms is the word *promiscuous*, which is used nowadays almost exclusively of people who have multiple sexual partners, in the sense 'sleeping around' or 'changing partners indiscriminately'. Students reading *Paradise Lost* for the first time – the fortunate few who still get the opportunity – are sometimes taken aback to read that when Satan first called his followers to him after their being cast into hell, the leaders responded to his summons "While the promiscuous crowd stood yet aloof" (1.380): to those who know only the current sense, it sounds as if the crowd are about to have an orgy but haven't yet broken the ice. But the *promiscuous* crowd is simply one that is 'mixed up and disorderly', or, if you like, *miscellaneous*: the two words are from the same Latin root, *miscere* 'to mix'.

Milton is famous for his Latinisms. Not only are Satan's followers a "promiscuous crowd"; they are also said to have "a horrid front" (1.563), which means not that they have ugly mugs (though it's clear that they didn't retain their former beauty after their expulsion from heaven), but that their front rank is bristling with spears (from the Latin verb *horreo* 'to bristle', or, of the hair, 'to stand on end'). So old fogies who describe Johnny Rotten's hairdo as "horrid" may be displaying a lamentable intolerance of pop culture, but at least they're being Etymologically Correct; if they go one further and call it "horrible", they're suggesting it's so awful that it makes their own hair stand on end!

LAVATORIES, TOILETS AND RESTROOMS

The first time I visited Gloucester Cathedral I was staggered by the splendour of that part of the cloisters described as the *lavatorium*: a long, narrow room with a magnificent, low, fan-vaulted ceiling, a two-light window at each end, and eight two-light windows letting light in from the garth (the open part of the cloisters). A stone ledge with a long trough in front of it, at about thigh height (rather like the manger in a cowshed), runs along the wall backing on to the garth; and beneath each of the eight windows there's a hole in the trough. I looked at this arrangement and envisaged the monks seated in this lavatory, eight at a time, one per hole, and I couldn't help thinking, "Well, it's a splendid room, but I don't know about this communal living – not much privacy here!"

Then I read the guide-book and had to blush at my own error. The monks wouldn't have been seated there because it wasn't a *lavatory* in the sense in which we use it today: it was the place where they washed their hands before eating. There used to be a water tank on the ledge behind the trough, with spigots to let the water out into the trough; the holes in the trough were to let the dirty water drain away. It's called a *lavatory* or *lavatorium* precisely because that word means, literally, 'a place for washing', from the Latin *lavāre* 'to wash', with the ending *-ory* (Latin *-orium*) denoting 'a place' (as in *dormitory* 'a place for sleeping').

How has the word now come to denote a place for excreting rather than a place for washing? Simply through euphemism: there are certain subjects, about which human beings are generally a bit coy, notably excretion, sex, and death; rather than speak directly about these things they tend either to use crude, jokey terms for them or else, as in the present instance, to use euphemisms. So, *lavatory*, which, as we've seen, originally meant 'wash-place', came to mean instead 'excreting-place'. When that happens, you have to find a new term for a wash-place, such as *bathroom*. But this word has followed the same path in America as *lavatory* in England: if American visitors ask you for the bathroom and you show them to a room containing a bath but not a *throne* (a comic euphemism) or (as they'd say) a *john*, they will not be amused – which is perhaps why *bathroom* is now giving way in America to another euphemism, *restroom*. As to why the *john* should be as widely used a term in America today as the *jakes* was in Elizabethan England, it's hard to say; but I'd guess that both uses are equivalent to the common application of the pet form *Jack* to contrivances "which in some way . . . save human labour" (*Jack*, II, senses 7–27 in *OED*), like the *jack* with which one levers up a car to change a tyre.

As for the popular English term *loo*, lexicographers are unsure of its origin. I used to favour either of two explanations, both taking it as a euphemism: one of these derives it from the French *lieu d'aisance* (literally 'place of easement', which is self-explanatory); the other from the French phrase *gardez-vous de l'eau* ('watch out: water!'), said to have been uttered as a cry of warning by people throwing out the night soil on to the street in the days before houses had running water and – another euphemism – *WC*s ('water closets'). Ross dismisses these explanations (along with five others) in his detailed essay on the subject; but his own preferred theory, that the word is somehow derived from *Waterloo*, strikes me as no more convincing than some of the explanations he rejects.

The usual term in Australia, particularly for an exterior *convenience* (yes, another euphemism) used to be a *dunny* (a word not to be found in *OED1*). Most authorities derive *dunny* from the English dialect word *dunnekin* 'an open cesspool' (*EDD*), of which the origin is uncertain, but which *OED2* and the *New Shorter Oxford* connect with *dung*. If they're right, *dunny* is a rare example of a word that isn't, or (for as long as its origin was generally known) wasn't, a euphemism. But there's no call for us to get smug about down-to-earth Aussies calling a spade a spade, because *dunny* has now been almost totally eclipsed in Australia by *toilet* (a word that's difficult for middle-class English migrants to come to terms with, since in England it belongs to a lower-class sociolect). This is yet another euphemism, derived from French *toilette* 'dress', a reference, I assume, to the re-arrangement of clothing that this function necessitates. (No wonder children are puzzled by survivals of the old sense in such combinations as *toilet box*, *toilet set*, and *toilet water*!)

There's nothing new about this coyness. In the thirteenth-century poem *The Owl and the Nightingale*, the owl accuses the nightingale of being a dirty beast because it likes to sing in the bushes surrounding the *roomhouse* (591–6). *Roomhouse* combines a euphemism with a joke: the adjective *room* meant 'spacious' (it's the same word as our noun *room*, meaning 'an enclosed space in a building'): spacious is, of course, exactly what this place usually is not (which is why one sometimes sees notices on doors in private houses declaring it to be *the smallest room*).

No one ever calls this place by its right name, which is, of course, the *shithouse*. But it's curious that that word has had its own functional shift, and has entered the colloquial language as an adjective and an adverb rather than a noun. When I gave one of my colleagues the other day the standard Australian greeting, "G'day mate; how are you going?", he replied, without batting an eyelid, "Shithouse: how are you?"

This may have come as a surprise, but Bill Scammell (at that time Chancellor of the University of Adelaide) bettered it with a story about his days in the RAAF during the War. "There was an Irishman in the same squadron as me," he began. (No, this is not an ethnic joke: it's a linguistic one.) "He said to me, one day, 'Well, Bill, and what kind of a day have you had today?'

I'd had a lousy day, as it happened, so I replied, with some feeling, 'Shithouse!'

He turned to the room at large, and he said, 'Did you hear that piece of swank? This feller says *shit'ouse* with *two* haitches!'"

ATCHISON

LET

"Unhand me, gentlemen./ By heav'n, I'll make a ghost of him that lets me." So cries Hamlet to Horatio and Marcellus as they try to restrain him from following his father's ghost (1.4.61–2). I think this must be one of the very rare occasions where, by happy chance, a modern misunderstanding actually improves the force of the original. Modern audiences (unless they've studied the play in detail) are bound to think that *lets* means 'allows', that Hamlet is longing to kill someone, and that he's threatening to do so if given half a chance. Read like this, "lets me" has a sort of grim irony in keeping with the black humour of "I'll make a ghost of" for "I'll kill". But most editors insist that *lets* here means 'hinders', so that what Hamlet is saying is "I'll kill anyone who tries to prevent me from following" (and some directors, to make it clear that this is the sense intended, change "him that lets me" to "him that stops me" or "him that keeps me").

Is this, like *fast*, an example of a word that can have two opposite meanings in use at the same time ('to prevent' and 'to allow')? It looks like it; but in fact it isn't so. What we have here are two verbs that were originally distinct in pronunciation and spelling, but which, through gradual sound change, have become indistinguishable. The first of these two verbs was in Old English *lǣtan* 'to allow', with a single -t- in the middle preceded by a long vowel similar to the sound in the first syllable of American *daddy*. Had the vowel not been shortened over time, this would have produced *leet* rather than *let* in modern English, just as OE *slǣpan* has produced MnE *sleep*. The second verb was in Old English *lettan* 'to hinder', with a short e followed by a double -tt- in the middle: this combination would have been pronounced much like that in MnE *set to*.

Let in the sense 'hinder' is now virtually obsolete, except in fossilized phrases such as *without let or hindrance* (which is, strictly speaking, a tautology), or in specialized uses such as the *let* in tennis (often – wrongly but understandably – thought to be *net*), where a serve has to be taken again, since the ball has been hindered in its passage by touching the top of the net. I've heard it said that a *French letter* is so named because it acts as a hindrance between the sperm and the ovum: that's an ingenious suggestion, but one that's not borne out by the dictionaries, where this combination is entered (for example, in the *New Shorter Oxford*) amongst the *letters* that have to do with writing, as if (though this isn't spelled out) a French letter were an intimate means of communication favoured by the French.

As for the other verb, the usual sense in current English, 'allow', was just one of a wide range of possible meanings in former times: *OED* records seventeen different senses for this verb, not including phrasal uses such as *let alone, let be, let go, let loose*, etc. These senses are grouped in three main branches: the first has to do with 'leaving', the second with 'allowing', and the third with 'behaving'. Most of the 'leaving' senses are now obsolete, but one or two survive, such as to *let* a property to a tenant, i.e., to leave it for someone else to occupy in exchange for rent. More of the 'allowing' senses survive: apart from 'allow' itself, we still have the imperative use in *let's* do such-and-such, and even an old causative use that was very common in Chaucer's day, but which now survives only in the phrase *to let (someone) know something*.

None of the 'behaving' senses survives, except in the phrase *to let on*, i.e., 'to pretend' (the other sense of *let on*, 'reveal', seems to me to belong with the 'allowing' senses: if you *let on* that such-and-such is the case, you 'allow it to be seen' that it is so). But the 'behaving' senses were very common in Middle English. Fans of *Sir Gawain and the Green Knight* will be familiar with them from several memorable occurrences of the phrase *let as*, meaning 'behave as if, pretend'. When his beautiful hostess pays him an early morning visit in his bedroom, while her husband is out hunting, Sir Gawain at first "let as he slepte" ('pretended to be asleep', 1190), hoping she would go away; when this ploy fails, he "unlouked his yye-lyddes and let as hym wondered" (literally 'unlocked his eyelids and behaved as if he were amazed', 1201). The lady in her turn "let lyk a[s] hym loved mych" ('behaved as if she loved him dearly', 1281). No wonder the poor bloke had such difficulty preserving his chastity!

LEWD

This word *lewd* has a rather mysterious origin: no one can say exactly what it's derived from, although the *OED* has a nice little essay on its etymology, saying that it ought to come from ecclesiastical Latin *laicus*, but apparently doesn't.

Why should it come from *laicus*? Because *laicus* is the Latin word for 'lay' referring to members of the *laity* as opposed to members of the clergy, as in *layman*, *lay sister*, *lay brother*, and so on; and that is also the sense in which *lewd* (originally *læwed*) is first recorded in English: *lewd* or *læwed* people in medieval England were not ones who slept around or spent long hours propping up the bar telling dirty jokes; they were simply members of the laity.

This sense is nicely illustrated by the famous lines from the General Prologue to the *Canterbury Tales* describing Chaucer's Parson:

> This noble ensample to his sheep he yaf,
> That first he wroghte, and afterward he taughte.
> Out of the gospel he tho wordes caughte,
> And this figure he added eek therto,
> That if gold ruste, what shal iren do?
> For if a preest be foul, on whom we truste,
> No wonder is a lewed man to ruste;
> And shame it is, if a prest take keep,
> A shiten shepherd and a clene sheep.   (I 496–504)

If gold rusts, what'll happen to iron? If a priest, the shepherd, is covered with shit, how can you expect one of his sheep, a *lewd* person – a member of the *laity* – to stay clean?

But how did this innocent word acquire its current sense, 'obscene, indecent, dirty-minded'?

Well, its history is not unlike that of *knave*. Education was not universal in the Middle Ages: the clergy were generally educated – they had to know Latin, after all – but amongst the laity it was only the rich who could afford an education for their children. Most lay people, accordingly, were uneducated, and so *læwed*, meaning 'lay', came to be synonymous with 'uneducated, unlearned'. In just the same way, in reverse, the word *læred*, meaning 'educated, learned', came to mean 'clerical, belonging to the Church', because it was for the most part only the clergy who were educated. The two words were frequently joined as an alliterating pair, *læred* and *læwed*, meaning either 'the clergy and the laity' or 'the educated and the uneducated': it isn't always easy to tell from the context exactly which of the senses is intended, and very often it doesn't matter, because in either case the phrase is probably being used as a periphrasis for 'everybody', which includes all people irrespective of the state of their education or their association with the Church.

But, human nature being what it is, rich, upper class, educated snobs tend to look down on the uneducated and the lower classes, as if their low station in society were a reflection of a lack of intelligence or a lack of moral sensitivity. It is then fairly predictable that a word meaning 'uneducated' will come in time to mean 'lower class or base; ignorant or stupid; ill-mannered, unprincipled, or worthless' (*OED* senses 3–6); and thus eventually, through a concentration on one particular lack of principle, it will come to mean (as the *OED* puts it, somewhat archaically) 'lascivious or unchaste' or (as we would say) 'dirty-minded' or, in its current sense, 'lewd'.

LICKING THINGS INTO SHAPE

One of my mother's favourite expressions, when something was annoying her, used to be that she would pretty soon *lick it into shape*. I always took this to mean that she would knock it into shape – not that my mother was an aggressive woman (far from it), but that she always enunciated the phrase with such vigour that it never occurred to me that it might mean something else. And indeed, in the West Indian English that my mother spoke (having grown up in Barbados), giving something a *lick* was more likely to involve smacking it with the hand than caressing it with the tongue. Both senses are acceptable in standard English, of course; but my impression is that the flagellatory sense of the noun *lick* is closer to the surface in West Indian than in British English, as, for example, in Lord Kitchener's Calypso, "Cricket Champions":

> England must understand
> We are the champions
> Sobers come back and give dem
> Plow-two, plow-tow
> Two six
> England must understand
> We are the champions
> Holford carry
> And hit em
> Pow-tow, pow-tow
> More licks

– that is, in short, Sobers and Holford were knocking the stuffing out of England (though the tables have lately been turned).

But even without a West Indian background I think that most people today, if asked what image was called to mind by this phrase, *licking something into shape*, would say, a schoolmaster or a sergeant-major with his cane, or perhaps a carpenter with his hammer. And yet the phrase has nothing originally to do with beating, or punishment, or discipline. On the contrary, its origin is of the gentlest imaginable: it derives from the medieval belief concerning bears and their new-born cubs, as described in T.H. White's *Book of Beasts*:

> For they say that these creatures produce a formless foetus, giving birth to something like a bit of pulp, and this the mother-bear arranges into the proper legs and arms by licking it. This is because of the prematurity of the birth. In short, she pups on the thirtieth day, from whence it comes that a hasty, unformed creation is brought forth. . . . The period of gestation is short. . . . This is why the precipitate childbirth creates shapeless fruits. They bring forth very tiny pulps of a white colour, with no eyes. They gradually sculpture these by licking.   (pp. 45–6)

In short, literally, they lick them into shape. And it was thought that the bear herself got her name (Latin *ursus*) from the action of licking her cub into shape to enable it to begin its life: "Vrsus fertur dictus quod ore suo formet fetus, quasi orsus", says Isidore (*Etymologiae* 12.2.22); that is, 'the bear (*ursus*) is said to be so named because she shapes the foetus with her mouth (*ore suo*), as a beginning (*orsus*)'.

On this belief White comments, in one of his wonderfully humane footnotes:

> There was a reasonable substratum of truth for the medieval belief. Bear cubs really are born blind and hairless, and remain so for no less than five weeks. Naked, born in a jealous seclusion which made observation almost impossible, and constantly licked by their dam as bitches clean their puppies, the idea that the cubs were produced as a kind of mola was not absolutely preposterous. "The cub comes forth involved in the Chorion," says Sir Thomas Browne, "a thick and tough membrane obscuring the formation, and which the Dam doth after bite and teare asunder, (so that) the beholder at first sight conceives it a rude and informous lumpe of flesh, and imputes the ensuing shape unto the mouthing of the Dam".   (p. 47)

How different the mother bear's care for her cubs from the kind of licking that appears to be endemic in hierarchical institutions, and that is otherwise known, for reasons too obvious to need explanation, as *brown-nosing*!

LONG WORDS BOTHER ME

Jeremiads about the decline of literacy and prophecies about the impending death of English are nothing new: they've been going on for centuries. Yet the language survives – changed, of course (as witnessed by almost every item in this book), but remarkably resilient. Should we worry about change, then? Or should we embrace it? Or just shrug our shoulders and say it's inevitable?

My own view is curiously schizophrenic. As someone who teaches the history of the language, I cannot but recognize that change is inevitable: today's error (as I've said before) is tomorrow's accepted form. But as one who has to correct my students' essays, I cannot let sentence fragments, or comma splices, or false agreements between subject and verb, or other such egregious errors pass unnoticed and unpenalized. I am speaking, of course, about written English. Unlike the majority of callers on talkback radio, I am not much troubled by changes in speech habits. The spoken language has life only on the tongues of its speakers; they will do with it what they wish; and what people do with it – irrespective of their educational level – is marvellously inventive. Writing is different: it is not learned naturally, like speech (except perhaps by the exceptionally bright); it has to be taught; its rules must be mastered and internalized if it is to be wielded with power. Articulacy is power, and it is part of the work of English teachers to help their students acquire that power with the written word.

Each period has its own axe to grind about falling standards of literacy. So what are today's worries, and how seriously should we take them? Three things strike me in particular: the educational theories about the teaching of English in schools that have held sway since the late 1960s at least; the impact of contemporary critical theory on the language used in the humanities since about the mid 1970s; and, more recently, the insidious spread into all areas of human experience of the language of business management.

As a schoolboy, in common with everyone else of my generation, I was taught grammar as a formal subject. Parsing was the name of the game. What is the subject of this sentence? What is the predicate? What part of speech is this word? What is the main verb? Is this a main clause or a subordinate clause? Can this clause stand as a sentence in its own right? Why? (Or why not?) How would you punctuate this sentence? Where would you start a new paragraph? How do you turn this bit of dialogue into indirect speech? What happens to the tenses of the verbs when you do? And so on, and so forth. Some pupils found it boring; some found it difficult; but most learned to construct sentences of which the meaning was relatively clear. But by the time I trained to be a schoolteacher myself, the sixties were in full swing and had been so for several years: Elvis had swung his pelvis both before and after his time as a G.I.; James Dean had inspired a generation of young rebels; Bob Dylan had told us how the times they were a-changin'; the Beatles had conquered the world's youth with their music and shocked the parents with their long hair; Woodstock was happening; it was time to let it all hang out; and the educational theorists decided to get with it. Don't teach formal grammar: it bores students to tears! Don't correct their errors: it kills their spontaneity! Don't set formal essays: let them do 'intensive writing'! Get them to jot their ideas down on paper as fast as they come! Don't worry about apostrophes and commas and all that: just help them get their creative juices running! They'll pick up all that other stuff in good time: you don't have to ram it down their throats!

The motive was good, of course; with educational reforms it usually is. But the results have been catastrophic. Students who leave school after an education like that are victims of a system that has failed – indeed, not even tried – to teach them the mechanics of the written word. They can't be blamed for not knowing the difference between *it's* and *its* if no one has ever told them, or made them see why it matters. It's not their fault if they don't know when to use a semi-colon rather than a comma, or why it turns the nouns into verbs if you put a comma after *eats* in "Eats shoots and leaves". And it's much harder to teach them at the age of eighteen or more than it would have been at ten or eleven. Can anything be done about this? Can the trend be reversed? Let's hope so. The huge success of Lynne Truss's little book on punctuation – all power to her! – shows how many people care about these things, and how much they care (and they can't all be apoplectic colonels or retired schoolmarms or crusty old pedants like me). And if public opinion gets strong enough, even the theorists – eventually – have to listen. (The Australian version of the story about the panda from which she takes her title, by the way, is "Eats, *roots* and leaves". I don't know whether that joke will be fully understood in most other English-speaking countries, since the sexual sense of *to root* is characterized in the *New Oxford Dictionary* as peculiar to Australia and New Zealand – and Ireland.)

The impact of contemporary critical theory on the humanities is a different kettle of fish. Somehow or other, by a process I've never understood (though the battle has raged all around me), the humanities were taken over in the seventies by the theories of fashionable French philosophers, especially Jacques Derrida and Michel Foucault. None caught the contagion more quickly or more deeply than departments of English in universities. One of the chief points of the theorists was that language was not a transparent window through which one could see a pre-existing world and describe it as it was, but a medium which affected the very way one perceived the world in the first place. They sought to draw attention to the materiality of language, to *defamiliarize* it (to use one of their own buzz words), to make people as aware of the language itself as of the supposed meaning it carried. The most obvious way of doing this was to write obscurely so that readers couldn't see *through* the language to something else but would have to look *at* the language in search of a meaning. Thus grew up the cult of difficulty in writing: the harder the reader had to work to find out what the writer was getting at, the more forcefully the point had been made. No doubt I'm oversimplifying; but that is because – as my students (probably) and the theorists (undoubtedly) would say – I am (like that Bear) "of Very Little Brain, and long words Bother me". In short, I have never come to terms with contemporary critical theory, because reading it gives me a headache. I have only one life, and I don't choose to spend it learning how to use an obscure vocabulary and a convoluted syntax to show how clever I am.

This sorry state of affairs continued until the mid nineties, with the theorists getting ever stronger. Then, suddenly, an enterprising academic who had not been fooled by the hype, Denis Dutton from the University of Canterbury in New Zealand, editor of the journal *Philosophy and Literature*, began to run an annual Bad Writing Contest in an attempt "to locate the ugliest, most stylistically awful passage found in a scholarly book or article published in the last few years." Certain categories of writing were excluded: "Ordinary journalism, fiction, etc. are not eligible, nor are parodies: entries must be non-ironic, from actual serious academic journals or books. In a field where unintended self-parody is so widespread, deliberate send-ups are hardly necessary." Entrants in the contest found some pieces of writing that were so bad as to beggar belief. I reproduce here one prize-winning entry (from several) for each of the years 1996–1998:

From the second contest, 1996:
It is the moment of non-construction, disclosing the absentation of actuality from the concept in part through its invitation to emphasize, in reading, the helplessness – rather than the will to power – of its fall into conceptuality.

From the third contest, 1997:
If such a sublime cyborg would insinuate the future as post-Fordist subject, his palpably masochistic locations as ecstatic agent of the sublime superstate need to be decoded as the "now-all-but-unreadable DNA" of a fast deindustrializing Detroit, just as his Robocop-like strategy of carceral negotiation and street control remains the tirelessly American one of inflicting regeneration through violence upon the racially heteroglossic wilds and others of the inner city.

From the fourth contest, 1998 (the winning entry for that year):
The move from a structuralist account in which capital is understood to structure social relations in relatively homologous ways to a view of hegemony in which power relations are subject to repetition, convergence, and rearticulation brought the question of temporality into the thinking of structure, and marked a shift from a form of Althusserian theory that takes structural totalities as theoretical objects to one in which the insights into the contingent possibility of structure inaugurate a renewed conception of hegemony as bound up with the contingent sites and strategies of the rearticulation of power.

This last sentence achieved a notoriety far beyond the usual academic circles when Dennis Dutton published it in the *Wall Street Journal* in an article headed "Language Crimes: A lesson in how not to write, courtesy of the professors". "To ask what this means," wrote Dutton, "is to miss the point. This sentence beats readers into submission and instructs them that they are in the presence of a great and deep mind. Actual communication has nothing to do with it." The ensuing furore is described by Mark Bauerlein in a review of a collection of essays published in 2003 in which the theorists defend themselves against the charge of *bad* writing by calling it *difficult* writing. They will, of course, convince no one but themselves: the rest of us will continue to see their labour as a prolonged act of mutual masturbation. The sad thing is that it will take a long time for their influence to work its way out of the system; in the mean time we are stuck not only with their language but with the dumbing down of syllabuses which their theorizing paradoxically brought about, such that in many "English" departments in the Western world it is possible to write essays on *Buffy the Vampire Slayer* or the film of *The Silence of the Lambs*, but not on Milton, Johnson, or Pope, who are no longer taught because they don't happen to be flavour of the month. "We no longer teach *Paradise Lost*," I mourn to my green tea; "we *are* paradise lost." – But Dutton gives me hope that all is not lost, quite.

There may be no obvious connection between the language of contemporary critical theory and that of the worlds of business management and of politics, but they have two things at least in common: the dressing-up of commonplace thought in inflated language and the attempt to hide meaning rather than to reveal it. Don Watson's book *Death Sentence* is a mine of examples of official-speak of the kind that now deadens our daily discourse. I borrow three of his many examples:

> While most discussions of knowledge management have treated commitment as a binary variable, underlying theory suggests otherwise. Commitment can be better represented in terms of a continuum ranging from negligible or partial commitment to the KMS, and from avoidance (non use) to meagre and unenthusiastic use (compliant use) to skilled, enthusiastic and consistent use (committed use) of the KMS. (p. 19)

> This requires a commitment to the provision of adequate data so that informed evaluation can occur. There must be a commitment to the provision of statistical information that will facilitate effective monitoring and evaluation strategies and a commitment to the implementation of changes that are identified as necessary following evaluation. (p. 77)

> Given the within year and budget time flexibility accorded to the science agencies in the determination of resource allocation from within their global budget, a multi-parameter approach to maintaining the agencies [sic] budgets in real terms is not appropriate. (p. 194)

It's enough to make one contemplate suicide, isn't it? "Continuing existence or cessation of existence: those are the scenarios. Is it more empowering mentally to work towards an accommodation of the downsizings and negative outcomes of adversarial circumstance, or would it be a greater enhancement of the bottom line to move forwards to a challenge to our current difficulties, and, by making a commitment to opposition, to effect their demise?" – as Hamlet might well have put it had he done an MBA.

Can we do anything about such pompous prose? Precious little, it seems, except send it up, and try not to write it ourselves. Laughter is perhaps the best weapon as well as the best medicine; and accordingly I leave both the last example and the last word to Sir Ernest Gowers, whose attack on jargon of all kinds (in this instance scientific jargon) is the wittiest I've encountered.

> Although certain broad zonational patterns are discernible in the geographical distribution of animals as well as in those of soils and vegetation, the mobility of animals and, in the case of some, seasonal altitudinal migrations mean that the zonation becomes indistinct.

"This," writes Gowers, "is from a published academic study. I have corrected both grammar and punctuation. It seems to tell us that animals move about more than plants do, and that when they have moved they are not in the same place as before."

LUST AND LUXURY

These two words, like *knight* and *knave*, demonstrate two opposite kinds of semantic development.

Lust was a perfectly innocent word in the Middle Ages: it just meant 'pleasure' or 'delight'. King Alfred's translation of Boethius tells us that Epicurus declared *lust* to be the "hehste (i.e., 'highest') good" (first quotation for sense I in *OED*). Epicurus certainly wasn't talking about lust in our sense: he meant that *pleasure* was the ultimate good. But since most of us long for the things that give us pleasure, it's easy to see how *lust* came to mean 'desire' or 'appetite': when Malory tells us that on a hot afternoon Sir Launcelot "had great lust to slepe" (6. I), there's no suggestion that Launcelot had Guenever on his mind: he was just exhausted by the heat and in need of a snooze.

In a similar way the cognate word *list*, which is probably more familiar nowadays in the compound *listless*, means 'pleasure' or 'appetite': when one is *listless* (i.e., one has lost one's *list*) one mooches around without energy, showing no desire or inclination to get involved in anything. When the Wife of Bath complains of her fifth husband that "He nolde suffre nothyng of my liste" (*CT* III 633), she's not saying he couldn't put up with her sexual advances; she means that he wouldn't allow her to do the things she enjoyed doing, like visiting her friends (see *gossip*).

But since, for most of us, our strongest desires are situated "between the navel and the knee" (as D.H. Lawrence put it, I believe, though – shocking, unscholarly confession! – I have lost the reference and have failed to track it down in any dictionary of quotations), it doesn't usually take long before a word meaning 'appetite' comes to designate specifically sexual appetite; and given the long history of fear and disapproval of the sexual appetite in the Western world, it's not unusual for such words to acquire overtones of what the *OED* calls "intense moral reprobation", as with the commonest use of *lust* today (*OED*, *lust*, noun, sense 4, the "chief current use").

Luxury, on the other hand, has gone exactly the opposite way: it *used* to mean specifically 'lechery' or 'lust' (in the current sense). This was the standard sense for Shakespeare, whose characters tend to use the word with undisguised loathing, as when the ghost of his dead father urges Hamlet not to let "the royal bed of Denmark be/ A couch for luxury and damnèd incest" (1.5.82–3): he's not suggesting Hamlet should throw away his mother's satin nightgowns or stick a needle in the waterbed, but that he should stop her sleeping with his (the dead king's) usurping brother, Claudius. This disgust comes out just as strongly in *King Lear*, in the mad scene with Gloucester, when Lear says, with evident sarcasm, in that infamous speech in which he goes on to describe women as centaurs, "Let copulation thrive. . . . To't luxury, pell-mell,/ For I lack soldiers" (4.5.112–16).

Nowadays, on the other hand, it's used innocently enough of anything that pleases the senses — fine wine, good music, silk underwear, a comfortable chair, whatever takes your particular fancy. How did such a censorious word lose its sexual connotations? I don't think that question can be answered; all we can say is that this is one example of that relatively rare phenomenon that linguistic historians call *amelioration* (cf. *knight*); the more usual process is that of *degeneration* or *pejoration*, as demonstrated by *lust* (cf. *knave*).

MIRTH AND MERRIMENT

The association between *mirth* and laughter is so strong in current English that the two are generally taken to be synonymous; and most readers today would be likely to think that Byron is indeed using them synonymously in *Don Juan* when he writes, "Let us have wine and women, mirth and laughter,/ Sermons and soda-water the day after" (2.178). But the words have not always been interchangeable in the way that they are today. When Shakespeare has Beatrice say, in *Much Ado*, that she was "born to speak all mirth and no matter" (2.1.308–9), mirth is evidently a *cause* of laughter, not the laughter itself. Similarly in one of Feste's well-known songs in *Twelfth Night*, laughter and mirth are closely associated without being the same thing:

> What is love? 'Tis not hereafter,
> Present mirth hath present laughter.
> What's to come is still unsure.
> In delay there lies no plenty,
> Then come kiss me, sweet and twenty.
> Youth's a stuff will not endure.   (2.3.46–51)

He doesn't say, mirth *is* laughter, but that it *hath* it, that is, that it *includes* it. In the context of Feste's song *mirth* means 'pleasure or enjoyment' (as perhaps it still does, in spite of what modern readers think, in the quotation from *Don Juan* with which we began): the argument is that, just as laughter is a natural concomitant of enjoying oneself or feeling happy, so kisses proceed naturally from being in love – so let's get on with it! Feste's song is a celebrated expression of what literary critics call the *carpe diem* theme ('seize the day'): "Gather ye rosebuds while ye may" (as in Robert Herrick's celebrated appeal 'To the Virgins, to Make Much of Time'); eat, drink and be merry, for tomorrow ye die (Luke 12: 19; Isaiah 22: 13).

In this context *be merry* doesn't necessarily mean 'crack jokes'; it means 'enjoy yourself, have fun'. It's not hard to see the etymological connection between *mirth* and *merriment*: both are derived from the Old English adjective *myrig* 'merry', which as applied to things meant originally 'giving pleasure, pleasing', and as applied to people meant 'feeling pleasure, joyful' – which, of course, often leads to laughter. (Lexicographers think that the word is connected ultimately with an adjective meaning 'short', the connecting idea being that we generally do pleasurable or entertaining things to shorten time; see the etymological comment under *merry* in *OED*.)

But before it became synonymous with laughter, *mirth* could suggest pleasure of any kind, according to the context. In religious contexts, for example, it tended to mean 'eternal bliss, or the joy of heaven': on the Day of Judgement, we are told, "The goode to hevene the weie shullen take,/ Where joye and merthe shal nevere slake" (*Sidrak* L9333–4). This doesn't mean that the inhabitants of heaven spend their whole time cackling with laughter; it means that their *joy* is ceaseless: in this context *mirth* is synonymous with *bliss*.

In amatory contexts, on the other hand, *mirth* suggested sexual pleasure, as in the memorable lines describing the cavortings of Alison and Nicholas in the carpenter's bed (in Chaucer's Miller's tale) while Alison's hapless husband, the carpenter himself, lies asleep in the loft:

> Ther was the revel and the melodye;
> And thus lith Alison and Nicholas,
> In bisynesse of myrthe and of solas,
> Til that the belle of laudes gan to rynge,
> And freres in the chauncel gonne synge.   (*CT* I 3652–6)

Doubtless there was some giggling going on; but there's more involved in the "business of mirth and solace" than mere tickling. And in *Sidrak and Bokkus* I have even come across the phrase *chamber mirth* (literally 'bedroom pleasure') used as a euphemism for sexual intercourse by a scribe who found in his exemplar the naughty word *swive*, and who was too coy to repeat it (see *fun* and *glee*). So editing is not *all* drudgery: it has its *mirths*.

MOOD AND MOODY

One of Glenn Miller's best-loved pieces – still often heard today, more than half a century after his death – was called "In the Mood". The jaunty music (see *gentle*) gives a clear indication that the *mood* implied in the title is a good mood: if you're *in the mood* (with no specification of what you're in the mood for), it's a safe bet you're in the mood for fun. But if you're in *a* mood (without further specification), it's just the opposite: to be *in a mood* is invariably to be in a bad mood. How strange, yet how characteristic of the inexplicable oddities of language, that the difference between the definite and the indefinite article can reverse the meaning of the phrase!

But before it came to mean 'frame of mind' (as it does today), the word *mood* (OE *mōd*) was used to mean the mind itself, or the thought, heart, or feeling. King Alfred, in his famous letter to his bishops urging them to look to the education of the young, claims that the English of his time had lost the knowledge and the wealth of their forefathers because, although they could see the path left by their predecessors, "we noldon to thæm spore mid ure mode onlutan", that is, 'we would not bow down to the path with our mind'. Similarly Ælfric, in his homily on King Oswald, tells us that whatever gifts Saint Aidan received, he would divide them amongst the poor and needy "mid welwillendum mode", 'with a very willing spirit'.

In Old English poetry *mōd* is frequently used in compound nouns or adjectives indicating the subject's state of mind. Thus the speaker in *The Wife's Lament* is miserable because she can never get any rest from her "modceare" 'mindcare, heartache'; the solitary exile in *The Wanderer* is described as "modcearig" 'having care in his mind, troubled in heart'; and scholars are unlikely ever to stop wrangling about whether the "ofermod" attributed to the Essex warrior, Byrhtnoth, in *The Battle of Maldon*, was a good thing, indicating laudable pride, or a bad thing, indicating excessive *mōd*, i.e. 'overconfidence, overweening pride'.

As for the adjective *moody*, it has always been something of a two-edged sword. If *mood* is a good thing, then to have it is good; if not, not. So, in Old English, "modig" was applied to God (in *The Phoenix*) in the good sense 'high-spirited or noble-minded' and, in the sense 'brave or bold', to warriors like Ælfere and Maccus in the *Battle of Maldon* or like Beowulf himself in *Beowulf* (lines 502, 670, 813); but it could also mean 'proud or arrogant', as in the nicely alliterative phrases "mære and modig" 'famous and proud', describing Nebuchadnezzar in *Daniel*, or "modig and medugal" 'flown with insolence and wine', describing the drunken Holofernes in *Judith*. What it boils down to, I suppose, is that you *can* have too much of a good thing: to have plenty of mind/heart/ spirit is desirable; to have too much is not so good.

Well, as Glenn Miller's music reminds us, we still have some good senses for the noun; but the senses for the adjective have degenerated and weakened almost beyond recognition. *Moody* people in Anglo-Saxon times were full of *mood*; today they are full of *moods*, that is, as the *New Shorter Oxford* has it, 'subject to or indulging in moods of bad temper, depression, etc.; sullen, melancholy'.

NAMES (1): CULINARY TERMS

One not unusual way for words to acquire new uses or senses is through the process known as the commonization of proper nouns. In this process, as its name implies, a proper noun (that is, a person's own name, spelled with a capital letter) becomes a common one (spelled with a lower case letter), applied to other people or things.

The best known examples of this process are probably culinary ones, in which a certain type of food gets named after the person who popularized it. A *sandwich*, the *OED* tells us, is "Said to be named after John Montagu, 4th Earl of *Sandwich* (1718–1792), who once spent twenty-four hours at the gaming-table without other refreshment than some slices of cold beef placed between slices of toast." It doesn't take much generalization before a *sandwich* comes to denote (as the *OED* somewhat ponderously puts it) "An article of food for a slight repast, composed of two thin slices of bread, either plain or buttered, with a layer of sliced meat, usually beef or ham (or, in later use, of almost any savoury comestible) placed between; frequently with specifying word prefixed, as *ham, egg, watercress sandwich*."

Once proper nouns have been commonized in this way, they behave just like other common nouns, and can acquire new uses, through functional shift, as parts of speech other than nouns. So, nowadays we can use *sandwich* as a verb, meaning 'to squeeze something tightly in between two other things', or indeed as an adjective, as in a *sandwich course*, which is a period of study *sandwiched* between two periods of work (or vice versa).

A nice antipodean equivalent is Australia's favourite dessert consisting of meringue topped with whipped cream and fresh fruit (originally specifically passion fruit), which we all know as a *pavlova* (or a *pav* for short). This, the *Macquarie* dictionary tells us with nice detail, was "invented in 1935 by Herbert Sachse, 1898–1974, Australian chef, and named by Harry Nairn of the Esplanade Hotel, Perth, after Anna *Pavlova*, 1885–1931, Russian ballerina." Chauvinistic Australians who look the

word up in the *Australian National Dictionary* will be dismayed to find a quotation (from Sydney's *Bulletin*, 28 May 1985) claiming that the pavlova is in fact *New Zealand*'s "No. 1 indigenous dessert . . . created there after a visit by Pavlova in 1926" (nine years earlier than the date for Australia given in *Macquarie*). Well, there's evidently a fierce dispute as to exactly when and where this dish was created, but at least we all know who it's named after.

These examples are both from personal names, but the same thing can happen with place-names. A *hamburger* takes its name from the German city of *Hamburg* (just as a *frankfurter* takes its name from *Frankfurt*): it's short for *Hamburger steak*, that is, steak in the Hamburg fashion. But this word also gives us a lovely example of folk etymology in action: since it's the name given to meat cooked in a particular way, it's easy enough to see how people who didn't know the geographical origin of *hamburger* assumed that *ham* indicated the kind of meat used. But since this is usually beef rather than ham, it's only a short step to the development of the alternative term *beefburger*, and from there to *cheeseburgers*, *chickenburgers*, *fishburgers*, and, in New Zealand (but not, surprisingly, Australia), *lamburgers*.

NAMES (2): POLITICAL TERMS

My previous examples of commonized proper nouns all had to do with food. But food is not a necessary ingredient (if I may be forgiven the execrable pun).

A *boycott*, for example, is named after Captain C.C. Boycott (1832–97), who was the land agent for the Earl of Erne in Ireland. The Earl's tenants were so incensed by Captain Boycott's refusal to reduce their rents that they refused to deal with him (they *boycotted* him, as we'd now say, availing ourselves of functional shift to use the noun as a verb): he was the recipient of the treatment that was subsequently named after him. I couldn't help thinking, when the English cricketers were touring Australia some years ago, in the days when Geoffrey Boycott was still opening the batting for England, that if he just hung on for a few more years the verb *to boycott* might develop a new sense, 'to play or act defensively, to stonewall'; but he evidently didn't hang around for quite long enough for that to happen.

But commonized names can indeed change their meanings like that, or develop new ones, in just the same ways as other words do. The best example I can give of this – one that has changed its meaning in our own time – is the word *chauvinist*. To most of us today a *chauvinist* is a violent antifeminist, almost invariably a man; and we're probably most familiar with the adjectival use of the word in the disparaging phrase *a male chauvinist pig*. (I'm never quite certain whether, in that phrase, a *pig* is, or originally was, specifically a policeman, or whether it just means any ill-mannered slob; and I don't suppose it matters very much: the tone of contempt in which the phrase is used tends to be the same either way.) But this current sense is some way from the original one.

Nicolas Chauvin of Rochefort, from whose name the word derives, was "a veteran soldier of the First Republic and Empire [of France], whose demonstrative patriotism and loyalty," the *OED* tells us, "were celebrated, and at length ridiculed, by his comrades". After the fall of Napoleon the name *Chauvin* was "applied in ridicule to old soldiers of the Empire, who professed a sort of idolatrous admiration for his person and acts". It was "popularized as the name of one of the characters in Cogniard's famous vaudeville, *La Cocarde Tricolore*, 1831 ('Je suis français, je suis Chauvin')"; thus it came to be applied "to any one smitten with an absurd patriotism, and enthusiasm for national glory and military ascendancy".

A *chauvinist*, then, is originally someone who is aggressively and blindly patriotic. From there, through the normal process of generalization, *chauvinism* comes to mean violent support for any cause, not necessarily that of one's country, or, as the *Collins* dictionary neatly puts it, "smug irrational belief in the superiority of one's own race, party, sex, etc." Then, through re-specialization, we get the concentration on one particular cause – that of one's sex – and on one particular sex. Thus, eventually, *a chauvinist* comes to be thought of as specifically a *male chauvinist pig*, a man who thinks that men are superior to women.

NAMES (3): TRADE TERMS

It's not only personal names and place-names that can become commonized: the same thing can happen also to brand names and trademarks. A *biro* has become the standard name for a ballpoint pen, irrespective of who its manufacturer is. It was originally, however, the trademark in Britain of a particular brand of ballpoint pen, named after its Hungarian inventor, Lászlo József Biró (1900–85).

An *esky*, to give a local example, is a term in general use in Australia and New Zealand for a portable container for keeping food and drink cool. This, too, was the trademark for one particular brand, which was marketed so successfully that the brand name (an allusion, presumably, to the cold climate of the Eskimos) became the generic term for all such containers.

A *hoover*, similarly, was originally one particular brand of vacuum cleaner; but soon it became a synonym for any vacuum cleaner, whoever made it, so that we can now talk without contradiction about, for example, "an Electrolux hoover". This word has also given us a verb (through functional shift), so that we can talk about *hoovering* the carpet. And it's retained the specific sense of vacuum cleaning even though the parent company (named after its proprietor, W.H. Hoover, d. 1932) makes a wide range of other household goods such as washing machines, dishwashers, and deep freezers. (It looked in the 1990s as if the scandals concerning another famous American with the surname Hoover, that is, J. Edgar Hoover, would add an entirely different set of meanings; but that appears not to have happened.)

One thing that can be confusing for travellers is to come across the same brand name, or a common noun derived from an identical brand name, with different meanings in two different countries. I experienced this difficulty myself, to my great confusion and embarrassment, when I first moved to Australia from Britain, on my very first day in my new job. The senior secretary showed me around what was then the Department of English Language and Literature at the University of Adelaide, asked me solicitously whether I was happy with my *office* (which I would have called my *room* or my *study*), and proceeded to offer me various supplies essential to the academic life: rough paper, typing paper, departmental letterhead, pencils, (yes) *biros*, and so forth (these were the early seventies, in the days before paper clips were treated as if they were made of gold); and then she floored me completely by asking me, in a perfectly straightforward manner, "And would you like some *durex*?"

Well, now, this was my first university appointment, and although I had indeed heard about academics *having it off* with their students, as the term then was (*sexual harassment* had scarcely been heard of in those days, though I dare say it happened; and AIDS was buried distantly in the future); and although I liked to think of myself as reasonably liberal-minded, I have to say that I was more than a little taken aback to be offered (as I thought) free condoms – and by the departmental secretary, at that. I suppose this train of thought must have been visible on my face, because, after a moment of stunned silence on my part, the secretary laughed delightedly and said, "Now don't get me wrong: I'm offering you what *you* would doubtless call *sellotape*!"

But I think even this experience is capped by the story told me by June Whitaker about the rose named after the Duchess of Shropshire. (In fact she named someone else, but it struck me as safer to use a fictional name than a real one, and where better to make her duchess of than the county I grew up in?) "Don't you know why it's named after her?" she asked.

"No. Tell me."

She replied, without batting an eyelid: "Good in a bed; better against a wall!"

Doubtless this story will offend the more PC amongst my readers. "It treats women as sexual objects," they will say. "You shouldn't have repeated it." To this I would reply that it was told me by a woman (and with great relish); that she struck me not as a woman cowed by the internalization of male values, but as a free spirit, speaking for herself; and that to censor stories involving sex and women is a retrograde step, reducing women to the level of puppets who cannot fend for themselves. Victim feminism (as it has come to be called) is more oppressive than the oppression it sets out to attack.

NAMES (4): SAINTS' NAMES

Maudlin and *tawdry* are adjectives derived from saints' names, both now expressing disapproval.

Maudlin is an English adaptation of *Madeleine*, the French form of the name *Magdalen* or *Magdalene*, from the biblical *Mary Magdalene*, i.e., 'Mary from Magdala'. In the biblical context her name is normally pronounced with four distinct syllables (*Mag-da-lee-nee*), but the colleges named after her at Oxford and Cambridge both have the vernacular pronunciation, *maudlin*, in spite of their retaining the Latin spelling with the medial -*g*-.

Mary Magdalene is the woman "out of whom went seven devils" (Luke 8: 2); and she is usually identified with the (unnamed) "sinner" of the preceding chapter, who washed Christ's feet with her tears and wiped them with her hair, to whom he said: "Thy sins are forgiven. . . . Thy faith hath saved thee" (7: 37–8, 48–50). Thus she "appears in Western hagiology" (as the *OED* succinctly puts it) as "a harlot restored to purity and elevated to saintship by repentance and faith"; and in medieval and renaissance art she is almost always depicted weeping, as a sign of her repentance. In time, however, the repentance got pushed into the background, and the focus remained on the tears themselves rather than on the penitence that produced them; so *maudlin* as an adjective came to mean 'weepy or tearful'; and so eventually, through the familiar process of degeneration, it comes to suggest insincere or self-indulgent emotion, cloying or mawkish sentimentality, emotion wallowed in for its own sake, as, for example, when one is drunk.

As for the adjective *tawdry*, which to us means 'showy, cheap and nasty', this comes from the name of the patron saint of Ely, the Anglo-Saxon Saint Ethelthrith or Etheldrida (of which *Audrey* is a later form). When you say *Saint Audrey* quickly, the -*t* gets detached from the *Saint* and attached incorrectly to the first syllable of *Audrey* (cf. *nicknames*), giving us the new word *tawdry*. Bede tells us that Saint Audrey died of a throat tumour; and that she believed it to be a punishment for her having worn jewelled necklaces in her youth. As a result of this belief, women took to wearing necklaces made from silk instead of jewels, and these silk necklaces were known, in Audrey's honour, as "Saint Audrey laces" or *tawdry laces*. They were also sold at the fair held in the Isle of Ely on her saint's day, and this of course led (as the *OED* puts it) "to the production of cheap and showy forms for the 'country wenches', . . . which at length gave to *tawdry* its later connotation".

Both these words, then, have a somewhat sad and perverse semantic history: they begin by commemorating the Magdalen's tears of penitence and St Audrey's renunciation of finery; they end up suggesting almost exactly the opposite: self-indulgent sentimentality and cheap ostentation.

NAMES (5): PLACE-NAMES

Place-names sometimes conceal surprising or amusing stories. *Pendle Hill* in Lancashire (famous from the witches) is made up of three words, one Welsh and two English. The first element is the word *pen*, a Welsh (or British) word originally meaning 'head' (as in Penzance, 'holy head'), thence 'top, or hill', and which I take to be related to Gaelic *ben* (as in Ben Nevis and Ben Lomond). In earlier times Pendle Hill was called *Pen Hill*. It looks as if the invading Anglo-Saxons asked the local Britons (presumably in sign language) the name of the nearby hill, and as if the Britons took the question to be, not "What is the name of that hill over there?" but "What do you call that thing over there?" They therefore replied "pen", meaning 'a hill'; but the people who had asked the question took the answer to be the name of that particular hill and accordingly called it *Pen Hill*, which means literally 'hill hill'.

Much the same thing appears to have happened with rivers. There are several rivers in England called "Avon". Now *afon* is the Welsh for 'river', so *River Avon* means literally 'river river': again it looks as if the invaders asked for the name of a particular river and receiving in reply the common noun for 'a river' took that to be the proper name of the river in question.

But that's not the end of the story for Pendle Hill: we still have the second syllable in *Pendle* to account for. What seems to have happened is that the name *Pen Hill*, when pronounced quickly or lazily, came to sound like "Pennle", or, with the addition of an intrusive medial /d/, "Pendle". That form, then, was taken as one word, and was thought to be the name of the hill; so *hill* was added again, giving us the current form, *Pendle Hill*, which means, of course, 'hill hill hill'.

I don't know of any name in Australia that can match Pendle Hill for tautology; but when it comes to the sound of a name, Australian Aboriginal place-names are in a class of their own, as in the second stanza of John Dunmore Lang's "Colonial Nomenclature" (1824):

I like the native names, as Parramatta,
  And Illawarra, and Woolloomooloo,
Nandowra, Woogarora, Bulkomatta,
  Tomah, Toongabbie, Mittagong, Meroo;
Buckobble, Cumleroy, and Coolingatta,
  The Warragumby, Bargo, Burradoo;
Cookbundoon, Carrabaiga, Wingecarribbee,
  The Wollondilly, Yurumbon, Bungarribee.

With names such as these it's the sound you revel in rather than the sense – unless you know the original languages and hence the meanings of the names. (Isn't it the sound of *Llanfairpwllgwynggyll* ... and the rest of it, right down to the *-gogogoch*, that tourists love to hear Welsh speakers say, whether or not they know its meaning, 'St Mary's Church in the hollow of the white hazel near a rapid whirlpool and the Church of St Tysilio by the red cave'?)

But you can't always be sure of the sound, as demonstrated by a delightful story my former colleague Alan Brissenden once told me about a little place in South Australia spelled E-U-R-E-L-I-A. He said this used to be an important railway station of which the pronunciation was disputed. (Its origin, by the way, is uncertain. It looks Greek to me – as Casca the conspirator might have said; some writers derive it from an Aboriginal word meaning 'place of the ear'; others offer no explanation.) There used to be two porters, Alan said, who would stand one at each end of the platform to greet arriving trains: as the train pulled in, one of them would announce, loud and clear, "You're a liar! You're a liar!", to which the other would reply, with equal clarity, "You really are! You really are!"

NEWFANGLEDNESS

Newfangled may look like a newfangled word (i.e., in the current sense, a novel word, one that has only recently been invented), but in fact it's no such thing: it's at least 600 years old. Chaucer is the first recorded user of the word in English: he spells it without the final -*d*, and he uses it to describe not a thing that is novel but a person (or an animal) that is fond of novelty. This sense of the adjective, together with the corresponding sense 'love of novelty' for the noun *newfangle(d)ness*, comes out clearly in a famous passage from the Squire's tale in which the deserted female falcon describes the fickleness of males:

> Men loven of propre kynde newefanglenesse
> As briddes doon that men in cages fede.
> For though thou nyght and day take of hem hede,
> And strawe hir cage faire and softe as silk,
> And yeve hem sugre, hony, breed and milk,
> Yet right anon as that his dore is uppe
> He with his feet wol spurne adoun his cuppe,
> And to the wode he wole and wormes ete;
> So newefangel been they of hire mete,
> And loven novelries of propre kynde,
> No gentillesse of blood ne may hem bynde.   (*CT* V 610–20)

That's to say, roughly, 'Men, by their very nature, love novelty, just as caged birds do. No matter how you pamper them, strawing their cages as if with silk, and feeding them sugar, honey, bread and milk, as soon as the door is left open the bird will kick over the cup and fly away to the wood to eat worms: they're so keen on newness in their food and love novelty so much by their very nature that no gentility of blood can restrain them'.

But males had no monopoly on instability in the Middle Ages (any more than they do now): another short poem, entitled by editors "Against Women Unconstant" and generally thought to be Chaucer's, begins:

> Madame, for your newefanglenesse
> Many a servaunt have ye put out of grace.
> I take my leve of your unstedfastnesse,
> For wel I wot, whyl ye have lives space,
> Ye can not love ful half yeer in a place,
> To newe thing your lust is ay so kene

— from which it's clear enough that here, too, *newefanglenesse* means 'love of novelty, lust (i.e., desire) for what is new'.

Two hundred years later Shakespeare is still using the words in this sense, as when he has Rosalind warn Orlando that, once married, she will be 'more newfangled than an ape, more giddy in [her] desires than a monkey' (*As You Like It* 4.1.143–5). But already, by his time, the sense has begun to be transferred to the thing that is new rather than to the person who desires it, as in the opening lines of Sonnet 91:

> Some glory in their birth, some in their skill,
> Some in their wealth, some in their body's force,
> Some in their garments (though new-fangled ill)

i.e., some glory in their clothes, even if they're hideously new-fashioned.

But it's not the *new* part of the word that looks odd to current readers, it's the *fangle* bit. Where does that come from? It's from the now archaic verb *to fang*, meaning 'to catch, grasp, or seize' (with the diminutive suffix -*le* as in *babble*, *nestle*, *twinkle*, etc.), hence the early sense, 'wanting to seize on what is new'. And, yes, the verb *fang* is indeed connected with the noun *fang*, as in a wolf's *fangs*, which are, of course, used to seize things with.

As for Lady Thatcher, her dentistry may look newfangled, but you can bet she hasn't lost her bite.

NICKNAMES

A *nickname* is not, as one might at first sight suppose, a name that has been stolen or *nicked* from somewhere else: it is, literally, an 'additional name'. The current form of the word, with the first element as *nick-*, is in fact a corruption of the earlier form *eke-name* (with the first element as *eke-*).

This word *eke* is probably best known today as a verb, in the expression *to eke out*, meaning 'to make (something) last longer' – whether by adding bits to it to make it go further or by using it sparingly. You might *eke out* a bottle of whisky, for example, by watering it down, or you might *eke out* an essay by padding it out with repetitions, or a speech by putting in lots of *ums* and *ers* and *well nows* and *finallys* and *in conclusions*. Portia in *The Merchant of Venice* gives us a particularly moving example of this use in the third of the casket scenes, the one in which it's Bassanio's turn to try to win her hand. By the terms of her father's will, she's not free to marry the man of her own choice: she must marry the one who himself makes the right choice from the caskets of gold, silver, and lead. She's passionately in love with Bassanio, longing for him to make his choice, so that, if he chooses the right casket, she can have him; but at the same time, she's trying to make him wait before choosing, so that, if he makes the wrong choice, she will at least have had his company for a couple of days before he chooses:

> I pray you tarry. Pause a day or two
> Before you hazard, for in choosing wrong
> I lose your company.   (3.2.1–3)

(That "choosing . . . I" is a lovely example of a *hanging participle* or a *wrongly attached participle*, by the way, or, as the Americans call it, a *dangling modifier*: the syntax makes it sound as if Portia, not Bassanio, is doing the choosing. But Shakespeare wasn't bothered by the injunctions of prescriptive grammarians: most of them came after his time.) Portia continues in this vein for another twenty-odd lines before remarking eventually on her own long-windedness:

> I speak too long, but 'tis to piece the time,
> To eke it, and to draw it out in length
> To stay you from election.   (3.2.22–4)

She's trying to break time down into little pieces, that is, to *eke it out*, to stretch it, to make it last for as long as possible before Bassanio chooses, in case he makes the wrong choice and she has to lose him immediately afterwards.

This is a disputed passage, by the way: some editors read *eche* for *eke* (which makes no difference to the sense, these being cognate forms of the same word, like *kirk* and *church* or *ditch* and *dyke*); some also read *peize* or *peise* for *piece*, deriving it from French *peser* 'to weigh'. The sense would then be that Portia is trying to weigh time down so as to make it go more slowly. This is one instance, however, where the scholarly battle makes little difference in the long run (except to the combatants): whichever readings one adopts, the general sense is still that she is trying to make the time before Bassanio makes his choice last longer.

An *eke*-name, then, is originally an *additional* name: your real name is *eked out* by having another name added to it, and in time this *ekename* may become a substitute for the original. But how did *ekename* become *nickname*? It's a simple case of incorrect word division: if you say "an ekename" quickly, the hearer can't tell from the enunciation whether it's "*an* ekename" or "*a* nekename". When the words were written down in the Middle Ages by people who had never seen them in writing, the *n* evidently got detached from the *an* and attached to the *eke*, giving us a *nekename*; and when the vowel sound in *eke* is subsequently shortened through fast or lazy pronunciation, we end up with today's form, *nickname*.

Incorrect word division along these lines is not at all uncommon, and it can happen either way. *Nuncle*, the Fool's affectionate name for King Lear (derived from *mine uncle*), shows the same process as *nickname*. An *adder*, on the other hand, was in Old English a *nædre*; and an *orange* is ultimately from Arabic *nāranj* (it had already lost its initial *n* in French before coming into English). Whereas with *nickname* the *n* has been detached from the indefinite article and added to the noun, in these last two instances we see the results of the reverse process: the *n* has become detached from the noun and added to the indefinite article.

OBNOXIOUS AND PERILOUS

If I were to suggest that the eye is the most *obnoxious* organ in the body, you would surely think I had taken leave of my senses. What could be more delightful, less obnoxious, than someone's eyes (unless their owner happens to be giving one a baleful or a venomous look)? Well, we shall see.

Several of the questions in *Sidrak and Bokkus* are concerned with superlatives: what are the most necessary occupations? which animals live longest? what is the best thing people can have? what the worst? and so on. One of these questions asks, "Whiche is the perilousest lym/ That manis body hath in hym?" (L7583–4), that is, 'What is the most perilous organ in the human body?' (*Lym* is the ancestor of MnE *limb*; but in the Middle Ages it didn't have to contain either a -*b* or a bone.)

I don't think one has to have a particularly one-track mind to anticipate that the answer will be the sexual organ, because that is the organ most likely to lead people into sin (whether in deed or only in thought), and thus into hell. It comes as something of a surprise, then, to find that the answer is the eye. The reason (at least, the first reason) given, on the other hand, is pretty much what one would expect from a medieval text: the eye is dangerous because it shows tempting things to the brain and heart; the heart desires them and thus falls into sin; it wouldn't have fallen into sin if the eye hadn't shown it such a tempting sight to start with.

So far, so good: the eye is *perilous* in the usual, active, sense: it is 'fraught with danger', that is, it puts people or things in danger. From this point of view, if one happens to be a stern moralist, one might indeed call the eye *obnoxious* in the current sense, because putting people in danger is a pretty 'objectionable' or 'odious' thing to do.

But the answer doesn't stop there. It goes on to say that the eye is *perilous* because it is "tendre and ethe to dere" (L7870), that is, 'vulnerable and easily hurt' – a comment that must surely remind admirers of Milton of the opening speech of the blind Samson in *Samson*

Agonistes, "why was the sight/ To such a tender ball as th'eye confin'd/ So obvious and so easy to be quench't?" (93–5). In this instance, then, the eye is *perilous* because it is *imperilled*; it is itself in danger: it is *obnoxious* in the earlier sense of that word, that is, 'susceptible to injury' (from Latin *ob-* 'in the way of' + *noxa* 'hurt').

But how can a word meaning 'vulnerable' come to mean 'offensive'? And how can a word meaning 'likely to cause danger' come to mean 'likely to suffer danger'? Quite easily in both cases. With *obnoxious* it's probably a case, as with *buxom*, of the sound influencing the sense: *noxious* exists in its own right as an adjective meaning 'harmful', as in *noxious waste* or *noxious weeds*; and *ob-* is a prefix that in a number of words, such as *obstacle*, *obstinate*, or *obfuscation*, has what one might call *objectionable* overtones. As for *perilous*, it's not so very rare for an adjective to have both active and passive senses: *suspicious* and *fearful* exhibit a similar capacity to mean both 'feeling suspicion' and 'open to suspicion', 'fearing' and 'feared'; and although *perilous* has not previously been recorded in the passive sense 'in danger', *OED* tells us that this sense is still found in certain dialects of the United States for the synonymous word *dangerous*, as in (sense 4, final quotation) "He's dangerous; they don't think he'll live".

THE OLD WAGGON AND THE DEATH OF ENGLISH DIALECTS

Compulsory education and the impact of broadcasting have a lot to answer for: between them they have pretty nearly wiped out the regional dialects that used to be so rich a feature of the language, not just in different countries of the world, but in different parts of every country where English is spoken. No one has done more to preserve the dialects from extinction than the poets who were brave enough to prefer their own local dialect to standard English, and amongst the dialect poets none more than Robbie Burns in the Lowlands of Scotland, John Clare in East Anglia, and William Barnes in Dorset. (Burns's Scots is a dialect of English: it is quite distinct from Scottish Gaelic.) It is curious that Barnes is not (yet) as well known outside his own county as the other two; but his time must come. I reproduce here one of his loveliest poems, "The Wold Waggon", in the spelling of the first edition of his *Poems of Rural Life in the Dorset Dialect* (1844). No single poem can be expected to show all the features of the dialect, of course, but this one gives a fair idea of the care Barnes took to get them right.

THE WOLD WAGGON

THE girt wold waggon uncle had
When I wer up a hardish lad,
Did stan' a-screen'd vrom het an' wet
In zummer, at the barken geät,
Below the elems' spreadèn boughs,
A-rubb'd by al the pigs an' cows.
An' I 've a-clum his head an' zides
A-riggèn up ar jumpèn down,
A-plâyèn, ar in happy rides
Along the liane, ar droo the groun'.
An' many souls be in ther griaves

That us'd to ride upon his riaves,
An' he an' al the hosses too.
'V' a-ben a-done var years agoo.

Upon his head an' tâil wer pinks
A-pâinted al in tangled links;
His two long zides were blue; his bed
Wer bended upward at the head;
His riaves rose gently in a bow
Above his slow hind-wheels below.
Vour hosses wer a-kept to pull
The girt wold waggon when 'twer vull,
The black miare *Smiler*, strong enough
To pull a house down by herzuf,
So big as took my biggest strides
To stroddle hafewoy down her zides;
An' champèn *Vilot*, sprack an' light,
That foam'd an' pull'd wi' al her might;
An' *Whitevoot*, liazy in the triace
Wi' cunnen looks, an' snowwhite fiace,
Bezides a bây oone, shart-tâil *Jack*,
That wer a triace-hoss ar a hack.

How many luoads o' vuzz to scald
The milk, *thik* waggon 'ave a-hal'd!
An' wood vrom copse, an' poles var râils,
An' bavins wi' ther bushy tâils,
An' loose-ear'd barley hangèn down
Outzide the wheels, a'most to groun',
An' luoads o' hây so sweet an' dry,
A-builded strâight an' long an' high,
An' hâymiakers, a-zittèn roun'
The riaves a-ridèn huome vrom groun',
When *Jim* gi'e'd *Jenny*'s lips a smack
An' jealous *Dicky* whipp'd his back,
An' mâidens scream'd to veel the thumps
A-gi'e'd by trenches an' by humps.

But he an' al his hosses too,
'V' a-ben a-done var years agoo.

There are a few words here that will be unfamiliar, or used in unfamiliar senses. A *hardish* lad is not a tough boy but a well-grown one. The *barken* is the farmyard; it's a dialect form of *barton* (OE *bere-tūn* 'barley enclosure'), related to *barn* (OE *bere-ern* 'barley place'). *A-riggèn up* is climbing up – "in play or wantonness" Barnes tells us in the Glossary to the 1844 collection; it's connected, according to the *OED*, with the noun *rig* 'a wanton girl or woman' ('of obscure origin'). The *riaves* of the waggon form the 'ladderlike frame work attached to the sides of a wagon to uphold the load extended laterally over the wheels' (Barnes's own definition, from the Glossary); in that part of Shropshire where I grew up, as my brother Robert reminds me, they're called *ripples* (with a different term, *gormers*, for the frames attached at the front and back ends of the cart). *Sprack* is a favourite adjective with Barnes; he defines it as 'lively' or 'active'; but its origin is unknown. So, also, is that of *bavin*, defined with great precision in *OED* as 'a bundle of brushwood or light underwood, such as is used in bakers' ovens, differing from a fagot in being bound with only one withe or band instead of two'; it's a word I had not met before reading this poem, but it's not, apparently, a dialect word.

The pronouns used of the waggon are *he* and *his*, not *it* and *its*. This is not, as one might at first suppose, a land-lubber's answer to a sailor's use of *she* and *her* for a ship; as Barnes explains in §43 of the Dissertation prefixed to the 1844 edition, "The masculine pronoun *he* or *'e* is still used in Dorset for inanimate nouns, as *he* was in Anglo-Saxon; in which language, as a consequence of its case-endings, many things without life were taken as of the masculine or feminine gender. Indeed it is sometimes said in joke that every thing is *he* but a tom cat, and that is *she*." The demonstrative pronoun used with the waggon is *thik*, not *that*; and again, the explanation is best left to Barnes (in §47 of the Dissertation): "*Theos* ['this'] and *thik* ['that'] are . . . applied only to individual nouns, and not to quantities of matter, which in Anglo-Saxon were of the neuter gender, and which we should still name as *this* or *that*. We may say *theos* or *thik* tree, or *stuone*, but it would be wrong to say *theos* or *thik* water or milk. It would be *this* or *that* water or milk."

The other notable grammatical features in the poem are all to do with verbs. In §53 and §54 of the Dissertation Barnes points out the non-emphatic use of the verb *to do* in the conjugation of verbs: "I da work" means simply 'I work'; but *did* with the infinitive forms the imperfect tense (for a repeated or habitual action) as opposed to the simple past (for a single action). So the waggon "did stan'" below the elms at the gate of the yard because that's where it always used to stand; if it had stood there just once, the verb would have been *stood*. Readers who had *was* drummed into them in primary school as the past tense singular of the verb *to be* may feel superior about "I wer up a hardish lad" and "his bed/ Wer bended upward", but Barnes points out that *wer(e)* is the regular form in his dialect (Dissertation, §49). The initial *a-* prefixed to past participles (*a-screen'd*, *a-rubb'd*, *a-ben*, *a-done*, etc.) is a survival of the Old English perfective prefix *ge-*, which, when it survives in standard English, appears as *y-*, as in the (now archaic) form *yclept* (§55); that prefixed to present participles, of which there are several examples in this poem (*a-riggèn*, *a-plâyèn*, *a-zittèn*, *a-ridèn*) is from a different source, Old English *on* plus the verbal noun (as in "Daddy's gone a-hunting"). The Dorset preference for *-ed* forms of the past tense and past participle (§15) is seen in this poem in *bended*, *a-builded* and *(a-)gi'e'd* (for *gived*); conversely *a-clum* shows the retention of a strong form of the past tense from Old English: *climb* belonged to the same class as *sing* and *ring* (see *ring, rang, rung*); its forms would have been *climb* (present, with a short *i*), *clamb* (past), *clumb* (past participle).

The first surprise in pronunciation is the initial *w-* in *old* in the title and the first line of the poem, making it look as if *old* were pronounced as in the Cots-*wolds* or Stow on the *Wold*, to alliterate with *waggon*. But this is one instance where Barnes's spelling is in fact misleading: elsewhere he says that the long *o* diphthong is (approximately) a combination of the sounds "ooh" and "uh", as in *boot* and *but*, so that *old* would have sounded something like "oould". This is better shown by the *uo* spellings in *luoads* and *huome* – and Barnes's frequent rhyming of *home* with *come* shows that the second element of the diphthong is indeed close to the short *u* sound in *come*. *Girt* in line 1 shows metathesis of the consonant and vowel in *great* (cf. *thrills* below). The word *het* (line 3) shows that *heat* has a short vowel, making an internal rhyme with *wet*; and *wet* rhymes with *gate*, the spelling *geät* together with the rhyme suggesting a pronunciation somewhere near "gi-et" or "gyet". If this sounds West Indian, it's less surprising than might at first be supposed: spoken English in the West Indies has been strongly influenced by Bajan pronunciation, and many of the early settlers in Barbados came from the West Country. This pronunciation is confirmed by the rhyming of *gate* with *let* in "The leäne" in Barnes's second collection of dialect poems; but elsewhere he rhymes *gate* with expected forms such as *late*, as well as with unexpected ones such as *beat*. It is impossible at this distance in time to know how exact these rhymes were; but it's a reasonable assumption that in all these instances the sound after the initial consonant approximated to "i-et" or "yet".

The long *a* diphthong in situations where the standard English spelling is *a*+consonant+*e* is consistently spelled *ia* in the 1844 collection, as in *liane, griaves, riaves, liazy, triace, fiace, -miakers* in this poem, suggesting that all such words in Barnes's Blackmore Vale dialect had the Bajan *a* (as we might now consider it). I am reminded of a limerick with an embarrassment of rhymes on this sound that my father used to recite – in broad Bajan – to tease my mother (who was born and brought up in Barbados, and who spoke all her life with a gentle Bajan accent). It's a sort of "How now brown cow" for Bajan speakers, used in the bad old days (but I presume no longer) to inculcate the RP pronunciation of long *a* in place of the Bajan equivalent:

> I once knew a young man called Tate
> Who had a date at eight eight,
> But I am sad to relate
> That this young man called Tate
> Was *late* for his date at eight eight.

In Barnes's 1844 spelling the *-ate* words in this limerick would all have been *-iate*: *Tiate, diate, reliate*, and *liate*. The odd word out is *eight*: though its vowel is indistinguishable in standard English from that in *late*, it derives from a different source, as does the diphthong in words now spelled with *ai* or *ay*, such as *rain* and *play*. The sounds in all these words have fallen together in RP, but they were originally different, and they remained so for Barnes. This is shown by his use of a circumflex over the *a* in such words: *tâil, pâinted, râils, strâight, mâidens, bây, hây* in this poem, *wâight* and *âight* (for *weight* and *eight*) in others. Recordings deposited in the Dorchester library by some of Dorset's few remaining dialect speakers show that the diphthong in these words that Barnes spelled with *âi* or *ây* in 1844 is somewhere between the vowel sounds in *day* and *die* – as in a Cockney rendering of "The rain in Spain stays mainly on the plain" or as in broad Australian "G'day".

Other long vowel or diphthong sounds in *The wold waggon* that may cause surprise are those in *half-way* (here *hafewoy*) and *ago* (here *agoo*, rhyming with *too*). That the latter was the normal pronunciation in the Blackmore Vale in Barnes's day is shown by his consistent spelling of *go* and *ago* with double *oo* and by the frequent rhymes of one of these words with the sound in *do*, *two*, *who*, etc. Whereas *half* and *laugh* invariably have their standard English spelling in the final collection of Barnes's dialect poems in 1879, they are never so spelled in the first collection, where the usual spellings, *hafe* (as here) and *lafe* or *lafe*, may be taken as a fair indication of the dialectal pronunciation. Similarly, the frequent rhyming of *(a)way* with *boy* (usually spelled *(a)woy/ buoy* in 1844) confirms the usefulness as a guide to pronunciation of the spelling *hafewoy*.

The *ar* for *or* spelling, used consistently in 1844 and seen in this poem in *ar*, *var*, and *shart*, reflects the pronunciation indicated by such rhymes in other poems as *storm/ harm*, *corn/ barn*, and *short/ heart*. But that the combination *ors* was not subject to the same rule can be seen here from the spelling *hosses* for *horses*. Barnes is completely consistent about this: *horse* is invariably *hoss* (sometimes rhyming with *across*); *Dorset* is always *Do'set*, not (as in some parts of the county today) *Darzet*. That Smiler was "strong enough/ To pull a house down by herzuf" establishes the pronunciation of *self*; and *stroddle* for *straddle* shows the interchangeability of short *a* and short *o* sounds in some words: *zot* is Barnes's normal spelling for *sat*, and John Bloom the miller (in "John Bloom in Lon'on", in the third collection) was famously partial to "a drap avore [his] nap".

Consonant sounds present fewer difficulties than vowels and diphthongs. The briefest glance will show that initial *s-* and *f-* are often voiced (as common in the south and west of England): *zot*, as we have just seen, and, in this poem, *zummer*, *zides*, *bezides*, *outzide*, and *vour*, *vull*, White*voot*, *vuzz*, *vrom*, and *veel*. Barnes makes it clear in his commentaries that this voicing occurred only in certain native English words, not in foreign imports. The assumption is not, of course, that Dorset people said to themselves, "I won't voice the *f* in *farm* because that's a French word", but that the voicing occurred early in the history of the dialect, and that it didn't affect words that were subsequently imported. The italics used for the initial sound in "*th*ik" were Barnes's way of indicating that the sound was voiced, as in *this*, not voiceless, as in *thick*; his spelling *droo* for *through* shows that the initial sound in *through* was, as it were, doubly voiced – first to the initial sound in *though* then to that in *dough*.

Consonant sounds are often lost, especially at the ends of words, as in *stan'*, *an'*, *groun'*, *wi'*, and the present participles ending in *-èn* for *-ing*: *plâyèn*, *spreadèn*, *jumpèn*, *hangèn*, etc.; and *gi'e'd* (for *gived*) shows that the addition of an inflexional ending does not necessarily mean that the consonant sound will be restored. That initial *h-* is often dropped (as in many other regional dialects) is shown by *'ave* and *'v*. The spelling *elems* shows that *elm* was disyllabic for Barnes (as *film* and *milk* still are in some pronunciations today); conversely elision of the second syllable is indicated by the spelling *Vilot* for *Violet*, a characteristically delicate name for a carthorse (albeit a light one), reminding me of *Blossom*, one of the two carthorses that still did occasional work on our farm when I was a boy.

How sad that so few of Britain's colourful dialects have been preserved with the ear and eye for detail that William Barnes bestowed on the language of his beloved Blackmore Vale! Almost all the others *'v* a-been a-done var years agoo.

POLICY, POLITICIANS, AND THE POLICE

These words are all derived ultimately from the Greek *polis* 'city, state', a word that survives as the second element in *metropolis* 'mother-city', *necropolis* 'corpse-city' (hence 'cemetery'), South Australia's aborted *Multi-Function Polis*, etc. Aristotle entitled his treatise on government *ta politika*, 'The Politics'; *politics* remains our word for the art of governing the state; *politicians* are those involved in that business; the affairs they deal with are called *political*; it is their business to promote and pursue that *policy* or plan of action that they deem best for the government of the country; the *police* are entrusted with the maintenance of law and order in the state; and both *police* and *politicians* are supposed to carry out their duties in a *politic* or judicious manner.

Those are the good senses; but, no doubt because government is anything but a straightforward business, most of the derivatives of *polis* have acquired bad senses that co-exist with the good ones. So a *politic* plan is likely to have more to do with pragmatism than with principle, and a *political* decision to have more to do with keeping one's own party in power than with the good of the country: thus *politic* comes to mean 'cunning', *political* to mean 'partisan'. As for *politicians*, even those that set out with the highest ideals are likely to find that they have to use questionable means to bring about their high-minded ends (as illustrated some years ago in the feature film, *The Candidate*): thus *politician* develops the sense 'a shrewd schemer; a crafty plotter or intriguer'.

It's this latter sense – the pejorative one – that is given as the first sense for *politician* in *OED*, though the first example in this sense is almost exactly contemporaneous with the first example under the neutral sense, 'one practically engaged in conducting the business of the state'. Indeed, it's not always easy to tell from the accompanying quotations which sense of the word is intended. When, for example, Shakespeare has Hotspur say of King Henry IV (Henry Bolingbroke),

> Why, look you, I am whipped and scourged with rods,
> Nettled and stung with pismires, when I hear
> Of this vile politician Bolingbroke,   (*I Henry IV*, 1.3.237–9)

which is he suggesting: that the King is a vile schemer or that he's a bad head of government? Probably the former (as *OED* has it); but since Hotspur's outburst has been provoked by Henry's power – the underhand way he acquired it, and the inequitable way he is using it – , the latter sense would fit the context just as well. And since *politicians* are more or less obliged to be devious in order to get and keep power, this is hardly surprising. (*Pismires*, by the way, is an old word for 'ants', so called, according to *OED*, "from the urinous smell of an anthill".)

That *politician* acquired the elevated sense 'statesman' in the sixteenth century and retained it until the nineteenth, but that it's now well on the way to re-acquiring the bad sense 'intriguer' listed first (and, for the moment at least, marked obsolete) in *OED*, is a nice comment on the quality of present-day politicians – some of whom, as we are from time to time reminded, would be better placed in the hands of the *police* than in houses of parliament. I don't think *politician* is quite so mild a snarl-word now as Brook suggested it was in 1958. But it does offer a nice demonstration of the capacity of single words to undergo both amelioration and pejoration, and to revert to older senses as well as to acquire new ones: *politician* has pretty nearly gone full circle.

PRECISION RULES, OK?

One of my secret vanities when I was a young man was that I had no obvious verbal mannerisms: I didn't say "sort of" every second word, or "you know" (as Prince Charles used to say when he was younger); and I don't think I used any of those other meaningless space-fillers that people frequently fall into. I used to be pretty proud about this – until I got my come-uppance at the advanced age of twenty-three, in a way that makes me blush to this day.

I was in Uganda, taking a Diploma in Education (in Teaching English as a Second Language) at Makerere University College in Kampala. We (the Dip.Ed. students) had been sent out on teaching practice towards the end of the course, and one of the lecturers had come out to observe us in action and to give us some feedback on how we were doing. (It was in fact Lionel Billows, that colossus of English Language Teaching whose recent death at the grand old age of ninety-five has given rise to some moving tributes in the TESOL journals. "We stand on the shoulders of giants," writes Alan Maley, "and Lionel was one of them.")

After the lesson Billows began with some positive remarks, and then said to me, "So far, so good, but – " ("Please, no! But me no buts!") "but you'd come over a bit better if you got rid of that irritating verbal tic of yours."

What? Surely not! This couldn't be true. He must have imagined it.

But he was insistent. "You end nearly every sentence with 'OK?' with a questioning inflection. Fair enough: you don't want to go too fast for the class; you want to make sure no one's left behind. That's good practice. But there are other ways of finding out whether a thing has been understood besides asking 'OK?' Think about it."

Well, I thought about it; and when I'd recovered a little from my mortification, it occurred to me that I could get some good pedagogical mileage out of this – and wouldn't that look good in my lesson-plan book? Nothing like a bit of self-criticism to impress your supervisors! If Billows had noticed it in the space of just one class, it was a safe bet that the boys would have noticed it, too, since I'd been teaching them for three weeks already.

Right, then: I'd admit it to them, and see if I could use it as a lever to cure one of *their* verbal tics. They were going to have to take an oral exam as well as a written one; any obvious verbal idiosyncrasies would be penalized. One fault that was almost universal amongst them (*fault*, that is, from the point of view of standard British English, though it must surely have become acceptable East African English by now – but my brief then was to prepare them for an examination still supervised by a British authority) – one fault, I say, was to begin every utterance with "anyway". They used it for a thinking-space, as a native English speaker might unconsciously use "um" or "well" (or "you know", if it comes to that). If you asked a boy his name, he'd be almost certain to reply, "Anyway, my name is Abraham Lincoln Musoke" (or whatever it was) – and he was going to be penalized for this in his oral exam. I'd had several goes at them about it, and it hadn't made a blind bit of difference.

Next morning I couldn't wait to get into that classroom. I went straight up to the blackboard and wrote "ANYWAY" in block capitals in the top left-hand corner and "OK" in block capitals in the top right. "Boys," I said, "we're going to have a competition. You know how I'm always getting at you for saying 'anyway'? Well, every time one of you says it from now on, I'm going to chalk up a mark here on the left and you're going to lose a point." Groans. "But it seems you're not the only ones who say things without knowing you're doing it. Mr Billows told me yesterday that I'm always saying 'OK?', so any time you catch me saying that from now on, one of you is to jump up, take a piece of chalk, and put a mark up here on the right, and I'll lose a point; and whichever side has lost the fewest points at the end of the lesson wins, OK?"

Gales of laughter. I started to think I was pretty damned smart: this was going to work.

Francis Xavier Kigozi in the front row jumped up, grabbed the chalk from me, and put a mark under "OK", to some titters and catcalls from the other boys.

"Eh? I haven't said it yet, surely?"

"Yes, you've just said it: 'Whoever has the fewest points at the end of the lesson wins, OK?'"

I put my head in my hands in despair and disbelief. Francis went to sit down and as he did so Jackson Bulumba raced forward from the back, took the chalk from him and started to write something else on the board. This time the laughter was thunderous. I turned round to see what he'd written, and there, at the top right-hand side of the board, beside "OK", I saw "PRECI" and, as I watched, he finished with "SELY".

"Oh, no! Don't tell me I say *precisely* as well, do I?"

This time the laughter was so uproarious that the history master came in from the next classroom to see what was going on. He was greeted by a blast of *OK*s, *exactly*s, and *precisely*s sufficiently strong almost to blow him back out through the door. I told him not to worry, everything was under control (er, sort of); we were just having a game about verbal mannerisms, and I was being beaten hollow, and the class was loving it.

That evening I compared notes with Cyprian Cele, one of the Ugandans taking the Dip.Ed. at the same time. We'd been sent to the same school for our teaching practice, and were sharing a house. (That was good: he was a scientist and a local; I was a foreigner and a language teacher; we got to talk about problems outside our own immediate field.) I told him about my exploits of the morning. He laughed almost as uproariously as the boys had done. "Anyway, Tom," he said, "I was looking forward to sharing a house with an Englishman. I thought it might help to improve my own English. But you know what? I think the only phrase I've learnt from you is '*Bloody Hell!*'"

PREPOSITIONS AT THE END OF A SENTENCE

There has long been, amongst sticklers for correctness in written English, a curious prejudice against ending a clause or a sentence with a preposition; but, as Sir Ernest Gowers says, in his forthright way, "No good writer ever heeded it, except Dryden, who seems to have invented it. . . . The very rule itself, if phrased 'do not use a preposition to end a sentence with', has a smoother flow and a more idiomatic ring than 'do not use a preposition with which to end a sentence.' "

The translators of the King James Bible were not afraid to end their clauses with prepositions. God's own speech in Jacob's dream of the ladder reaching to heaven ends with one: "I will not leave thee, until I have done that which I have spoken to thee of" (Genesis 28: 15); and Jesus himself says that he has "a baptism to be baptized with" (Luke 12: 50). The famous Fowler brothers used a preposition to end the first paragraph of their preface to *The King's English*, assuring those authors and newspapers whose inelegancies were frequently quoted that this was not meant to imply that they erred more often than others, but that it showed merely that they had been "among the necessarily limited number chosen to collect instances from" (p. 4). When a reviewer "condemned [the] book out of hand" because of the supposed gaffe of ending this sentence with "from" (p. 179), the response was the detailed argument to be found under the article "preposition at end" in H.W. Fowler's *A Dictionary of Modern English Usage*. The article ends with a fistful of delightful examples of clauses ending with prepositions, taken from most of the best writers of English from the fourteenth century to the twentieth. The list begins with Chaucer; it includes Shakespeare ("Such bitter business as the day Would quake to look on"); and it ends with Kipling ("Too horrible to be trifled with"). And the latest edition of Fowler's *Modern English Usage*, revised by Robert Burchfield, illustrates a number of circumstances "in which a preposition may or even must appear at the end of a clause or sentence" (p. 618). In the last word

discussed in this book – *wassail* – I have been emboldened by such powerful backing to use a preposition to end with!

Winston Churchill's famous marginal parody of the kind of artificial English that avoids putting prepositions at the end (a comment that I have not been able to trace to its source, though it is often quoted in books on usage) makes the point beautifully: "This," he is reputed to have written, "is the sort of English up with which I will not put". I think he would have enjoyed the story passed on to me by my former student, Trudy Brown, demonstrating that it is possible to end a sentence with five prepositions. "A child asked the babysitter to bring a book from downstairs and read her a bedtime story. When the babysitter returned with the wrong book, the child demanded furiously, 'What did you bring that book I don't want to be read to out of up for?' " (Both Gowers and Burchfield give a slightly different version of this anecdote, in which the sentence ends with a mere four prepositions.)

I am reminded of a punning anecdote reported to me by another of my former students, Fiona Pollock. "The sex-starved daughter of a prison governor offered a male prisoner whom she fancied the chance to escape from jail if he would sleep with her. He replied, 'It's a tempting offer; but I'm afraid it's against my principles to end a sentence with a proposition.'"

PROVERBS (1)

Proverbs and sayings are relatively stable in comparison with other aspects of language, doubtless because they are handed down from generation to generation in a fixed form – though, of course, the meaning sometimes shifts along with the sense of the individual words, as with *more haste less speed* (see *speed*); or the syntax may be misleading, as with *all that glisters is not gold*, which some take to mean 'nothing that shines is gold', whereas a little thought will show that the sense must be '*not everything* that shines is gold'.)

In view of this relative stability, it is no surprise to find that some of our comparisons and similes relating to the natural world, like *bright as the sun* or *as white as snow*, date back to Anglo-Saxon times and consist entirely of native English words. Chaucer gives us two such comparisons for blackness in a single line of the Miller's tale, preparatory to the famous anal kiss:

> Derk was the nyght as pich, or as the cole,
> And at the wyndow out she putte hir hole,
> And Absolon ...   (*CT* I 3231–3)

– well, Absolon, as everybody knows, got a mouthful of what he was least expecting. Comparisons like these are, one might say, *as old as the hills*.

Nevertheless, such sayings are not all *carved in stone*, or, as we might now say, *set in concrete*. One might suppose that, in a primarily oral culture, the wording would necessarily be fixed, as an aid to memory, whereas in our print culture exactness of wording would matter less, because memory is less crucial when there's a written script to consult. In fact, the reverse is true: the evidence suggests that it was the writing down that caused the fixation: sayings that appear in Old and Middle English with many variations are known today in one standard form, with only an occasional variant. Here, for example, are half a dozen versions from the Middle English period (all listed under E216 in Whiting's

Proverbs) of the saying known to us in either of two fixed forms *what the eye doesn't see the heart doesn't rue* (or *doesn't grieve*): "That eye ne seeth, herte ne reweth"; "Hert sun ['soon'] for-gettes that ne ei seis"; "At e nocht seis, hart nocht yarnis"; "that thyng whiche the eyen see not the herte coveyteth not"; a positive form, "That the ey seith the hert doith rewe"; and finally, almost the current version, "That which the eye seeth not, the hart doth not rue".

In other instances the idea is the same then and now, but the terms have changed. Where we say, in our urban society, that *walls have ears*, they said a few hundred years ago that *the field has eyes and the wood has ears* (Whiting F127); and where we might say that so-and-so is *as blind as a bat* or *as a mole*, the comparison then was *as blind as a bee* (Whiting B163).

Dictionaries of proverbs are full of surprises like this. One of their great attractions is the sayings we have now lost that could profitably be revived. One that grows on me more with each passing year and that I am sometimes tempted to use on my students has it that *one may the old outrun but not outrede* (Whiting O29), that is, roughly, 'you can outrun old people but you can't out-think them' (see also *rede*); to which, however, I'm afraid they might reply that *the greatest clerks are not the wisest men* (Whiting C291), or even, if they'd been studying the Middle English *The Owl and the Nightingale* with the attention that poem deserves, that there's no point *yawning against an oven*, that is, 'arguing against a bigmouth' (Whiting O59).

PROVERBS (2)

One of the pleasures of editing a previously inedited text is the discovery of words or meanings not recorded in any dictionary. This pleasure extends beyond individual words to include complete phrases; and some of these phrases may have a proverbial ring, though they are not recorded in any existing dictionary of proverbs. *Sidrak and Bokkus* is full of such phrases.

On what grounds do I claim that certain phrases have "a proverbial ring"? Well, sometimes the author of the work tells us plainly that the phrase is proverbial, as in " 'It was never olde manne,'/ As men saye in olde sayyng,/ 'That he ne was wight whill he was yyng' " (B9232–4), that is, 'There was never an old man who was not [i.e., who does not claim to have been] valiant in his youth'.

In other instances, though the author doesn't say the phrase is a proverb, the combination of moral teaching with pithy expression in an epigrammatic way suggests that this is so. There are several such sayings in *Sidrak* concerned with heat or fire, along the lines of *playing with fire* or *a burnt child fears the fire*. At one point we are told that "Whoso on the fire goos,/ He brenneth bothe foote and toos" (L4597–8): one is tempted to add, *like a cat on hot bricks*. At another point we are warned that "The more that a man a fire leith ynne,/ The more and the hotter it wole brenne" (L6469–70), i.e., 'The more you put on a fire the hotter it burns'. At still another we are told that a man who boasts of more than he's capable of is "As he that flesshe sethe wolde kunne/ At the hete of the sunne" (L4960–2), i.e., he's like someone trying to cook meat (or, as we might say, "fry an egg") in the heat of the sun. And hot news, we are told, is too hot for some tongues to handle: "That many mouthes woote ['know']/ On somme tunge it lieth ful hoote" (L8309–10).

Sometimes the syntactical structure is the same as that in a surviving proverb. *The X-er the Y-er*, as in *the more the merrier*, occurs in a comment that is as apt for our acquisitive society as it was for the fifteenth century: "Ever the more he may wynne,/ The more care he is ynne"

(L4891–2), i.e., 'the more you get, the greater your care'. The syntax of *a bird in the hand is worth two in the bush* is found in a passage suggesting that one light in front is worth two behind:

> if a man goyng be
> In derknesse, there he may not see,
> And a lanterne goo hym before,
> Thereof hath he light wel more
> Than thogh behynde hym folowed twoo
> And for the light of them he might misgoo.   (B10069–74)

And sometimes a family relationship is suggested as well as a syntactical one, as in "Coveytyse, nought for to lye,/ She is the doughter of envye" (B2531–2), i.e., 'Covetousness is the daughter of envy', on the same lines as *necessity is the mother of invention*.

My most treasured find is a saying that might well be applied to people who go on air or into print to broadcast their discoveries: "As seith to us an oolde auctour, 'He that himself preiseth in towne,/ With an hors tord men shullen him crowne'" (L4742–4), i.e., in brief, 'a boaster shall be crowned with a horse turd'.

PUMPERNICKEL

Folk etymology works in insidious ways. We're all prone to perpetrate it, and language teachers are no exception – as I discovered to my embarrassment when I got my first teaching post after finishing my Dip.Ed. The school was in the little bush town of Kitgum, in the north of Uganda, not far south of the Sudan border. I arrived bursting with zeal, stuffed to the gills with Piaget's theory of conservation and other such niceties, and looking forward to the challenge (yes, I had buzz words like that oozing out of every orifice) of being the first native English speaker to teach in the school, apart from the Headmaster – and he was Irish.

There were three weeks of term left when I arrived. "I won't put you into the boys' classes you'll be teaching next term," said the Headmaster; "we might as well let them finish the term with their present teachers. At least they're qualified English teachers. But I want you to take over the top girls' class straightaway: I've been teaching them myself, and I'm a biologist!"

This (as I subsequently discovered) was his way of saying that he wasn't going to let any of the local teachers get their hands on *his* girls. It was a newish government school, only two and a half years old, and was supposed to have been co-educational. But Father Russell had other ideas. (I never did find out by what curious twist of fate a government school had come to be run by an Irish priest belonging to an Italian missionary order: it was one of the many things I never got to the bottom of.) Thus it came about that the school had two campuses, one for the girls, on the site of a former primary school near the town of Kitgum itself, and another for the boys, two miles further out into the bush: the timetable had to allow for a twenty-minute difference in starting time between classes at the two campuses, so that teachers would have time to travel the two miles in between. (Anything to keep the boys away from the girls.)

I asked Father Russell what he'd been doing with his class of girls.

"We've been reading *Vanity Fair*."

I swallowed hard and said, with the arrogance of the newly qualified, that I thought Thackeray was too difficult for students of that level: shouldn't I drop it quietly and teach some grammar instead?

"Oh, you can't do that: we've reached chapter three! They're getting interested in the story."

Chapter *three?* And they'd been doing that, and nothing but that, for nine weeks? At that rate we wouldn't finish the book before my two-year contract was up. I decided that the only thing to be done was to race through the rest of the book at breakneck speed to get through it within the remaining three weeks of term; then from the beginning of the next term we'd be able to get back on track with the grammar syllabus I was supposed to be teaching.

So we started our gallop: the girls would read ten pages (or however many it was) in the evening, not stopping to look up every word in the dictionary, and we'd discuss those pages the next day in class. I'd try to make sure that they were getting the gist of the story and that any major difficulties were cleared up; and I thought that that was about as much as we could hope to achieve.

Now it happened that I had never read *Vanity Fair* myself. (Too modern for me: I'm a medievalist – as Father Russell might have said.) The edition we were using was an abridged one (which made our three-week target less impossible than it might otherwise have been for second-language learners), but it was somewhat sparsely annotated, so that I had quite a bit of explaining to do. It became apparent fairly soon that the names of some of the characters were puns that the pupils could not be expected to interpret without prompting. "Dr Swishtail" is an apt enough name for a schoolmaster who (evidently) ruled by the cane; "Dobbin" is a suitably unheroic name for a man who becomes the hero of "a novel without a hero", one who, besides, carries the scorns and burdens of the world on his shoulders with the patience of a carthorse; and so on.

Thus we staggered on until we came (in chapter 62) to the "little comfortable ducal town of Pumpernickel". Now, strange though it may seem, *pumpernickel* was a word I had never before encountered. It did not occur to me that this was a common noun that could be looked up in a dictionary: I assumed it was one of those self-explanatory punning names like *Swishtail* that Thackeray had made up to give the reader an instant idea of the character of its bearer. And it was obvious that

Pumpernickel, with its operas, its grand dinners, its ballrooms, and its gaming tables, was a place where people got through a great deal of money in a short space of time. And so, keen to put into practice one of the very few useful pieces of advice I'd picked up when my doing my Dip.Ed. – "never *explain* when you can *demonstrate*" – I borrowed some coins from the friendly American Peace Corps teacher who lived in the other half of our semi-detached quarters, and proceeded solemnly to demonstrate to my class that Pumpernickel was so named because, like a one-armed bandit, it would *pump* your *nickels* out of you, no matter how hard you tried to hold onto them.

When I took Ned back his coins that evening, he asked me what I had wanted them for. I smiled, with such modesty as I could muster, and told him how I had used them to demonstrate the meaning of *Pumpernickel*. He looked at me with a kind of pitying incredulity, and said, "I hate to tell you this, Tahm, but pumpernickel is a kind of *bread*!"

So that's what I had to tell my class the next day. But I wish I had thought to look it up in a dictionary, not only because it would have saved me from one of the foolishest of my follies, but also because the etymologies suggested by lexicographers are rather more interesting than my own folk etymology. The various *Oxford* dictionaries say only that it's a German word of uncertain origin meaning (originally) a 'lout' or a 'bumpkin'; but the more adventurous *American Heritage Dictionary* suggests that it derives from German *Pumper* "breaking wind" and *Nickel* "a goblin": if this is right, *pumpernickel* has a little devil in it that makes you fart. Now *that* I could have demonstrated without having to borrow the materials from my neighbour!

Rage and Outrage

Rage is ultimately from the same root as *rabies*: both nouns are descended from the Latin verb *rabere* 'to rave'; both had the sense 'madness, insanity'; but whereas *rabies* had only the specialized sense denoting the hydrophobia of a mad dog or of a human bitten by a mad dog, *rage* was used of insanity of any kind, irrespective of its source.

It's not difficult to see how the sense of *rage* expanded to include first the anger and loss of control that is associated with madness, and then the violent action that often accompanies furious or uncontrollable feeling. This development is easily traced in *King Lear*: when Lear wakes from sleep after the scene between the blind Gloucester and himself in his madness, the Gentleman (in some texts the Doctor) reassures Cordelia with the words "Be comforted, good madam. The great rage/ You see is killed in him" (4.6.72–3). The literal sense is that Lear's madness is cured; but it was a madness that, as we saw in the previous scene, included both fury and violence, as in his threat, "And when I have stol'n upon these son-in-laws,/ Then kill, kill, kill, kill, kill, kill!" (182–3).

The kind of violence, excess, or loss of control implied could vary according to the context. Dorigen in Chaucer's Franklin's tale bewails her husband's departure for days on end, but eventually "hir grete sorwe gan aswage:/ She may nat alwey duren in swich rage" (*CT* V 835–6). Here the context requires that *rage* mean 'grief'. Elsewhere it can mean sexual passion, as in Chaucer's comment on Antony that "love hadde brought this man in swich a rage" for the love of Cleopatra "That al the world he sette at no value" (*LGW* 599–602). And in other contexts it can just mean violent pain, as in *a rage of teeth* (one of those *terms of association* that was at one time mistakenly thought to be a collective term, with the meaning 'a set of teeth', whereas it is in fact a strong term for 'toothache').

As for *outrage*, its supposed connection with *rage* is spurious. It came into English via Old French *ultrage*, from Latin *ultra* 'beyond' with the noun-forming suffix *-agium*, which appears in English as *-age*, pronounced

'-idge', as in *homage, suffrage, usage,* etc. (see *OED*, s.v. -*age, suffix*); and just as *suffrage* is not *suff-rage* but *suffer-age,* so *outrage* is not *out-rage* but *ultra-age,* of which the literal sense is 'beyondness' or 'excessiveness', hence 'intemperance'. This is how the word is used in Middle English, as for example in the proverbial comment that one cannot lengthen one's allotted lifespan, "But with outrage man may lett/ The terme [that] God him hath sett' (*Sidrak* L2767–8), i.e., one can shorten one's life through excess. Since, however, the word looks like a combination of *out* and *rage,* that is what people took it to be; and it soon began to be used in the sense 'excessive anger' or 'extreme violence', as in the Duchess of York's cry in *Richard III* that her sons, having defeated their enemies, are now making war upon one another

> brother to brother,
> Blood to blood, self against self. O preposterous
> And frantic outrage, end they damnèd spleen,
> Or let me die, to look on death no more.   (2.4.61–4)

Nowadays, we still sometimes use the adjective *outrageous* in something like its early sense, 'excessive', for example in such innocuous comments as that so-and-so's fashion sense is *outrageous,* meaning merely that it is 'flamboyant'. But when we use the noun, in phrases such as "It's an absolute outrage", or the verb, in constructions such as "I am outraged at this behaviour", our intended meaning, I think, is that the thing we are commenting on is so far beyond the pale as to be *a cause of rage.* Purists may be *outraged,* but folk etymology wins again.

RANK

The adjective *rank* has almost entirely unpleasant or negative connotations in modern English. A *rank outsider* is, in social terms, a person so far outside the accepted circle as to be virtually persona non grata; in horse-racing or equivalent contests (like political elections) the long odds on a rank outsider mark that contestant as a no-hoper. A *rank smell* makes one's gorge rise; a garden that is *rank with weeds* is likely to be choked.

These unfavourable senses are long established. They are all present in Shakespeare: *rank* in *Hamlet* is a veritable snarl-word. The thought of what his mother herself describes as her "o'er-hasty marriage" to his uncle very shortly after his father's death (2.2.57) makes Hamlet think of the world as "an unweeded garden/ That grows to seed; things rank and gross in nature/ Possess it merely" (that is, 'entirely', 1.2.135–7). His obsession with his mother's sex-life makes him accuse her of living "In the rank sweat of an enseamèd bed" (that is, 'a greasy bed'), "Stewed in corruption, honeying and making love/ Over the nasty sty" (3.4.82–4). When she, in turn, accuses him of madness, he replies,

> Mother, for love of grace,
> Lay not a flattering unction to your soul
> That not your trespass but my madness speaks.
> It will but skin and film the ulcerous place
> Whilst rank corruption, mining all within,
> Infects unseen. Confess yourself to heaven;
> Repent what's past, avoid what is to come,
> And do not spread the compost o'er the weeds
> To make them ranker.   (3.4.135–43)

And when the usurping Claudius tries to pray for forgiveness for having murdered his brother, he is prevented by the consciousness of the vileness of his crime:

O, my offence is rank! It smells to heaven.
It hath the primal eldest curse upon't,
A brother's murder.   (3.3.36–8)

In such instances as these the word *rank* is associated with disease, corruption, weeds, foul-smellingness – anything, in short, that is disgusting. One might say, indeed, that the word is used of things that rankle – except that that would be a piece of gratuitous folk etymology: *to rankle* is not from *rank* with the suffix *-le* (as in *dazzle* or *giggle*); it comes (via Old French) from medieval Latin *dranculus*, a diminutive of *draco* 'a snake or dragon', and was used of wounds that festered with (as it were) the poison of a snake or the fire of a small dragon.

But what a degeneration there has been in the meaning of *rank* in the last thousand years! The word's senses in Old and Middle English were on the whole favourable. *OED* suggests that it may be connected with the OE word *rinc* 'a warrior': it was used of fighting men in the sense 'bold' or 'strong' (but no, it has nothing to do with the noun *rank* in the military sense of a group of soldiers: that's another sheer coincidence); it could also mean 'swift' or 'vigorous', 'full-grown' or 'mature', 'luxuriant' or 'copious', and various other things besides. The problem is that with all these qualities, though they may be desirable in moderation, an excess of them is not desirable. An excess of boldness can make one arrogant or rebellious; excessive luxuriance leads to growth that isn't wanted; and so on. So one finds that even in Old English pejorative senses existed alongside the favourable or neutral ones; and in that situation, as we have seen many times, it's almost invariably the more pejorative senses – the *ranker* ones, if you prefer – that survive.

READ AND REDE

The primary sense of the noun *rede* in Old English is 'advice or counsel', from which quickly developed senses such as those of 'a decision (taken after thought), a plan of action'. These senses are more or less lost in current English, except perhaps in fossilized phrases such as the proverb in which Ophelia admonishes Laertes to put into practice himself the brotherly advice he has given *her*:

> good my brother,
> Do not, as some ungracious pastors do,
> Show me the steep and thorny way to heaven
> Whilst like a puffed and reckless libertine
> Himself the primrose path of dalliance treads
> And recks not his own rede   (*Hamlet* 1.3.46–51)

– that is, 'and takes no notice of his own advice'.

They also survive, though less recognizably, in certain old-fashioned Anglo-Saxon names such as *Ethelred*, which means, literally, '(of) excellent counsel', i.e., 'intelligent, clear-thinking, or well advised'. The Anglo-Saxon king known usually today as *Ethelred the Unready* (i.e., 'the ill-prepared') and to earlier generations as *Ethelred the Redeless* ('the lacking in counsel') was in fact nicknamed by his contemporaries *Æthelræd Unræd*, a nicely punning paradox in which the structure of the two words is the same (adjectival prefix + noun), but the meaning is opposite: 'excellent advice: no advice' or 'clever fool' or 'intellectual idiot'.

The verb *to rede* had senses corresponding to those of the noun, of which the primary ones are (to quote *OED*) 'those of taking or giving counsel, taking care or charge of a thing, having or exercising control over something'. These senses and the spelling *rede* have not survived in modern English, except as archaisms, although they were common enough in Middle English, for example in prayers such as "so God me rede" (the literal sense of which is 'may God take care of me', and which was used in just the same way as the modern equivalent, "so help me God"), or in the goose's sharp advice to each of the lovesick male eagles in Chaucer's *Parliament of Fowls*: "I seye I rede hym, though he were my brother,/ But she wol love hym, lat hym love another!" (566–7), that is, roughly, 'If *she* won't love him, I advise him to love someone else!'

Our current sense of the verb, with its differentiated spelling *read*, appears to have come from the idea of a group of people putting their heads together to solve a problem: they are taking counsel or *rede* of one another: they are advising or *reding* one another, just as the birds are doing in Chaucer's *Parliament*. By a simple transference the problem itself, rather than the people considering it, then becomes the object of the verb: they are said to be *reading* the problem, that is 'considering' or 'solving' *it*, rather than advising one another. In this way to *read* something came to mean to 'find out the meaning' of it or to 'interpret' it; and the word was used in this sense particularly of dreams, signs, and riddles. Radio operators have found a new application for this old sense: their "Do you read me?" means 'Are you receiving and understanding my signal?'

When one recalls that literacy was not widespread in the Middle Ages, so that writing was to many people a mysterious thing that had to be interpreted to them by someone who understood it, it's not difficult to see how *reading* came to be applied specifically to the interpretation of written characters, or how, with the spread of literacy, we have come to use the verb with books, newspapers, and other written material as the object, without any consciousness of the underlying idea of 'interpretation'.

RING, RANG, RUNG

When a young man telephoned some time ago to speak to my elder daughter, Bec, and found she was out, he asked very politely if he could leave a message: "Please tell her I rung." Then he added, perhaps recollecting that he was speaking to an English teacher, "Or should that be *rang*?"

Well, if he wanted to be historically accurate (but perhaps it's a bit much to expect young men to be Historically as well as Politically Correct), it should indeed have been *rang*; but he had good cause for his uncertainty, because these days one increasingly hears *rung* rather than *rang* as the past tense of *ring*. And this is hardly surprising given the way changes in language happen – in pronunciation and grammar as well as in meaning.

In Old English there were many different classes of strong verb (verbs that form the past tense and past participle by changing the vowel of the stem, like *drive/drove/driven*, as opposed to weak verbs, which add -*d* or -*t*, like *live/lived*). But the tendency ever since has been towards simplification and standardization: the number of vowel changes in strong verbs is reduced; in some instances the vowel changes are abandoned completely and the verb becomes weak; and almost all newly-coined verbs behave like weak verbs, with no vowel changes. The past tense of *to fax*, to give just one example of a new verb, is not *fex*, *fox*, or even *fux*, but *faxed*.

The class of strong verb to which *ring* belongs (all members of which have -*in*- or -*im*- in the present tense) is in fact one of the more conservative: we still say "I sing, I sang, I have sung; I drink, I drank, I have drunk; I swim, I swam, I have swum"; but most of us don't say, "I swing, I swang, I have swung" (I'm told they still say *swang* in the North of England and Scotland, but I've never heard it); and we don't say "I climb, I clamb, I have clumb": we say "I climb, I climbed, I have climbed". The number of vowel changes has been reduced in *swing*; and *climb* has become a weak verb.

If we were to insist on historical accuracy, we would still be saying *halp* rather than *helped*; we'd be saying not *books* but *beech*; and we'd still be pronouncing *life* as *leef*, *bone* as *bahn*, and *house* as *hoose*. (This last, indeed, they still do in Scotland, as in that old joke about the Scotsman who went hunting in Canada and suddenly clapped eyes on a creature that looked like an overgrown deer with enormous antlers: "What's that?" he asked his host. "It's a moose," came the reply. To this the Scot is alleged to have responded, "If that's what your mice are like, I don't want to meet one of your cats.")

So I don't think the young man should be hung for not knowing whether it was *rung* or *rang* – or, er, should that be *hanged*?

Sad

> Since brass, nor stone, nor earth, nor boundless sea,
> But sad mortality o'ersways their power,
> How with this rage shall beauty hold a plea,
> Whose action is no stronger than a flower?   (Sonnet 65, 1–4)

How indeed? But there can't be any need for me to complete the sonnet: it's sufficiently well known that Shakespeare's answer to the ravages of time was to preserve his love's beauty in his writing. What I want to talk about is the way in which we are likely to misconstrue these opening lines because the meanings of some of the key words have shifted: unless we read the notes in an annotated edition, we're unlikely to notice the shifts in meaning, because the words make perfectly good sense with their current meanings, even though these are not the ones Shakespeare intended.

The two words I have particularly in mind are *rage* and *sad*. I needn't dwell on *rage*, since I've spoken about it before; I merely point out that whereas to us it is likely to imply anger, as if death had lost its temper and were destroying everything in existence in a fit of fury, in the context of the poem it is more likely to have the earlier sense of violence or fierceness in battle, without any suggestion of anger. This makes the line "How with this rage shall beauty hold a plea" all the more effective: are not adversaries who do you violence without emotion more sinister and more frightening than ones who have lost their temper and with it their control? As for *sad*, it is in current English inextricably linked with the idea of grief; so the line "But sad mortality o'ersways their power" will mean to us that there is nothing so durable that it is not subject to death, and that this is a cause of sorrow: we take the words "sad mortality" to mean something like 'sorrow-causing death'. Now this is perfectly reasonable, and it may be that this sense is lurking beneath the primary one; but I don't think it's the main sense required by the context.

Sad has an intricate and rather surprising history. It's related to the Latin word *satis* 'enough' as in *satisfactory* meaning 'sufficient or good enough'. In its earliest recorded uses in Old and Middle English it was synonymous with the cognate words *satisfied* 'having had enough' and *sated* 'overfull, weary, having had more than enough'. My Middle English book of knowledge warns, for example, that a man shouldn't visit his friend too often for fear that "He might make hym of hym sadde" (*Sidrak*, B9192), i.e., the friend might get sick of the sight of him. Similarly in the Harley lyric "With longing I am lad", when the speaker laments that he doesn't see enough of his beloved – "selden I am sad/ That semly for to see" – he doesn't mean it seldom makes him miserable to see her; he means he seldom (i.e., never) sees too much of her.

The word improves in meaning after this: it's one of those rare words whose semantic history (at least in the early part) shows amelioration rather than degeneration. After 'sated' come such senses as 'established, settled, steadfast, or constant', as in the description of faithful Griselda in Chaucer's Clerk's tale:

> But thogh this mayde tendre were of age,
> Yet in the brest of hire virginitee
> Ther was enclosed rype and sad corage;   (*CT* IV 218–20)

that's to say, not that she went around with a long face, but that her heart and mind were constant – as her husband, the dreadful Marquis Walter, duly discovered. From here we get such senses as 'dignified, sober, mature, serious, or trustworthy'. When Olivia describes Malvolio as "sad and civil" (*Twelfth Night* 3.4.5), she means that he's a sober, orderly sort of fellow; and when she sends for him shortly afterwards "upon a sad occasion" (3.4.18), this is not a reference to her being in mourning for her brother; it means that she has serious business to employ him on.

At this point we've more or less reached the summit of the word's pleasant senses; hereafter its development follows the more usual degenerative line. The absence of gaiety in the idea of seriousness leads on to that of the presence of sorrow, which gives us the normal current senses 'feeling or causing sorrow'; and from there we descend to such derogatory senses as 'deplorably bad', as in "a sad state of affairs".

Browning puns nicely on these two newer senses in the last two lines of his *Confessions* – "How sad and bad and mad it was – / But then, how it was sweet!": the speaker's love trysts may have been *sad* ('deplorable'), but he doesn't sound very *sad* ('unhappy') about it, even if he *is* on his deathbed.

And where in all this does Shakespeare's "sad mortality" belong? Contrary to current presuppositions, the context requires that *sad* here have primarily the earlier sense 'steadfast or trustworthy'. There's a sort of black humour in thus acknowledging death's reliability: the one thing we all know for certain about death is that, as Hamlet says, "If it be not now, yet it will come" (5.2.167–8); and so the opening lines of the sonnet I began with ask what hope there can be for a fragile and evanescent thing like beauty when even the toughest things (like brass and stone) succumb in time to the certainty of dissolution. "In this world nothing can be said to be certain," as Benjamin Franklin is reputedly the first to have said, "except death and taxes."

SEETHING AND SODDEN

What has *seething* to do with being *sodden*? It may seem hard to believe today, but these two words are different parts of the same verb: *seething* is the present participle, *sodden* the past participle, of the verb *to seethe*, of which the original meaning was 'to boil'.

A medieval recipe for blancmange (literally 'white food'), which in the Middle Ages was a savoury dish made from white meat or fish in a white sauce, begins "Take Capons and seeth hem. . . . Take Almands blanched; grynd hem and alay hem up [i.e., 'mix them'] with the same broth. Cast the milk in a pot. Waisshe rys ['Wash rice'] and do therto ['add to it'], and lat it seeth". One of the medieval proverbs discussed in an earlier item says that a man who boasts of more than he can perform is like a man "that flesshe sethe wolde kunne/ At the hete of the sunne" (*Sidrak*, L4960–2), i.e., he's like someone trying to boil meat (or "fry an egg", if you prefer) in the heat of the sun (see *Proverbs (2)*).

'To boil' is the sense the word has for Chaucer, too: the Cook in the General Prologue to the *Canterbury Tales* "koude ['knew how to'] rooste, and sethe, and broille, and frye" (I 383); and it can still be the literal sense for Shakespeare two hundred years later: the fountain in which one of Diana's maidens steeped Cupid's burning arrow in Sonnet 153 drew such heat from the arrow that it became "a seething bath" – not just 'turbulent', that is, but 'boiling'; and after the siege of Harfleur in *Henry V* the Constable of France wonders how the English can have become so valiant when their national drink is only "barley-broth" ('ale or beer'), which is made from "sodden water" (3.5.18–19), whereas the French, whose blood should be hot from drinking wine, ought as a result to be the braver. "Sodden water" sounds like a comic tautology to us, because, well, obviously water's wet, isn't it? We need the notes in a scholarly edition to remind us that *sodden* meant 'boiled'.

But by Shakespeare's day a figurative sense had developed for *seethe* alongside the literal one, so that the word could be used in any context suggesting heat, steaminess, or agitation. This is nicely demonstrated in an exchange between Pandarus and one of Paris's servants in *Troilus and Cressida*: Pandarus is in a great hurry to see Paris, "for", he says, "my business seethes", that is, so to speak, 'my business is boiling over with urgency'. The servant, who appears to have a fair idea what sort of business Pandarus has in mind, replies "Sodden business! There's a stewed phrase, indeed" (3.1.40–2): both the "sodden business" and the "stewed phrase" are allusions to the hot bath houses or stews that had a reputation for serving as brothels. About the nearest we could get to an equivalent in current English would be "Steamy business! Sounds like something you'd hear in a massage parlour"; but even so, we'd have lost the pun on *stewed*, because visiting a massage parlour (so I'm told) doesn't necessarily entail having a Turkish bath.

In current usage the figurative sense of *seethe* has almost entirely replaced the literal one: to seethe with some strong emotion is (as it were) to boil inwardly. "Seething with rage" and "boiling with rage" are exactly synonymous; but whereas the first is now well on the way to being a dead metaphor (since we have more or less forgotten the literal meaning of *seethe*, although we're aware that it's a strong word), the second is still very much alive, since it conjures up a mental image of a pot boiling over.

With *sodden* it's a question of a change of focus: in order to be boiled, a thing has to be put in water; when the focus changes from the heat of the water to its wetness, we have a new sense, 'wet through' (cf. *drenched*); and in this instance the original sense, of being boiled, has been lost completely.

What about the Australian *sod* or *sod(dy) damper*, 'a damper that has failed to rise', as in Jack Strapper's sole, repeated comment in Tom Ronan's *Vision Splendid*? –

> And Mart the cook the shovel took
> And swung the damper to and fro.
> "Another sod, so help me God,
> That's fourteen in a flamin' row."

The *Macquarie Dictionary* connects this with a *sod of earth* (from Middle Dutch or Middle Low German *sode* 'turf'), I suppose because of its taste or texture; but most authorities (the *Australian Concise Oxford Dictionary*,

Australian Dictionary of Colloquialisms, Australian National Dictionary, New Shorter Oxford) think it's called a *sod* because it's wet and doughy (i.e., in the modern sense, *sodden*). Like most etymological disputes, this can't be settled either way; but at least the authorities agree that, unlike *sod off* and related expressions, the words discussed here have *sod all* to do with *sodomy*.

SHAMEFACED

Readers of medieval religious literature are sometimes amazed by the adjectives applied to the Virgin Mary: not only is she described as *daft* and *buxom* (as we have already seen), but sometimes also as *shamefast* – and these are all intended as terms of praise.

The spelling of *shamefaced* in Middle English may also surprise us: the second element is not *-faced* but *-fast*. There is, in fact, no etymological connection with the word *face*; what we have here is the adjective *fast*, meaning 'firm, or firmly fixed', as in *steadfast*, which means literally 'fixed in one stead', i.e., 'in one place'.

But what does it mean to be 'firmly fixed in shame'? Well, *shame* (OE *sceamu*) has at root two complementary meanings: one is that of 'embarrassment or humiliation', usually produced through a sense of guilt or inadequacy; the other, not widely used today except in negative phrases such as *without shame*, is that of 'modesty or restraint', proceeding from the wish to avoid such embarrassment or humiliation. It's this latter sense that was originally the operative one in the compound *shamefast*: it meant 'having a deeply rooted sense of modesty', either in a good sense, 'modest or self-effacing', or in a not-so-good one, 'shy, timid', or (as we'd now say) 'lacking in self-esteem'.

It is, of course, in the good sense that the word is used of the Virgin Mary, for example, by the Lincolnshire priest Orm in the late twelfth century, who describes her as "Shammfasst, & daffte, & sedefull", that is, 'modest, and humble, and chaste' (see *daft and deft*). And this is also how Chaucer uses it in the Physician's tale, when the fourteen-year-old girl (significantly named Virginia) after whom the corrupt judge lusts is described (somewhat tautologously) as "Shamefast ... in shamefastnesse" (*CT* VI 55).

How do we get from this sense to the modern *shamefaced*, which can still mean 'modest or bashful' but which, I think, is more frequently used to mean 'ashamed' in the sense 'embarrassed about one's own behaviour'? There are two connections: one is, as I've said, that the word *shame* has always had as one of its root senses that of 'embarrassment or humiliation'; the other is that this sort of embarrassment has an irritating habit of making itself visible in the sufferer's *face*, often, of course, by way of blushing. This point is nicely made by the second of the two murderers sent to kill the Duke of Clarence in *Richard III* as he wrestles with his conscience before bringing himself to act. He complains that conscience

> makes a man a coward. A man cannot steal but it accuseth him. A man cannot swear but it checks him. A man cannot lie with his neighbour's wife but it detects him. 'Tis a blushing, shamefaced spirit, that mutinies in a man's bosom. It fills a man full of obstacles.... (1.4.131–6)

When one recalls that *face* would in Chaucer's day have been pronounced pretty much as in modern French rather than in Modern English (that is, with a vowel sound very much like that in Australian *car park* as opposed to the diphthong in Modern English *pay*), the possibility for confusion with *fast* (whether that's pronounced with a long *a* or a short *a*) is obvious. The current spelling (*-faced*), and the more usual of the current senses ('with shame showing in one's face'), are thus the result of perfectly understandable misinterpretation. This is as nice an example as one could find of the phemonenon that linguistic historians call folk etymology, that is, misinterpreting a word's meaning through confusing it with another word.

SHREWD

The adjective *shrewd* is another of those relatively rare words of which the senses have undergone amelioration rather than pejoration. It comes from the noun *shrew*, that little insectivorous mammal that looks like a mouse with a long sharp snout, but that isn't a mouse at all. Shrews had a bad press in the Middle Ages: their bite was thought to be poisonous, and they were considered harmful in other ways. So the noun came to be applied figuratively to humans: *a shrew* was a person (of either sex) who was malevolent or evil; the meaning was 'villain' or 'rascal'. Thus Chaucer's Wife of Bath, accusing one of her first three husbands of having said that women keep their vices hidden until after they are married and only then allow them to be seen, comments "Wel may that be a proverbe of a shrewe!" (*CT* III 284); and a few lines later she hurls the word at him as a term of abuse: "olde dotard shrewe!" (291, nicely rendered in the *Riverside Chaucer* as 'senile scoundrel'). I am not sure by what sexist manoeuvring the word came to be attached specifically to sharp-tongued women, but we can see this sense developing already in the *Canterbury Tales*, where, alongside the Wife of Bath's use of it of her husbands, the Pardoner's use of it for the first of the three rioters in his famous tale of the three men who set out to kill Death (VI 819), and the Canon's Yeoman's use of it for the devil, "that ilke shrewe" (VIII 917), we have the Host's comment on his wife, that "of hir tonge, a labbyng shrewe is she" (IV 2428).

With all these unpleasant meanings for the noun, it's not surprising that the adjective *shrewd* (whether it comes directly from the noun or indirectly via the verb *to shrew* meaning 'to curse') should have unpleasant meanings to match. Thus the earliest recorded sense of the adjective is 'evil': the Wife of Bath gives us an example once again, in her comment on "shrewed Lameth [i.e., Lamech] and his bigamye" (III 54). Shakespeare is still using it in the sense 'evil' or 'malicious' two hundred years later, for example when one of the fairies in *A Midsummer Night's Dream* calls Puck "that shrewd and knavish sprite/ Called Robin

Goodfellow" (2.1.33–4), although the meaning here is perhaps slightly weaker – *mischievous* in the current playful sense – since the "shrewd and knavish" tricks Puck is accused of here are no worse than frightening the village maidens, stopping the beer from having any froth and the cream from turning into butter (see *bootless*), and so on.

When applied to animals or things, *shrewd* was just as depreciatory as when it was applied to people. A *shrewd animal* was bad-tempered or vicious; *shrewd news* was bad news, as in Portia's comment when she sees Bassanio's reaction to the letter bringing the news of the loss of Antonio's ships: "There are some shrewd contents in yon same paper/ That steals the colour from Bassanio's cheek" (*The Merchant of Venice* 3.2.241–2); *a shrewd turn of events* was a turn for the worse; *a shrewd wind* was a biting wind; and *shrewd words*, needless to say, were abusive.

Alongside all these bad senses there developed early on the sense 'cunning' or 'keen-witted' – probably via the notion of sharpness that goes back to the shape of a shrew's snout and the reputation of its bite. But whereas sharpness may be undesirable in a wind or in a spouse's language, it's generally thought to be advantageous as a quality of the mind. Thus 'cunning' becomes 'artful', 'artful' becomes 'astute', and thus we come to the chief current sense, in which the originally derogatory sense of 'cunning' has given way to the more flattering senses of 'sharply perceptive, clever and judicious' (*New Shorter Oxford*). I am not quite sure, though, that the word has entirely lost the negative associations with which it began. We may, indeed, feel admiration for a person who knows how to drive *a shrewd bargain*, but it's likely to be a fairly grudging sort of admiration – especially if we are the other party to the bargain; and I don't think we're being unambiguously complimentary when (in Australia or New Zealand) we call someone *a shrewdie*.

SILLY

Silly is a somewhat patronising word in current English: if we say "Don't be silly", or if we describe someone as "a silly Billy" or "a silly moo", there are implications of childishness as well as foolishness; we speak of *the silly season* when the media are even fuller than usual of mindless trivia; people who *play silly buggers* are indulging in what Eric Partridge nicely calls 'provocative horseplay', or, if you prefer, they're fooling around like children or pretending to be stupid. It's only if the captain of the cricket team asks you to field at *silly point* or some equally suicidal position that you might begin to think this word is serious.

But what a sad descent for a word that in Old English meant 'happy' or 'blessed' (as the cognate word in German, *selig*, still does), from the noun *sæl* 'happiness, prosperity, good fortune'! This sense is very common in the Old and Middle English periods, as in Troilus's plea to death to end his sorrows when he hears he must lose his beloved Criseyde:

> O deth, that endere art of sorwes alle,
> Com now, syn I so ofte after the calle;
> For sely is that deth, soth for to seyne,
> That, ofte ycleped, cometh and endeth peyne, (*TC* 4.503–4)

that is, 'blessed is the death that comes (when repeatedly called upon) to end one's misery'. Closely allied to this sense of happiness is that of blessedness or holiness: thus *sely* is commonly applied to saints and martyrs. But goodness implies innocence, and innocence all too often implies weakness or helplessness. It is often difficult to tell which of these senses the word carries in any given instance. Thus when Chaucer's Custance is wrongly accused of murder in the Man of Law's tale, she is miraculously saved from the accusation by a hand from heaven that knocks out her accuser's eyes, accompanied by a voice that declares her innocence:

Greet was the drede and eek the repentaunce
Of hem that hadden wrong suspeccioun
Upon this sely innocent, Custance.   (*CT* II 680–2)

What exactly does "sely" mean here? I have seen it glossed variously as 'blameless' (Cawley), 'holy' (the *Chaucer Glossary*), 'innocent or blessed' (the *Riverside Chaucer*), and 'weak, helpless, defenceless, or hapless' (*MED*). These different glosses illustrate nicely one of the recurring problems that beset lexicographers, that of deciding which of several possible contemporaneous meanings a word may have in a given instance, when it is quite likely that the author intended to conjure up the whole complex of associated meanings: in this instance Custance's holiness, her virtue, her innocence, her being blessed by divine favour, and (had it not been for divine intervention) her helplessness.

So far, so good: these senses are all more or less favourable (though helplessness has little to commend it if one does not happen to be blessed with divine favour). But innocence is not far removed from naivety; naivety implies simple-mindedness; simple-mindedness is a close cousin to stupidity – and, well, there we are. One of the signs that these meanings are all closely related is, I think, that they may all be found contemporaneously in the Middle Ages. Thus Chaucer's Custance may be *sely* in a wide variety of the good senses, but "sely John", the hapless carpenter in the Miller's tale who believes Nicholas's fantastic story of a second Noah's Flood (*CT* I 3404, 3423, 3614), is a gullible simpleton: he may be superficially pious, but he is also well on the way to being *silly* in the modern sense.

Most of the intermediate senses are present in Shakespeare's time as well as Chaucer's. The "silly women" on whom Valentine urges the outlaws to "do no outrages" in *The Two Gentleman of Verona* (4.1.69–70) are not idiots: they are defenceless. The "seely beggars" whom King Richard imagines sitting in the stocks (*Richard II* 5.5.25–6) are not fools: they are pitiable. The "silly sooth" of the song Orsino asks Feste to sing is not stupidity (*Twelfth Night* 2.4.45): it is the simple truth. When we say sheep are *silly* we may today be implying that they have no brains, but it is unlikely that Shakespeare had any such thoughts when he had his Henry VI ask, in his famous panegyric on the life of shepherds,

> Gives not the hawthorn bush a sweeter shade
> To shepherds looking on their seely sheep,
> Than doth a rich embroidered canopy
> To kings that fear their subjects' treachery?   (*3 Henry VI* 2.5.42–5)

These sheep are not mentally deficient: they are merely defenceless – which is why they need a shepherd. The baby Jesus is likewise in need of protection in the first stanza of "New Prince, new pompe", by the Jesuit priest Robert Southwell (who was executed in 1595, a victim of the religious persecution of the late sixteenth century, and has recently been canonized):

> Behold a silly tender Babe,
>   In freesing Winter night;
> In homely manger trembling lies,
>   Alas a pitteous sight.

The claim is not that Jesus is an imbecile, but that, as a baby born in a cowshed on a freezing night, he is vulnerable: his plight demands pity and sympathy. (The poem appears as hymn 143 in *The Cambridge Hymnal* and as carol 170 in *The Oxford Book of Carols*. In the first instance *silly* is glossed as 'simple, naive, innocent'; in the second the compilers evidently got cold feet about the word, because they have replaced it with *simple*, which they call "its modern equivalent". I think both books are wrong. *Silly* can indeed have these meanings, as we've seen, but it's not simplicity or innocence that's in question here, it's vulnerability: the baby is "tender"; the night is "freesing"; he lies "trembling" (i.e., 'shivering'). The modern equivalent in this context is not *simple* but *poor*: "Poor little thing," one might say, "he must be frozen!") And Robert Burns is using a similar sense some two hundred years later in his much-loved "To a Mouse" (subtitled "On Turning Her up in Her Nest with the Plough, November, 1785"): "Thy wee bit housie, too, in ruin!/ Its silly wa's the win's are strewin!" (19–20). The walls are not stupid (or simple, or naive, for that matter): they're fragile – which is why, having been exposed by the plough, they're being blown away by the wind.

But our sense was already present in Shakespeare's day, as when Iago calls Roderigo a "silly gentleman" for wanting to drown himself on

discovering that Desdemona is married (*Othello* 1.3.307), or when Hippolyta declares, in *A Midsummer Night's Dream*, that the workers' play of Pyramus and Thisbe is "the silliest stuff that ever I heard" (5.1.209). The inconsistent spelling, sometimes with -ee-, sometimes with -i-, suggests that the pronunciation was variable in Shakespeare's time: sometimes long, as in OE, sometimes short, as in MnE. It would have been useful if one spelling had been kept for the good senses and one for the bad, as with *deft* and *daft*; but, though modern editors sometimes try to make this distinction (as suggested by the two examples of *seely* quoted earlier), and even though *OED* gives each of the two forms a separate entry, the original-spelling edition of Shakespeare's works shows that he uses the spellings interchangeably.

It just seems to be an inescapable fact of human nature that we consider innocence and simplicity childish, ignorance culpable, and defencelessness contemptible: thus words like *innocent, simple, daft, lewd*, and, yes, *silly* acquire their pejorative senses; and when that happens their good senses are usually lost.

SLEDGING

This is a term I had never encountered before coming to Australia, except in the innocent sense 'tobogganing, riding on a sledge' (a sense connected ultimately with the verb to *slide*). In Australia, however, it's a term used specifically of cricket: it's defined by Gerry Wilkes in his *Dictionary of Australian Colloquialisms* as "the taunting of a batsman by members of the opposing team in order to undermine his confidence", a definition with which George Turner concurs in the *Australian Concise Oxford Dictionary*; and the *Collins* and *Macquarie* dictionaries are in broad agreement. None of these dictionaries offers any suggestions as to the origin of the term, but Bruce Moore, who defines it nicely in the *Australian Oxford Dictionary* as attempting 'to break the concentration of a person batting etc. by abuse, needling, etc.', takes it to derive from 'using a sledgehammer on'. (To needle someone with a sledgehammer may seem a paradoxical concept: perhaps it's a reflection on the subtlety of Australian needling.)

This use of the term as applied to cricket is one that annoys Ian Chappell, who remarks, in his forthright manner:

> Fieldsmen, 'heaping abuse and ridicule on the batsman', what a load of bollocks. That's where the pundits really come unstuck and display their ignorance of the game of cricket.
> Any batsman (of District level, never mind Test standard) will immediately pull away if a fieldsman is chattering while he's facing up.

To this one can only reply, "Well of course the batsman will pull away if fielders are daft enough to talk after the bowler has started his run up; but which dictionary said anything about the abuse occurring *then*?" The words "while he's facing up" are Chappell's own addition, and I assume he's put them there in an attempt to discredit the current use of the term by suggesting that cricketers just don't behave like that. (Pull the other one, Ian. Who are you trying to kid? It may not be cricket, but it's common knowledge that – like shit – it happens.)

However, Chappell does offer an explanation of the origin of the term, and it's so far-fetched that, since truth is stranger than fiction, it seems to me that it may well be correct: "I was there the day the term 'sledging' was coined", he writes. "Grahame ... Corling was a fast bowler for NSW and Australia in the early sixties ... who ... used to swear in mixed company before it became fashionable." On one occasion when he described a party, in mixed company, as "all f ... ed up" (*sic*), another NSW player told him that he was "as subtle as a sledgehammer". Thereupon Corling was instantly nicknamed "Percy" after the singer Percy Sledge (whose song "When a Man Loves a Woman" was a big hit at the time). "From that moment on," says Chappell, "any cricketer in Australia who made a faux pas in front of a lady was said to be a 'sledge', or guilty of 'sledging'".

This, of course, has nothing to do with cricket as a game; but it isn't hard to see how a term current among cricketers and meaning, roughly, 'to say rude things in the wrong place', could have been transferred to the cricket field in the sense in which it's now commonly used.

Did Bruce Moore get the idea of a sledgehammer (which connects this kind of *sledging* ultimately with the verb *to slay*, i.e., 'to kill') from Chappell's anecdote, or did he come up with it independently? It's hard to know; but, either way, this new kind of *sledging* neatly illustrates two things about language: (1) how uncertain the origins of colloquialisms can actually be; (2) how impossible it is for anyone to control what words and phrases mean: expressions come to mean what the majority of people believe they mean, irrespective of what their first users may have intended them to mean.

But what on earth can have motivated the publishers to censor Corling's language in this anecdote? (I assume it was the publishers: one can scarcely think Chappelli himself would have been so pusillanimous.) Did they really suppose, after giving us the *bollocks*, that we couldn't face the *fuck*?

SOTSHIP

One of the obsolete words that I should most dearly love to revive is the word *sotship*, meaning 'stupidity', which doesn't appear to have survived in English beyond the fourteenth century. Students of Middle English are most likely to meet it in a famous passage for the year 1127 in the *Peterborough Chronicle* describing the machinations of the terrible Abbot Henry of the abbey of St Jean D'Angély in France, a daughter-house of Cluny. He was given the abbacy apparently for no better reason than that he was a relation of King Henry I of England and of the Count of Poitou; but he was such a bad abbot that the monks rebelled against him and booted him out.

At that point, says the chronicler, "him trucode" ('there failed for him') "ealle his mycele cræftes" ('all his great tricks': *mycel* is the ancestor of our word *much*, used as an adjective meaning 'great'; *cræftes* is literally 'acts of craft', hence 'tricks'); "nu him behofed thet he crape in his mycele codde in ælc hyrne" (this clause is full of traps for the unwary translator: to the disappointment of most of my students it means not, as one might suppose, 'now it behoved him to crap into his great cod-piece' but 'now it behoved him that he should creep into his great bag [i.e., bag of tricks], into each corner [of it]': *crape* has nothing to do with defecation; it's the past subjunctive of *creep*, which was at one time a strong verb, that is to say, it formed its past tense by changing the vowel as opposed to adding a *-d* or a *-t* (see *ring, rang, rung*); and although *codd* is indeed the same word as the first element of *cod-piece*, it's here used in the general sense 'bag' as opposed to the specific one, 'bag in which you put your genitals').

And why did Abbot Henry have to creep into each corner of his great bag of tricks? Why, [to see] "gif thær wære hure an unwreste wrenc thet he mihte get beswicen anes Crist and eall Cristene folc" (to see, that is, 'if there were even one evil trick [left] with which he might yet once [more] deceive Christ and all Christian people'). But, failing to find one, "Tha ferde he into Clunni, and thær man him held thet he ne mihte ne east na west" ('Then he went to Cluny, and there he was held so that he could [go] neither east nor west'). "Sæde se abbot of Clunni thet hi heafdon forloron Sancte Iohannis mynstre thurh him and thurh his mycele sotscipe" ('The abbot of Cluny said that they had utterly lost St John's monastery (see *forlorn*) through him and through his great *sotship*', that is, 'his great stupidity').

What an expressive word, *sotship*! It's derived from the French noun *sot* meaning 'fool, dolt, blockhead', with the addition of the English suffix *-ship* as in *mateship*. The stem survives in the participial adjective *besotted* 'rendered foolish with infatuation'; it also survives as a word in its own right in the phrase *a drunken sot*, where the sense has been influenced by the sound of a word like *sodden* (see *seething*) to suggest someone rendered foolish by being soaked in drink. But alas, that we have lost the word *sotship* itself: it so aptly sums up the goings-on in the public service and on university committees, does it not?

SPEED

When we use the word *speed* in current English, whether as a noun or as a verb, what we are talking about is swiftness of motion. This must, I think, be the sense underlying the relatively new use of the word as the name of the drug *speed*, which is reputed to be able, however temporarily, to reduce fatigue and to increase mental activity – in short, to *speed you up* for a while (see the quotation for 1970 in *OED* under sense 7 of the noun; cf. senses 11d and 13f of the verb).

In Old English, however, the noun had the senses of 'wealth, prosperity, success, etc.', and the verb meant 'to prosper or succeed'. When Ohthere told King Alfred that he was a very "spēdig" man, he didn't mean he could run a hundred yards in ten seconds: he meant (as he goes on to explain) that he was very well off for livestock, which was the commodity by which his people measured their spēd, i.e., their wealth. And when the cuckoo in Chaucer's *Parliament of Fowls* offers to speak "for comune spede", it's offering its opinion for the common profit, for the good of all.

Some of these old senses survive, fossilized, in proverbs and sayings. *God speed* (short for *God speed you*) meant 'may God assist you; may you succeed'; *God speed the plough* meant 'may God grant your ploughing success', i.e., 'may you have a good crop'. *More haste less speed* used to puzzle me terribly as a child. I took it to be a wish ('we want more haste and less speed'), and I couldn't work out why hurry should be more desirable than swiftness. Later, when I realized it was a statement, not a wish ('the more you have haste, the less you'll have speed'), I took the meaning to be 'the more you *try* to hurry, the less quickly you will actually go' – and I think that's probably the sense in which most people use it today, although the original sense was 'the more you hurry, the less likely you are *to succeed*'.

It's not difficult to see how words denoting success come in time to denote swiftness, since the first so often depends upon the second. This is nowhere more obvious than in the first of these sayings, *God speed*.

One says it to people setting out on a journey, and it's a pretty fine line between wishing them a successful journey and hoping they don't get hijacked or delayed in a traffic jam.

Can proverbs change their meanings, then, as words do? Well, yes: the phrasing remains fixed, because the sayings are learned by heart and passed on by word of mouth; but when the meanings of the words change, so too must the meaning of the saying (see the two items on *Proverbs*, above).

SPELLS AND SPELLING

Why is it that when racehorses or greyhounds are given a rest from racing they are said to be *having a spell*, whereas when bowlers in a cricket match are *having a spell* they have stopped resting and have begun to bowl? And what has either of these uses to do with *witches' spells* or the *spelling* of words that schoolteachers (and pedants like me) complain about when our students make mistakes?

Well, we are dealing here with several different words that just happen to share the same (yes) *spelling*: *OED* records no less than five different nouns with the form *spell*. Two of these are relatively uncommon (a dialect word meaning 'a splinter' and a Dutch word meaning 'a theatre'); since I've never encountered either of these except in the pages of a dictionary, I shall say no more about them. As for the other three, one is a noun from Old English meaning 'a speech or story' (there doesn't seem to be any connection with *spiel*, which is an adaptation from a German verb meaning 'to play'); one is from a verb of unknown origin (originally with the form *spele*) meaning 'to take someone's place'; and one is a colloquial shortening of *spelling*, as nicely demonstrated by the first quotation for this sense ("There were eighteen horrid false spells . . . in one short note that I received from him").

But is there no connection between any of these three? In fact there is: two are related, one apparently not. The basic sense of the OE noun *spell* (still in use in Scotland) was, as we have seen, 'a speech or a story'. Students of Old English are likely to encounter the word first in Ohthere's account to King Alfred of his voyage round the northern tip of Norway to the White Sea: "Fela spella him sædon tha Beormas, ægther ge of hiera agnum lande ge of thæm landum the ymb hie utan wæron" ('The Karelians told him many stories, both about their own land, and about the lands that were around them'). The *gospel* is a contraction of OE *gōd spel(l)* 'good story, good news' (the Good News Bible, whatever one may think of the translation, is well named etymologically): the shortening of the long o in gōd ('good') was assisted over time through folk etymology by the mistaken (but perfectly understandable) assumption that the first element was 'God', giving gospel the meaning 'news about God' or 'message from God' (as brought out in the title of the hit musical, Godspell). A specialized sense of the same word spell is that used in magic spell or witch's spell, that is, a set form of words recited in order to bring about a desired effect, like John the Carpenter's night-spell in Chaucer's Miller's tale (CT I 3480) or (though he would have been scandalized to hear it termed a spell) the Reverend Eli Jenkins's regular sunset prayer in Under Milk Wood:

> O let us see another day!
> Bless us all this night, I pray,
> And to the sun we all will bow
> And say, good-bye – but just for now!   (p. 58)

In time, through focus on the magic effect of this kind of spell, the idea of words or speech may disappear altogether: one may fall under a person's or a place's spell without a word having been uttered. But when it comes to the spelling of a word we are back with speech again, at least to start with: the earliest sense of this verb to spell is 'to read out letter by letter', hence to interpret. When we are told that Shakespeare's Beatrice "never yet saw man,/ How wise, how noble, young, how rarely featured,/ But she would spell him backward" (Much Ado 3.1.59–61), we are to understand that she manages to say rude things about them whatever their good qualities may be. From reading aloud or with difficulty, or from subvocalization (i.e., saying the words silently as one reads), we come to the idea of saying aloud the individual letters of which a word is made up, hence to spelling in the current sense, where speech may once again be forgotten if one is talking about writing.

As for the bowlers and the racehorses, their spells are from the other root, originally spelled spele, meaning 'to take someone's place'. The earliest senses of the noun given in the New Shorter Oxford are 'a set of workers taking a turn of work to relieve others' and 'a turn of work taken by one person or group to relieve another', both of which we would now call a shift (but that's another story). By a change of focus the idea of doing something for someone else is lost and the time involved is foregrounded; thus a *spell* comes to mean a fixed period of whatever it may be: of good or bad weather; of ill health (if you're an American); of a game of rugby (if you're an All-Black); of action (if you're a bowler); and, if you're a horse, a dog, or an Australian, of rest.

SPILLS

To spill is an Old English verb that meant originally 'to kill or destroy'. The Viking messenger who is sent to speak to the English defenders in *The Battle of Maldon* (the poem commemorating the English defeat at Maldon in 991, in the reign of Ethelred the Redeless – see *read* and *rede*) suggests that the English would do better to buy the Vikings off than to fight them: "Ne thurfe we us spillan", that is, 'We do not need to kill one another', he says, "gif ge spedath to tham" 'if you speed to that extent', that is, 'if you have enough wealth [to pay us with]' (see *speed*).

In this sense the word is frequently found in Middle English in the collocation *save or spill*. The knight–rapist in Chaucer's Wife of Bath's tale was condemned to death and would have been executed had not the Queen – to the consternation of some critics – interceded for him; thereupon King Arthur "yaf hym to the queene, al at hir wille,/ To chese wheither she wolde hym save or spille" (*CT* III 897–8), that is, Arthur 'handed him over to the Queen to decide, entirely as she pleased, whether she would spare him or have him put to death'. A slightly weaker sense than 'kill', probably influenced by the similar-sounding *spoil*, is 'ruin' or indeed 'spoil', as when, in the Prologue to her tale, the Wife of Bath explains how she always managed to have the upper hand over her first three husbands in their quarrels:

> I koude pleyne, and yit was in the gilt,
> Or elles often tyme hadde I been spilt.
> Whoso that first to mille comth, first grynt;
> I pleyned first, so was oure werre ystynt.   (*CT* III 387–90)

'I knew how to complain, even when I was in the wrong, otherwise I'd often have been ruined. The one who reaches the mill first grinds first: I complained first, and that put a stop to our warfare.'

Intransitively *to spill* meant 'to die'. When quick-handed Nicholas in Chaucer's Miller's tale grabs Alison by the *queynte* and says "Ywis, but if ich have my wille,/ for deerne love of thee, lemman, I spille" (CT I 3277–8), he's not talking about premature ejaculation: he means 'If I can't have you I'll die'. Whether knowingly or not, Chaucer is here echoing the poet of the earlier *Dame Sirith*, in which the cleric, Wilkin, claims that he loves the married woman, Margery: "Ich hire love! Hit mot me spille/ Bot Ich gete hire to my wille" 'I love her! It'll kill me if I don't get her as I desire [or, to do what I want with]'.

The current sense involving liquids comes about through the association between killing and loss of blood, probably via the phrase *to spill blood*, 'to shed blood or to cause blood to be shed'. Again, Chaucer provides an example, when the Parson warns that judges who condemn murderers to death must do so "nat for delit to spille blood but for kepynge of rightwisnesse" (CT X 571).

In the phrase *thrills and spills* we have a relatively recent use of the noun (recorded only from the mid-nineteenth century) in which the sense has nearly come full circle: this kind of *spill* doesn't involve liquids: it involves solids that fall, as when a rider falls from a horse, or when someone falls from a bicycle or a skateboard. (It has no relation to the kind of *spill* – a long piece of thickish or card-like paper – with which my father used to light his cigarettes from the open fire on a winter's evening: that's from a different origin entirely.) As for the most recent kind of *spill* in Australia, this is not (as one might be forgiven for supposing) a party at which as much booze ends up on the floor as goes down gullets: it has to do with a different kind of party, a political party: it's 'the declaring of a number of offices in the party vacant as a result of one vacancy occurring' (*Dictionary of Australian Colloquialisms*). This has nothing to do with the wetness of politicians: the implication is that if the vessel's leaking, or the applecart's been upset, you'd do better to empty it completely and start again with a fresh lot.

SPITTING THE DUMMY

Someone asked me a while ago if I could explain the origin of the expression *to spit the dummy*. I had to confess not only that I couldn't explain its origin but, worse, that (then) I had never even heard it and so had no idea what it meant. Worse still, I couldn't find it in any dictionary, Australian or British. This suggested to me that it must be a pretty recent expression that might well be current in speech, but hadn't yet made its way into the dictionaries. (It has since made it into the *Australian Oxford Dictionary*, but with no explanation of its origin.)

I asked my younger daughter, Sarah, if she could enlighten me, because people of her generation are generally a shade quicker than people of mine when it comes to keeping up with linguistic fashion. "Yes, of course I know what it means, *dummy*," she replied, with a pointed pun and her customary deference to my age and wisdom: "it means *to chuck a wobbly*."

It must have been apparent from my face that I wasn't any the wiser, because she added, with fine condescension, "*You'd* probably call it *flying off the rocker* or some such antiquated expression. It means 'to lose your temper', OK?"

I took a deep breath, and asked gingerly if she had any clue as to its origin. She rolled her eyes piteously heavenwards, and said, "Well, it's obvious, isn't it? – The noise you make when you explode with rage is exactly the noise a baby makes when it spits out its dummy: P-Ter!"

It struck me afterwards that there was a nice connection between Australian *spitting the dummy* and British *flying off the rocker*: rockers and dummies are both devices for keeping babies quiet, and when babies get separated from their pacifiers, all hell breaks loose. And since both expressions are used figuratively of adults, it seems clear that there's something patronizing or belittling in their use: the implication must be that the person in question has lost control and is behaving like an ill-tempered baby. This is confirmed by the entry in the *Australian Oxford Dictionary*: in addition to the primary sense, 'to be very angry',

Bruce Moore offers a secondary one, 'to give up ... prematurely', quoting as an example "when he realised he couldn't win, he spat the dummy, gave the race away".

As for *throwing a wobbly*, I confess I wasn't game to press my dear daughter on that one, for fear that she might have spat *her* dummy at *me*. But people have evidently been throwing wobblies for long enough for that expression to get into print, because I found it in three dictionaries (the *New Shorter Oxford*, *Collins*, and *Macquarie*) – and in the last, interestingly enough, it's classed as a New Zealandism. (I now find it also in a fourth, the *Australian Oxford*, where it's classed as an Australianism.) The wobbliness, I suppose, is a reference to the trembling with which rage is sometimes accompanied; and again it seems to me that, as with the other expressions, there's a certain scorn on the part of the user for the person who has thus visibly lost control.

But as for why, when they lose their temper, the British do it by *flying off the rocker* (or *off the handle* – but that's another story), New Zealanders (if the *Macquarie* is right) by *throwing a wobbly*, and Australians by *spitting the dummy*, I think one would have to ask a sociologist rather than a lexicographer.

SPORTING WORDS

It is amazing how the greyest of grey administrators and the most static of couch potatoes will talk today about *keeping the ball rolling* or *running with the ball*, about *keeping their eye on the ball* or being *behind the eight ball*, about making sure there's a *level playing field* or starting *a whole new ball game* – and one can't help feeling that in many cases the speaker wouldn't have the faintest idea what shape the ball was supposed to be or how many others there might be apart from the *eight ball*, so much has the language of sports and games invaded the general vocabulary of even the least sports-minded amongst us.

If you ask for an estimate these days, you're more likely to be offered a *ballpark figure* than a rough idea; if it's nowhere near the figure you had in mind, the chances are that you'll think it came *out of left field*. The likelihood is that neither you nor the person you're speaking to has any idea that both these terms are from baseball; and it's entirely possible that this conversation takes place in a country where baseball is a minority sport or is not played at all, and that neither of you has ever watched a game. (A *ballpark* is a baseball ground; if an estimate is *in the ballpark* or if it's a *ballpark figure*, it's one that's within the area covered by the ground, i.e., it is at least within the bounds of possibility. *Left field* is the part of the field to the left of the batter when he faces the pitcher, but it has never been clear to me why something from that side should be considered surprising or difficult – which shows how much I know about baseball.)

Sport is a rich source of terms for defeat, difficulty, and failure, as it is for terms denoting crushing victories. If you're *snookered*, you're in a very awkward position, because (originally) you can't take a direct shot at any of the permitted balls. It isn't difficult to see which game this term comes from (though no one knows the origin of the word *snooker* itself); but most of us have had times when we felt *stymied*, with no knowledge that this term is from golf (you're *stymied* when you can't get a clear shot at the hole you have to sink your ball in because there's another ball in the way – and no one knows the origin of *stymied*, either). If you score a *hole in one*, on the other hand, you're doing exceptionally well; and everyone knows this term is from golfing, even when they use it to mean achieving sexual intercourse on the first date. A *hole in one* is also known as an *ace*; but if you've been *aced* you've been on the receiving end of a serve in tennis (or some other racquet game) that was so good that you couldn't get near it, so your opponent won that point with a single shot. (*Ace* came into English via Old French from Latin *as* 'a unit or unity'; it was used of the face of a die with a single dot marked on it; thence it passed into card games for a card with only one spot – considered the highest-ranking in most card games; thence it passed into ball games. So this word had a long history in a variety of games before it made its way into the general vocabulary.)

Cricket is one of the richest sources of sporting terms in general use – at least in Britain and the former colonies. To *hit someone for six* is pretty much the same as to *KO* them in boxing (i.e., to *knock* them *out* – and, yes, I'm using the singular *they*, or, in this case, *them*: it's so much more convenient, unobtrusive, and – dare I suggest? – *natural* than to have to keep saying *him or her*, or *he or she*, or *s/he* or some other such self-conscious locution). To *bowl someone a bumper* or *a bouncer*, or, for that matter, *a googly*, is to bowl them a difficult or a dangerous ball, hence to pose them a serious problem (and will a *doosra* soon be added to the list of possibilities?); but to bowl them a *dolly* is to give them an easy ball and hence to risk being *hit for six* oneself. In a similar way, if a batsman hits a *dolly*, it's an easy catch. But this is a term that has entered sport from the common language rather than vice versa: a *dolly* is an easy ball (whether bowled or hit); it's like a child's plaything, a *doll* with the diminutive suffix *-y*. *Doll* is in its turn a pet name for *Dorothy*; it was used in the sixteenth century as a name for a mistress; thence it became used, as the *New Shorter Oxford* puts it, for 'a small model of a human figure, usually child or woman, for use as a toy'. So a *dolly* in a cricket game can be expected to be both childish and easy.

To go *in to bat* for someone is to take up the battle on their behalf (though this might equally originate from baseball or softball or some other game in which a ball is struck with a bat); but to *bat on a sticky wicket* is indubitably from cricket, and meant originally to bat on a rain-affected wicket on which the ball spun or seamed prodigiously, hence to face extremely difficult conditions. To do something *off one's own bat* is to do it on one's own initiative, or spontaneously, and I assume (but am not certain) that it's from cricket, though it might equally be from baseball. If you're *caught* or *caught out* before the ball hits the ground after you've hit it, you're dismissed, hence, apprehended making a mistake (but the similarity between the sporting and the general sense here may be pure coincidence). If you're *stumped*, you're bamboozled in a different way. I had always assumed that this was another cricketing term, but the dictionaries are unanimous in telling me that it's a farming term of North American origin, used of the bind you found yourself in when you were clearing new ground and your plough came to an abrupt halt when it hit a *stump* hidden below the surface of the ground. Obviously what's needed in these circumstances is a crafty Australian invention like the famous *stump-jump plough*!

SUBJUNCTIVES

When people sing "God save the Queen", they are not making a statement but expressing a wish: the meaning is not 'God saves (or does save) the Queen' but 'May God save the Queen' or 'Please, God, will you save the Queen'. Here, in the (British) National Anthem, are preserved (or, if you like, *saved*) both an early meaning of the word *save* and an early form of the verb. The sense is not 'rescue' but 'protect, look after, keep safe': *safe* is the adjective, *save* the cognate verb: the sense is 'Please God, protect the Queen and keep her safe'. As for the form ('God save' as opposed to 'God saves'), this is what grammarians call the *subjunctive mood* (as opposed to the normal or *indicative mood*) of the verb. The indicative is used for plain statements ("Music is the food of love": statement of fact), the subjunctive for wishes or hypotheses or other matters of doubt or uncertainty ("If music be the food of love [but we can't be certain that it is], play on").

Where Johnson a hundred and fifty years after him only occasionally has a subjunctive after *if* or *though* – as in his famous question, "If Pope be not a poet, where is poetry to be found?" – Shakespeare almost invariably has one, not just in the opening line of *Twelfth Night*, but everywhere else as well, because what follows these words is necessarily hypothetical: "If this be error and upon me proved/ I never writ nor no man ever loved" (Sonnet 116); "If it be true that good wine needs no bush" (*As You Like It*, Epilogue); "If it were done when 'tis done, then 'twere well/ It were done quickly" (*Macbeth* 1.7.1–2); "murder, though it have no tongue, will speak/ With most miraculous organ" (*Hamlet* 2.2.594–5); "if this letter speed/ And my invention thrive, Edmond the base/ Shall to th' legitimate" (*King Lear* 1.2.19–21); and so on. Inexperienced actors are inclined, when learning their lines, to substitute the equivalent indicative forms, because those are what we'd use today: "murder, though it has no tongue"; "if this letter speeds and my invention thrives" – when that happens directors, if they are (whoops! – I mean "If they be") like me, will lose their cool.

Since Shakespeare's day, the subjunctive in English has increasingly been expressed by *may, might, would*, and other auxiliaries, followed by the infinitive of the verb, rather than by a different form of the verb. Why has the old form more or less died out? Probably because, except in cases like *be* and *is*, its form has become indistinguishable from that of the indicative. In the present tense it's only in the third person that it makes any difference: I, we, you, and they *run*, but he, she, or it *runs*. So, if the subjunctive is *run*, we can't tell, when I, we, you, or they *run*, whether *run* is indicative or subjunctive; but if he, she, or it *run*, we know that that form is subjunctive, because we're expecting the form *runs*. And we know, too, that the writer is remarkably old-fashioned, because everyone today would say *runs*, even after *if*: you don't need a different form of the verb to express a hypothesis when the *if* has already expressed it. So rare has the old subjunctive become (except in American English, which in this – as in many other linguistic matters – is more conservative than

202

British English) that teachers sometimes fail to recognize it, as both my daughters have found out, to their annoyance and disgust, when their teachers have corrected them into error. "It was as if the whole world were silent" the elder wrote in a school essay; "If this were so" the younger wrote in an essay at university: the teacher in each instance 'corrected' the already correct *were* to the colloquial *was*.

Alas, those teachers revealed their own ignorance, albeit that their intentions were good. (Nice word *albeit*: like *goodbye*, 'God be with you', it has a fossilized subjunctive in its midst.) Well, I suppose the subjunctive is on its last legs, but *be* that as it may, I'd go on using it if I *were* you: it gives such innocent pleasure to linguistic dinosaurs like me.

SURPRISE, SURPRISE

It's amazing how many of our words indicating surprise are actually dead metaphors whose literal meaning is much stronger than we now recognize. *Amazed*, for example, originally meant literally 'stunned', i.e., 'rendered unconscious, knocked out, knocked senseless'. But the verb *to stun* itself, though it retains this sense in some contexts (as when one is *stunned* by a blow on the head) is losing its force in other contexts through hyperbolic overuse (as in such expressions as "you look stunning!"). The graphic Australianism, *like a stunned mullet*, seems to me finely balanced between the literal and the figurative: when we say that's what someone looks like, all we mean is that they look very surprised; but the literal sense is not yet quite dead, and the comparison retains its force precisely because it does still call to mind the image of a fish that's been bashed on the head.

But I'm telling only half the story when I say that *stunned* meant literally 'knocked senseless'. In fact it's one of a whole cluster of words (like *astonished*, *astounded*, and the archaic *astonied*) that are derived, via Old French *estoner* (modern French *étonner*) from Latin *tonāre* 'to thunder': all these words originally meant 'struck by a thunderbolt' hence 'knocked witless'. Milton is consciously calling the etymological roots to mind when he has Satan comment to Beëlzebub that their companions, having been expelled from Heaven, are lying "astonisht on th' oblivious Pool" (*PL* 1.266). He doesn't just mean they're a bit surprised to find themselves in Hell: he means, precisely, that they've been struck by thunderbolts, the weapons with which the Son of God has driven them from Heaven (6.824–66). The pool is called "oblivious", by the way (though this causative sense is not listed separately in *OED*), because it *causes* forgetfulness, like the "sweet oblivious antidote" that Macbeth wishes the doctor could give his wife to "Raze out the written troubles of [her] brain" (5.3.44–5), whereas we tend now to use *oblivious* only of people who are unaware of what's going on around them. But Milton is exceptional. For other writers these words had all lost their thunder – if I may be forgiven the obvious pun – before being taken into English: the earliest senses for all of them recorded in *OED* retain the idea of unconsciousness, but not that of the thunder that is its etymological cause.

And what of *surprise* itself? Is there a dead metaphor lurking there? Indeed there is. This is from French *surpris(e)*, the past participle of *surprendre*, which is from medieval Latin *superprehendere*. The stem, *prehendere*, meant 'to grasp, seize, or catch hold of', as it still does, intellectually, in *comprehend*, and both intellectually and physically in *apprehend*. If one was *superprehended* (or *surprised*), one was seized or caught hold of to an excessive degree by, say, an emotion or an illness. This is still, I think, the most prominent sense in the opening line of Wordsworth's moving sonnet on the death of his daughter, Catherine:

> Surprised by joy – impatient as the Wind
> I turned to share the transport – Oh! with whom
> But thee, deep buried in the silent tomb,
> That spot which no vicissitude can find?

I am not sure where the element of unexpectedness comes from with *surprise*. There doesn't seem to be any etymological reason for it; yet it has been there in English from the beginning, and indeed it's now the chief sense: when we're *surprised*, it's because something unexpected has happened. It takes a lexicographer to use the word in its older sense, 'caught', as one of my then students, Meredith Whitford, pointed out to me one day, when we were discussing Wordsworth's sonnet. When Noah Webster's wife caught him cuddling the maid and said she was surprised at him (Meredith told me), Webster is alleged to have replied, "No, my dear, it is I who am *surprised*; you are merely astonished."

TERMS OF ASSOCIATION (1)

At a meeting of the Board of the Faculty of Arts some time ago the then Dean caused some amusement by remarking that he had just returned from a conference of deans in Queensland at which, on the last evening, the delegates had had a friendly competition to see who could come up with the most appropriate term to describe a gathering such as theirs (in imitation of that well known trio, *a jam of tarts*, *a flourish of strumpets*, and *an anthology of pros*). The term that won the prize, he said, was a *drudgery of deans*. I was reminded of a similar contest at a conference of the New Chaucer Society, at which my own *chest of Chaucerians* (which contains a pun on two different kinds of *chest*, one meaning 'box or casket' as in modern English, the other meaning 'strife, contention, wrangling, etc.') was defeated (to my chagrin) by someone else's *parliament of Chaucerians* (which, of course, is a nice allusion to Chaucer's *Parliament of Fowls*, in which human contentiousness is satirized through the wranglings of a bevy of quarrelling birds).

Expressions like these, of course, are all attempting to suggest two ideas at the same time: on the one hand, that of a gathering of people; on the other, that of the quality that distinguishes them from other people, and that most nearly defines their character or their occupation. Deans work hard (we hope); Chaucerians squabble (we observe).

This game of finding appropriate terms for describing groups is in fact a very old one, dating back at least as far as the fifteenth century: several manuscripts survive from that period containing long lists of terms for groups, both of animals and of people, some of which are still in use in current standard English, such as a *herd of deer*, a *flock of sheep*, a *swarm of bees*, a *shoal of fish*, and so on. (It's much simpler in Australia, where almost any company is called a *mob*.) These are all obviously collective terms, although some of them are actually more precise than they may at first appear. A *covey of partridges*, for example (from French *couver* 'to incubate or hatch'), means strictly speaking a group consisting of the two parent birds and their young, like a *brood of chickens*; and the same is true of an *eye of pheasants*, from OF *ni* (modern French *nid*) 'nest', with incorrect word division (cf. *nickname*). A *team of horses* or of *oxen* is not just any old number but specifically the number harnessed to one's cart or one's plough.

A *gaggle of geese*, on the other hand, is indeed an indeterminate number, and the name, taken obviously from the noise geese make, is not just alliterative but onomatopoeic. As for some of the other terms found in the medieval manuscripts, scholars have pointed out that these weren't originally collective terms at all: they can't have been, because some of them are used of non-gregarious animals: a *sloth* or a *slowness of bears* refers to the apparently lumbering movement of a bear (although readers of John Irving's *The Hotel New Hampshire* will know that bears – even old ones – can in fact run "surprisingly fast"); a *skulk of foxes* alludes to the sneaky way a fox slinks around the hen-house, and a *labour of moles* to the hard work of tunnelling. Terms like these must have been intended to denote the distinguishing characteristic of a given species, as opposed to a group of individuals of the species, and for that reason scholars have come to call them 'terms of association' rather than 'collective terms'; but because they appeared in manuscripts in the same lists as collective terms, they were thought to be collective terms, too, and those that have survived, like a *pride of lions*, are used as if that's what they were. Ignorance and misunderstanding are powerful influences in linguistic change.

TERMS OF ASSOCIATION (2)

The terms from medieval lists discussed in the last item are all to do with animals; but there are many others (like the hypothetical *drudgery of deans*), that have to do with people. Some of these are quite amusing, and of great interest as indicators of medieval attitudes.

Dislike of the regular clergy comes out strongly in terms such as an *abominable sight of monks* and a *superfluity of nuns*; and readers of Chaucer's *Canterbury Tales* will recognize familiar territory when they come across a *skulk of friars*, who are thus equated with foxes, a *lying of pardoners*, and an *untruth of summoners*. The legal profession comes in for some stick, too, with a *sentence of judges*, and a *damning of jurors*, which implies that they are more likely to *condemn* than to acquit the accused; but an *execution of officers* probably means only (as Hodgkin suggests) that the officers are carrying out their orders, not that they're chopping people's heads off.

Women are the subject of some antifeminist jibes in the lists, as is usual in medieval literature: a *gaggle of women* and a *gaggling of gossips* speak for themselves; a *nonpatience of wives* looks like the complaint of a henpecked husband; and a *multiplying of husbands* echoes the Wife of Bath's comment that what some people think women want most is "oftetyme to be wydwe and wedde" (*CT* III 928). A *rage of maidens*, on the other hand, probably suggests not that young women are always losing their temper, but, since *rage* is used also of colts, that they're frisky and enjoy a bit of fun. (There may well be some sexual innuendo here, implying that maidens may be less maidenly than they seem, since the verb *to rage* in Middle English not infrequently carries sexual overtones, as in the Miller's tale, when "hende Nicholas/ Fil with this yonge wyf to *rage* and pleye,/ Whil that hir housbonde was at Oseneye" (*CT* I 3272–4); but one can't be sure of this, because there's no context to appeal to other than that of the list itself.) But the satire is not all directed at women: husbands who can't (or won't) believe that their wives have been unfaithful look pretty foolish in an *uncredibility of* cuckolds, in which the -ble of uncredible evidently carries an active rather than a passive sense (cf. comfortable and visible), so that we would say an incredulity of cuckolds.

Some of the terms, particularly those dealing with occupations, give revealing insights into social history. A venture of shipmen reminds us how precarious trade was in days when shipwrecks were commoner than oil-spills (as in The Merchant of Venice, when Antonio's ships are reported to have foundered: "Hath all his ventures failed? What not one hit?", i.e., 'hit the mark, succeeded', 3.2.265). A temperance of cooks may be an ironic comment either on heavy-handedness in the seasoning or tempering of food or on "the not infrequent alcoholic propensities of otherwise first-class cooks" (as Hodgkin puts it) – as nicely demonstrated some years ago by the cook's consumption of lemon essence in the Australian feature film Sunday Too Far Away. One of my favourites is a promise of tapsters, i.e., people serving drinks, who promise faithfully that they'll serve you next, and never do. This will remind Shakespeareans of the joke played by Prince Hal and Poins on Francis the drawer (another name for tapster) in Henry IV Part I:

> I prithee do thou stand in some by-room, while I question my puny drawer to what end he gave me the sugar, and do thou never leave calling 'Francis!', that his tale to me may be nothing but 'Anon!'   (2.5.28–32)

It may also remind Australians and New Zealanders of a certain age of the bad old six o'clock swill, when serious drinkers (I'm told) would get half a dozen beers lined up on the bar – if they could get near it – at five to six, because the law forbad the sale of drinks after closing time, but not the drinking of those already bought.

THRILLS

The word *thrill* has a curious history, both semantically and phonetically. The noun is descended from Old English *thyrel*, formed from a combination of the preposition *thurh* 'through' with the diminutive suffix *-el* (as in modern English *chapel* or *tunnel*). But what is a *through-el*, a 'little through'? It's 'a hole, an opening, or a perforation': something that's been pierced through or that allows things to pass through. A *nostril* (formerly *nose-thirl*) is, literally, a 'nose-hole'. The word could also function as an adjective with the sense 'pierced' or 'having a hole'. One of the Old English *Riddles*, to which the innocent solution is 'a key', begins "Wrætlic hongath bi weres theo,/ frean under sceate. Foran is thyrel", that is, 'An amazing object hangs by a man's thigh,/ master under the clothes. At the front it has a hole....' I don't suppose readers need any help in supplying the alternative solution.

The OE verb *thyrlan*, formed from the noun, meant 'to pierce, to penetrate, to make a hole in, to pass into or through'. In a famous passage in the early Middle English *Ancrene Wisse* ('Guide for Anchoresses') the author compares Christ's battle with death on the Cross to that of a knight fighting in a tournament to win the love of his lady: as the knight's shield is pierced in the tournament, so Jesus allows his body to be "ithurlet" for the love of humankind. The nameless knight injured in the tournament in Chaucer's Knight's tale has his breast-bone "thirled" by a spear (*CT* I 2710); if the pronunciation had been then as it is now, he might have said, without a trace of sarcasm, "I am thrilled".

The current pronunciation is the result of a sound change known as *metathesis*, which involves the transposition of a consonant and the adjacent vowel. This is not at all an unusual change; it can happen either way and at any time. A *bird* was in OE a *brid*; *to run* is ultimately from OE *iernan*; there are people today who think *presume* is pronounced *perssume*.

As for the current senses of *thrill* (both noun and verb), they are, of course, figurative: to be *thrilled* is to be, as it were, 'pierced by emotion'; a *thrill* is the piercing sensation one feels when an emotion passes *through*. The emotion in question is now almost invariably one of excitement or happiness, but in earlier use any kind of emotion could be described as *thrilling*. The messenger reporting the death of the Duke of Cornwall in *King Lear* says that when Cornwall had torn out Gloucester's eyes, "A servant that he bred, thrilled with remorse, . . . Flew on him, and amongst them felled him dead" (4.2.41–4), that is, 'A servant whom he [Gloucester] had brought up, moved [literally 'pierced'] by compassion, attacked him [Cornwall] and killed him in their midst'. Similarly when Juliet is about to drink the sleeping potion that will make her family think she has died, she confesses to herself (using the verb intransitively), "I have a faint cold fear thrills through my veins/ That almost freezes up the heat of life" (*Romeo and Juliet* 4.3.15–16). Strictly speaking – if one recalls the etymology of *thrill* – "thrills through" is tautologous, since it means, literally, 'passes through through'. But who, apart from crusty old pedants, is ever bothered by tautology? I am only too aware, when I cross out the *right* in the *right throughout* to which some of my students are so attached, that they are the ones who will win this battle in the long run: they've got the numbers.

Well, the verb may surprise us with its amelioration, but the noun is more predictable with its degeneration: in colloquial usage *a thrill*, except in the phrase *thrills and spills*, usually means *a sexual thrill*, and – how completely the etymology has been forgotten! – a sexual thrill doesn't necessarily involve penetration.

VISIBLE

People who work with medieval manuscripts not infrequently come across a word that can't be found in any dictionary, or a word used in a sense that is not elsewhere recorded. What do they do in such cases? How do they decide whether that word or that usage is genuine, or whether it's a scribal error?

I spent many years working on an edition of *Sidrak and Bokkus*, a previously inedited book of knowledge in Middle English verse, translated from Old French prose. It's a sort of medieval "one thousand and one questions you always wanted to ask, and never dared" cast in the form of a question-and-answer dialogue between a heathen king (Bokkus) and a learned philosopher (Sidrak) who has converted him to belief in the Trinity. After his conversion King Bokkus plies Sidrak with a barrage of questions covering every conceivable topic from the shape of angels to the copulation of dogs.

Not surprisingly, this being a medieval composition, the first questions are about God: has God always existed? is God everywhere? what was the first thing God made? and so on. One of these opening questions asks "if it might bene/ That God of heven mighte be sene". The reply begins:

> God is visible, that warne I the,
> And eke invisible so he,
> For al thing he may se
> And he may not ysen be.   (L1939–42)

God is *visible*, that is, *because he can see everything*; but he is *invisible* at the same time *because he himself cannot be seen*. There's no problem about *invisible*: it carries the expected sense, 'not able to be seen'. But what of *visible*? If God is visible *because he can see everything*, the context demands that *visible* have an active sense 'able to see' or 'all-seeing' instead of its usual passive sense, 'able to be seen'.

I was very puzzled by this because I couldn't find this active sense in any English dictionary (or in any French one either). It seemed to me impossible for a word ending in *-ible* or *-able* to have the active sense 'able to *do* something', since every such word I could think of had the passive sense 'able to *be* something*ed*': *audible* = 'able to be heard', *doable* = 'able to be done', *lovable* = 'able to be loved', *unthinkable* = 'not able to be thought', and so on. How, then, could *visible* mean 'able to see' rather than 'able to be seen'?

Eventually it occurred to me to look up the suffixes *-ible*, *-able*, and *-ble* in *OED*, and there at last, under *-ble*, I found one of those miniature essays that make the book not just a source for looking things up in but a joy to read. It points out that adjectives ending in *-ble* "were originally active as well as passive", and it gives as examples of the active sense such words as *comfortable*, *companionable*, *durable*, and *suitable*. A *suitable* job isn't one that is able to be suited: it's one that suits the person who's in it or who's applying for it.

So: *visible* can indeed mean 'able to see' as the context demands. But what we cannot tell without other examples is whether this was a standard sense in Middle English and in Old French (from which the translator has taken the word directly), or whether the author and the translator were simply playing with the word, on the analogy of other words ending in *-ble*. This is a question that must remain (in the usual sense) *unanswerable*.

WAR WORDS (1)

Wars cause indescribable misery in human terms; almost their only positive effect is linguistic, through the enriching of the vocabulary.

The First World War (to give only a few examples) gave us the *Anzacs* (originally specifically members of the Australian and New Zealand Army Corps, and subsequently any Australian or New Zealander), along with the many combinations in which the word came to be used, like *Anzac Day*, *Anzac biscuit*, *Anzac memorial*, and the *Anzac legend*. It also popularized *diggers* (a word formerly used in Australia of gold-diggers and in New Zealand of gum-diggers, i.e., people employed to dig up fossilized kauri gum); and trench warfare gave a new meaning to the word *dugout*, which had previously been used of canoes, and, in America, and also in South Australia's own mining town of Burra, of hovels burrowed into the sides of banks or hills.

The German air raids during the 1940 *blitzkrieg* of the Second World War (from *Blitz* 'lightning' + *Krieg* 'war') gave wide currency to one particular kind of *blackout* (a term adopted from the theatre, meaning in this instance a period in which lights were put out so as not to be visible to aircraft); they've also left us a short form that survives both as a noun – to have *a blitz* on something – and a verb – *to blitz* it. Advertisements today tell us that "There's only one Jeep"; but a *jeep* with a lower-case initial became the common term for a vehicle with emergency four-wheel drive, named after the *GP* ('general purpose') vehicles in the American army. Michael Atchison will no doubt be delighted by the suggestion in the *New Shorter Oxford* that the word's spread may have been influenced by the popularity of Eugene the Jeep, "a shape-changing character of great resourcefulness and power introduced into the cartoon strip 'Popeye' in 1936". It's curious that this handy little word has more or less been ousted in its general application by the more cumbersome (though admittedly more specific) *four-wheel drive*; and perhaps also that it has never (so far as I know) been used of that other kind of *GP*, a General Practitioner.

I don't think the Vietnam War is far enough behind us yet for many of its terms to have lost their horrific overtones in the same way as *blitz* or as *Catch-22*, from the title of Joseph Heller's first novel, published in 1961, in which (as David Crystal succinctly puts it in the *Cambridge Encyclopedia*) "US airmen seeking leave from active service in World War 2 on grounds of mental derangement are judged ineligible to apply, since such a request proves their sanity. Hence 'Catch-22' signifies any logical trap or double bind". The horrors of Vietnam, like *defoliation* and *Agent Orange* (named after the orange rings round the containers in which this herbicide was kept), and the cynical euphemisms of the Gulf War, like *collateral damage* (i.e., the killing of innocent civilians who just happened to get in the way), are still too close for such terms to have lost their sting, though they have certainly entered the common language.

One would think that the same would hold true for terms connected with nuclear warfare, and I think for many of them, like *mushroom cloud*, *nuclear deterrent*, and *radiation sickness*, it does. How extraordinary, then, that the Bikini Atoll in the Marshall Islands in the Pacific, the site of twenty-three US nuclear tests between 1946 and 1958 (including that of the first H-bomb), should have given its name to that 'scanty two-piece

215

beach garment worn by women and girls' (*New Shorter Oxford*), which folk etymologists would have us believe is so called because it has two pieces! They take the first syllable of *bikini* to be the prefix *bi-* 'two' (as in *bicycle*, *bilateral*, etc.); and this belief has given rise to the parallel name *monokini* for a bikini that has only one piece. But lexicographers and linguists insist that a bikini gets its name from the atoll because of the explosive effect it has on ogling males.

WAR WORDS (2)

The Mother of all Battles can, I think, claim the rare distinction for a foreign idiom of having been accepted into colloquial English virtually overnight. Its acceptance was doubtless hastened by the satisfaction with which his mainly English-speaking enemies were able to turn the phrase against Saddam Hussein, the man who made it famous, and who, before his fall, was regarded in the West as the *daddy* of all dictators (with the possible exception of Idi Amin): Saddam was himself, in the first Gulf War, made to suffer the *mother* of all defeats instead of inflicting such a defeat (as he'd threatened) on his enemies. Thus, in war, one's language can turn against oneself, like a rocket that *homes in* on the launcher instead of the target (like a *homing pigeon*, that is: not *hones in*, as some think, though I dare say that will catch on, on the assumption that the phrase derives from the *honing* that's required to produce accuracy – not a bad assumption at all, as folk etymology goes). Most of us, if we're honest, would concur with Hamlet in thinking that it's a "sport to have the engineer/ Hoist with his own petar" (3.4.206–7), that is, 'raised aloft (i.e., blown up) by his own bomb'. (Alas that these lines, the earliest recorded example of this saying, being found only in the second Quarto, are excluded from the Wells–Taylor *Complete Works!*)

It would be remiss of me if I failed to point out, in passing, that *petar* (or, as we'd now say, *petard*) is derived from the stem of the French verb *péter* 'to break wind' with the diminutive suffix *-ard*, as in *bastard*: a *petard* or small bomb is thus jokingly (perhaps disparagingly) called 'a little fart'. Hence (as Ewart Shaw and Laine Langridge were kind enough to point out to me) the stage name "Le Petomane" adopted by the Frenchman Joseph Pujol (1857–1945), who had such extraordinary control of his rectal muscles that he made a career of playing symphonies with musical farts.

Euphemisms do not have quite the proverbial or familial ring of the *Mother of all Battles*, but they are an inevitable by-product of warfare, and they seem to be no less successful in working their way into standard speech. Who could have predicted that Hitler's gruesome *Endlösung* would work its way into standard English as the *final solution*? or that the media would accept and reproduce the allies' glossing over of the killing of innocent civilians in the Gulf War with the seemingly innocuous phrase, *collateral damage*? or would help to preserve that contradiction-in-terms, *friendly fire*, as if getting killed by one's own people were somehow preferable to being shot by the enemy? or that the recent genocides in Rwanda and Bosnia should come to be called *ethnic cleansing*, as if, when one were exterminating people of a different race, one were doing something useful like disinfecting the bathroom?

Expressions like these are perhaps inspired by sick humour, though one suspects that their originators are completely humourless. But there are others in which the humour is very much to the fore – brave attempts to make light of difficult circumstances. One of my favourites is *snafu*, an acronym formed by American servicemen from the initial letters of "Situation Normal: All Fucked Up" (I'm told that there's an alternative version ending "all fouled up", but it isn't hard to imagine which of the two the troops would have been more likely to have in mind). This is not heard much nowadays: I think we could profitably revive it for use in politics, education, and the public service. Another that I am frequently asked about (for obvious reasons) is *gone for a burton*, of which the origin is not certainly known, but which is generally agreed to have originated in the RAF and to have something to do with *Burton ale*, brewed in Burton-on-Trent. The *New Shorter Oxford* defines it fairly widely as 'killed, destroyed, ruined, or lost', all of which senses it now covers; and although *OED* is surely correct in saying that "None of the several colourful explanations of the expression is authenticated by contemporary printed evidence", I must confess that I rather like the colourful explanation given to me recently by an anonymous caller on talkback radio, which accords reasonably well with that given in *Brewer's Dictionary of Phrase and Fable*. She said that the phrase was originally used specifically of aircraft lost at sea: if the plane disappeared into the water (alias the drink), its pilot could be said to have permanently *gone for a burton*.

WASSAIL

"Nay, but this dotage of our General's/ O'erflows the measure". So begins *Antony and Cleopatra*, with Philo's disgusted commentary on Antony's infatuation with Cleopatra. This opinion is echoed by Octavius, who complains bitterly about the news from Alexandria, that, instead of preparing for a war against Pompey, Antony "fishes, drinks, and wastes/ The lamps of night in revel" (1.4.4–5). Antony, in short, is having a good time when his allies are getting ready for war, and they don't like it. No wonder Caesar urges him (albeit not to his face) to leave his "lascivious wassails" (1.4.56)! It's pretty clear from the context, in which Antony's present life of luxury is contrasted with his former heroism in having uncomplainingly survived a time of famine when he was forced to drink "The stale of horses and the gilded puddle/ Which beasts would cough at" (1.4.61–2), that to Octavius *wassails* is a contemptuous word.

The same can be said for Hamlet's use of the word in describing the behaviour of his uncle, Claudius:

> The King doth wake tonight and takes his rouse,
> Keeps wassail, and the swagg'ring upspring reels,
> And as he drains his draughts of Rhenish down
> The kettle-drum and trumpet thus bray out
> The triumph of his pledge   (1.4.8–12)

– that's to say, roughly, 'The King's staying up late tonight, boozing, merry-making, and dancing; and every time he has a drink, a drum is beaten and a trumpet blown'. (This, by the way, is the custom that Hamlet declares famously to be "More honoured in the breach than the observance", 1.4.18.)

Both these contexts suggest that for Shakespeare *wassailing* implied drinking to excess. Perhaps it still does, although I'm inclined to think that for us the emphasis is on the good cheer rather than the drunkenness: certainly it's associated with drink, but I think it now implies festivity rather than debauchery, as in the burden of the Christmas carol "Now joy be to the Trynyte": "Wassaill, wassayll, wassaill, syng we/ In worship of Cristes nativite".

But what is the origin of this term, *wassail*? *OED* has one of its delightful mini-essays on the topic, pointing out that it is formed from the combination of two separate words in Old English or Old Norse, the imperative (or one form of the imperative) of the verb *to be* followed by an adjective meaning 'whole' or 'hale' or 'healthy'. The form in OE would have been *wes hāl*, that in ON *ves heill*; the OE form of the verb combined with the ON form of the adjective produced in ME the hybrid phrase *wæs hæil*; and when the verb and the adjective are run together and the *h* of *hæil* is lost, we have the modern form *wassail*.

And the meaning? Well, the phrases *wes hāl* and *ves heill* meant literally 'be healthy'; they were used as a formula for greeting or on parting, expressing a wish for the health of the person addressed. Just as we would now say (in Australia) "G'day", i.e., literally, 'May you have (or I hope you have) a pleasant day', or as American sales staff invariably say as you depart, "Have a nice day", so they said in Anglo-Saxon times "Wes hal", i.e., 'May you be healthy'. At some time this standard greeting appears to have become specifically a drinking formula: as you drank a person's health in Middle English times, you said "Wæs hæil", 'Be healthy' – an exact equivalent of current English "Good health" or "Your health". The standard reply (no longer in use) was "Drinc hæil", 'May you drink good health (or good luck)'.

Once the connection with drink is established, the rest follows. *Wassail* becomes, by semantic transfer, the name of the drink with which (or in which) healths were drunk, especially 'the spiced ale used in Twelfth-night and Christmas-eve celebrations' (*OED*), and thus, by another transfer, not the drink itself but the action of drinking it, especially of drinking a lot of it, and so to the revelry we began with.

NOTES AND REFERENCES

Parenthetic references are given in the text to works cited frequently; those works are listed separately, following the references for individual items given in the notes below. Except when otherwise stated quotations from Chaucer are from the *Riverside Chaucer*; those from Shakespeare are from the *Complete Works*, ed. Wells and Taylor. Where quotations are cited from dictionaries, the bibliographical details of the original source are not repeated.

EPIGRAPH
The exchange between Owl and Pooh is from chapter 4 of *Winnie the Pooh* (1926), "In which Eeyore loses a tail and Pooh finds one", quoted from *Winnie the Pooh* © A.A. Milne. Copyright under the Berne Convention. Published by Egmont Books Limited, London and used with permission.

ACKNOWLEDGEMENTS
For *come-uppance* see *OED*, *come, v.*, 74.l, and *marry, int.*, 2.c.

The most detailed books on semantic change known to me are:
J. Copley, *Shift of Meaning* (London, Oxford University Press, 1961).
Geoffrey Hughes, *Words in Time: A Social History of the English Vocabulary* (Oxford, Blackwell, 1988).
Gustav Stern, *Meaning and Change of Meaning, with Special Reference to the English Language* (1931; repr. Bloomington, Ind., Indiana University Press, 1965).
R.A. Waldron, *Sense and Sense Development* (1967; 2nd edn, London, André Deutsch, 1979).

The following books all contain helpful chapters or sections on semantic change:
Charles L. Barber, *The Story of Speech and Language* (New York, Thomas Y. Crowell, 1965), pp. 239–56.

Albert C. Baugh and Thomas Cable, *A History of the English Language*, 3rd edn (London, Routledge & Kegan Paul, 1978), pp. 307–12.

Henry Bradley, *The Making of English*, rev. Simeon Potter (London, Macmillan, 1968), pp. 108–43.

G.L. Brook, *A History of the English Language* (London, André Deutsch, 1958), pp. 165–97.

Robert Burchfield, *The English Language* (Oxford, Oxford University Press, 1985), pp. 113–23.

Simeon Potter, *Our Language* (1950; rev. edn, Harmondsworth, Penguin, 1966), pp. 104–16.

Thomas Pyles and John Algeo, *English: An Introduction to Language* (New York, Harcourt, Brace & World, 1970), pp. 225–32.

Thomas Pyles and John Algeo, *The Origins and Development of the English Language*, 3rd edn (New York, Harcourt Brace Jovanovich, 1982), pp. 238–59.

A complete book devoted to folk etymology is *Folk-Etymology: A Dictionary of Verbal Corruptions or Words Perverted in Form or Meaning, by False Derivation or Mistaken Analogy*, by A. Smythe Palmer (1883; repr. New York, Greenwood Press, 1969).

The word *enthusiasm* is studied in close detail in Susie I. Tucker, *Enthusiasm: A Study in Semantic Change* (Cambridge, Cambridge University Press, 1972).

ASHTRAYS, MOTORBIKES, AND AUSTRALIAN TERMS OF ABUSE

Quotations from the *Dictionary of Australian Colloquialisms* are taken from the following entries: *couldn't blow the froth off a glass of beer, homing pigeons, kick, mean, paper bag, revolving door, short of a sheet of bark, useful/useless.*

The formula "one thing short of something" is recorded also in John Ayto's *Twentieth Century Words* (Oxford, Oxford University Press, 1999), s.v. . . . *short of a* . . . , a reference I owe to Chris Bright.

Examples from talkback radio are taken from a session with Philip Satchell on ABC Radio in Adelaide, 22 August 2002.

BUXOM

For comments on the clang association see Pyles and Algeo, *English*, p. 226.

CLODS, CLOTS, AND CLOUDS

"Now springes the spray" is quoted from *Medieval English Lyrics: A Critical Anthology*, ed. R.T. Davies (London, Faber, 1963), p. 77.

Ohthere's words to King Alfred are quoted from *Bright's Old English Grammar & Reader*, p. 189/48–50.

COCKS AND ROOSTERS

Hugh Rawson's comments are from his *devious derivations* (New York, Crown Publishers, 1994), pp. 14, 46.

"I have a gentil cok" is quoted from *Middle English Lyrics*, ed. Maxwell S. Luria and Richard L. Hoffman (New York, Norton, 1974), p. 77.

For "process-orientation" and "performance-orientation" see chapter 9 of Beatrice Faust's *Women, Sex and Pornography* (1980; repr. Ringwood, Vic., Penguin, 1981), pp. 96–106.

COMFORTABLE

"The Destruction of Sennacherib" is quoted from *Byron: Poetical Works*, ed. Frederick Page, new edn, corrected by John Jump (London, Oxford University Press, 1970).

DAFT AND DEFT

A fuller discussion of the sense development of *daft* and *deft* may be found in my "Defining *Daftness*", *Medieval Literature and Antiquities: Studies in Honour of Basil Cottle*, ed. Myra Stokes and T.L. Burton (Cambridge, Brewer, 1987), pp. 165–74.

DANGEROUS

For further discussion of the meaning of *daungerous* in the Wife of Bath's Prologue see the gloss to line 514 in the *Riverside Chaucer*, and my "The Wife of Bath's Fourth and Fifth Husbands and Her Ideal Sixth: The Growth of a Marital Philosophy", *Chaucer Review* 13 (1978), 34–50, especially p. 42 and p. 49, n. 21.

DEER AND WORMS

"To his Coy Mistress" is quoted from *The Poems and Letters of Andrew Marvell*, ed. H.M. Margoliouth, 3rd edn, rev. Pierre Legouis with the collaboration of E.E. Duncan-Jones (2 vols, Oxford, Clarendon Press, 1971), vol. I, pp. 27–8.

ELEPHANTS

For Bill Bryson's suggestion about the origin of *Elephant and Castle* see his *Mother Tongue: The English Language* (1990; repr. London, Penguin, 1991), p. 195.

FART

The cuckoo song is quoted from *Early Middle English Verse and Prose*, p. 110.

For the various senses suggested for the word *verteth* see (1) *Early English Lyrics: Amorous, Divine, Moral and Trivial*, ed. E.K. Chambers and F. Sidgwick (1907; repr. London, Sidgwick, 1921), p. 4; (2) Theodore C. Hoepfner, "Sumer is icumen in", *Explicator* 3.3 (1944), 19–20, item 18; (3) Hans Platzer, "On the Disputed Reading of verteth in the 'Cuckoo Song'", *Neuphilologische Mitteilungen* 96 (1995), 123–43; (4) Carleton Brown, *English Lyrics of the XIIIth Century* (Oxford, Clarendon Press, 1932); Huntington Brown, "Sumer is icumen in", *Explicator* 3.3 (1944), 33–5, item 34; Eston Everett Ericson, "Bullock Sterteth, Bucke Verteth", *Modern Language Notes* 53 (1938), 112–13; and *OED*.

Rosemary Greentree's suggestion, together with a summary of scholarly debate about the word *verteth*, is in *Explicator* 61.4 (Summer 2003), item 1.

The remarks on the "The explosion of energy in the combination of kick and crepitation" are from Huntington Brown, p. 35.

FAST

The legend of *Saint Kenelm* may be found in *Early Middle English Verse and Prose*, pp. 96–107.

FORLORN

For the quotation from the *Peterborough Chronicle* see *Early Middle English Verse and Prose*, p. 208/198–9.

Keats's "Ode to a Nightingale" is quoted from *John Keats,* ed. Elizabeth Cook, The Oxford Authors (Oxford, Oxford University Press, 1990).

Pope's dictum is in *An Essay on Criticism*, line 365, quoted from *Alexander Pope*, ed. Pat Rogers, The Oxford Authors (Oxford, Oxford University Press, 1993).

FUN AND GLEE
For the fluctuating fortunes of the noun *glee* see the introductory comment in *OED*.

Johnson's definition is quoted in *OED*, s.v. *glee*, n., 3.a., quotation for 1755.

The quotation from the Cock and the Fox is from *The Poems of Robert Henryson*, ed. Denton Fox (Oxford, Clarendon Press, 1981), *Fables*, lines 518–19. Fox translates these lines, " 'As far as chamber sport . . . he was enfeebled' ", commenting that "A preponderance of the cold and dry elements causes impotence" (p. 217).

GIN AND ENGINES
The Fox and the Wolf is quoted from *Early Middle English Verse and Prose*, pp. 65–76.

GLOTTAL STOPS
Tom McArthur's account of the Glaswegian schoolboy may be found in his essay "Wee Jimmy and the dugs: or, where do *you* stand in the classroom?", chapter 6 in his *Living Words: Language, Lexicography and the Knowledge Revolution* (Exeter, University of Exeter Press, 1998), pp. 77–88. The story of Wee Jimmy and his struggle with glottal stops, under the title "Better butter", is on pp. 79–80.

GOSSIP
Sermo Lupi ad Anglos is quoted from *Bright's Old English Grammar & Reader*, p. 14/62; *The Fox and the Wolf* from *Early Middle English Verse and Prose*, pp. 65–76.

HAPAX LEGOMENA
A full collection of hapax legomena in *Sidrak and Bokkus* is printed in my note, "Some Fifteenth-Century hapax legomena", *Die Sprache* 33 (1987), 112–13.

HEAD

For Johnson's comment on concatenation, from the preface to his English Dictionary, see *Johnson: Prose and Poetry*, selected by Mona Wilson, 2nd edn (London, Rupert Hart-Davis, 1957), p. 311.

For *head* as an example of radiation see Simeon Potter, *Our Language* (1950; rev. edn, Harmondsworth, Penguin, 1966), pp. 110–11.

KNIGHT AND KNAVE

For *purr-word* and *snarl-word* see G.L. Brook, *A History of the English Language*, p. 168.

The Pentecostal oath is quoted from Sir Thomas Malory, *Le Morte D'Arthur*, ed. Janet Cowen (2 vols, Harmondsworth, Penguin, 1969), vol. 1, pp. 115–16.

LAVATORIES, TOILETS, AND RESTROOMS

The connection with *Waterloo* is suggested in A.S.C. Ross, "Loo", *Blackwood's Magazine*, 316 (1974), 309–16.

LICKING THINGS INTO SHAPE

Lord Kitchener's calypso may be heard on *lord kitchener: classic kitchener*, vol. 1, Words and Music by A. Roberts (n.p., Ice Music, 1993). [931102]

LONG WORDS BOTHER ME

The full title of Lynne Truss's book is *Eats, Shoots & Leaves: The Zero Tolerance Approach to Punctuation* (London, Profile Books, 2003).

Winning entries in the Bad Writing Competition, together with the rules of eligibility and Dutton's comments on the prize winners, may be found on the internet at <http://aldaily.com/bwc.htm>.

The quotation for 1996 is from Paul Fry, *A Defense of Poetry* (Stanford, Stanford University Press, 1995).

The quotation for 1997 is from an article by Rob Wilson. Dutton comments: "This colorful gem appears in a collection called *The Administration of Aesthetics: Censorship, Political Criticism, and the Public Sphere*, edited by Richard Burt "for the Social Text Collective" ([Minneapolis], University of Minnesota Press, 1994). Social Text is the cultural studies journal made famous by publishing physicist Alan Sokal's jargon-ridden parody of postmodernist writing. If this essay is Social Text's idea of scholarship, little wonder it fell for Sokal's hoax."

The quotation for 1998 is from an article by Judith Butler, Professor of Rhetoric and Comparative Literature at the University of California at Berkeley. The article, entitled "Further Reflections on the Conversations of Our Time", appeared in the scholarly journal *Diacritics* (1997).

Dutton's article "Language Crimes" appeared in the *Wall Street Journal* on 5 February 1999, p. W11.

Bauerlein's review is in *Philosophy and Literature* 28.1 (2004), 180–91; the collection of essays he takes apart is *Just Being Difficult? Academic Writing in the Public Arena*, ed. Jonathan Culler and Kevin Lamb (Stanford, Stanford University Press, 2003). Lest it be thought that I am simply jumping on the bandwaggon now that the tide appears (at last) to be turning, I must point out that I have been decrying the dumbing down of English syllabuses for some years – as in my lament that so few people (other than reviewers) would be likely to read John K. Hale's brilliant book, *Milton's Languages: The Impact of Multilingualism on Style* (Cambridge, Cambridge University Press, 1997); see *Parergon*, New Series 16 (1999), 236–9.

The full title of Don Watson's book is *Death Sentence: The Decay of Public Language* (Sydney, Random House, 2003). The bibliographical details of the three examples taken from this book (as given there) are as follows: (1) from "Role of Commitment and Motivation in Knowledge Management Systems Implementation: Theory, Conceptualisation, and Measurement of Antecedents of Success", by Yogesh Malholtra (Syracuse University of Management) and Dennis F. Galletta (Joseph M. Kratz Graduate School of Business); (2) a speech for the Human Rights and Equal Opportunity Commission; (3) faxed to Watson by an informant in the Department of Finance.

The final quotation is from chapter 11 of Sir Ernest Gowers's *The Complete Plain Words*, 2nd edn, rev. Sir Bruce Fraser (Harmondsworth, Penguin, 1973), p. 280. Gowers is too courteous to say where he found this hilarious example. For some unaccountable reason the editors of the 3rd edition (Sidney Greenbaum and Janet Whitcut) have deleted it.

LUST AND LUXURY

Launcelot's "lust to slepe" is quoted from Sir Thomas Malory, *Le Morte D'Arthur*, ed. Janet Cowen, vol. 1, p. 194.

MIRTH AND MERRIMENT

Don Juan is quoted from *Byron: Poetical Works*, ed. Frederick Page.

MOOD AND MOODY

Page and line references for the following quotations in this item are to *Bright's Old English Grammar & Reader*: King Alfred's explanation of England's decline, p. 181/31–2; Ælfric's comments on St Aidan, p. 242/59; "modceare" in *The Wife's Lament*, p. 345/40; "modcearig" in *The Wanderer*, p. 324/2; "ofermod" in *The Battle of Maldon*, p. 363/89; "modig" in *The Phoenix*, p. 319/10, and in the *Battle of Maldon*, p. 365/80; "modig and medugal" in *Judith*, p. 349/26. *Daniel* (line 105) is quoted from *The Junius Manuscript*, ed. George Philip Krapp, The Anglo-Saxon Poetic Records 1 (New York, Columbia University Press, 1931), pp. 109–32.

NAMES (4): SAINTS' NAMES

For Bede's account of Saint Audrey see Bede, *Ecclesiastical History of the English People*, trans. Leo Sherley-Price, rev. R.E. Latham, rev. edn (London, Penguin, 1990), 4.19.

NAMES (5): PLACE-NAMES

"Colonial Nomenclature" is quoted from *The Colonial Poets*, ed. G.A. Wilkes (Sydney, Angus and Robertson, 1974), p. 13.

Llanfairpwllgwynggyllgogerychwyrndrobwllllantysiliogogogoch is the full name of the famous Welsh village. The translation is David Crystal's in *The Cambridge Encyclopedia*.

Rodney Cockburn, in *What's in a Name? Nomenclature of South Australia* (1908, 3rd edn, [Adelaide], Axiom Publishing, 1990), describes the derivation of Eurelia as "elusive". Geoffrey H. Manning, in *The Romance of Place Names of South Australia* (Adelaide, published by the author, 1986), says "It is an Aboriginal name applied to a dam on Oladdie station, and in the Jadliaura tribal dialect means 'place of the ear'." (I am indebted to Chris Bright for this reference.) The same derivation is given by R. Praite and J.C. Tolley in *Place Names of South Australia* (Adelaide, Rigby, 1970). Manning reports the same story about the porters at Eurelia, as does A.W. Reed in *Place Names of Australia* (Sydney, A.H. & A.W. Reed, 1973). According to Manning and Reed the correct pronunciation is "You really are".

NICKNAMES

The various readings of *eke* and *piece* in Portia's speech are listed in most modern critical editions of *The Merchant of Venice*, such as those by Jay L. Halio for The Oxford Shakespeare (Oxford, Clarendon Press, 1993), and M.M. Mahood for The New Cambridge Shakespeare, updated edn (Cambridge, Cambridge University Press, 2003).

THE OLD WAGGON AND THE DEATH OF ENGLISH DIALECTS

William Barnes published three collections of dialect poems: *Poems of Rural Life in the Dorset Dialect: With a Dissertation and Glossary* (1844), *Hwomely Rhymes: A Second Collection of Poems in the Dorset Dialect* (1859), and *Poems of Rural Life in the Dorset Dialect . . . Third Collection* (1862). There were at least two editions of each collection before all three were republished in one volume under the title *Poems of Rural Life in the Dorset Dialect* in 1879. The spelling of the 1844 edition is very much more helpful as a guide to pronunciation than the simplified spelling adopted in later editions, and the grammar of the dialect is closer to that of the descriptions in Barnes's various grammars and glossaries than that of his later collections. The value of the 1844 edition, as a guide to both pronunciation and grammar, seems not to have been fully appreciated. I have in preparation a new edition of this important first collection, together with a guide to pronunciation.

For the sense 'strong, robust, well-grown' for *hardish* see *EDD*, s.v. *Hard*, adj., sense 4. The four illustrative quotations are all from the southwest: one from Wiltshire, two from Somerset, and one (this example) from Dorset. This sense is not in *OED*.

According to *EDD* the term *raves* (Barnes's *riaves*) is common throughout the Midlands and the southwest; *ripples* is recorded only in Warwickshire, Shropshire, and Herefordshire; *gormers* only in Nottinghamshire and Yorkshire. No etymologies are offered for any of these words. Only the first of these three words is found in *OED*, as a variant of *rathe*, 'of obscure origin; perh[aps] the base of *raddle, n.*,' related to modern French *ridelle*.

Of the present participle prefixed by *a-*, to form what Barnes calls the "Present Actual" tense ("I'm a-meäkèn, &c."), he remarks "The affix *a-* in this tenseform is not the same as the -*a-* of the perfect participle, but it is the Saxon-English preposition *on* with the verbal noun" (*A Grammar and Glossary of the Dorset Dialect*, Berlin, A. Asher, 1863, p. 26).

For the early settlement of Barbados and the influence of Bajan pronunciation on that of the other Caribbean islands see the *Dictionary of Jamaican English*, ed. F.G. Cassidy and R.B. Le Page, 2nd edn (Cambridge, Cambridge University Press, 1980), pp. xl–xlii.

Other examples of rhymes and spellings noted in this item may be found in the following poems (all from the 1844 collection unless otherwise stated):

The rhyme *home/come*:"Bringèn oon gwâin o' Zundays","The white road up a*t*hi*r*t the hill", "Eclogue: A bit o' sly coortèn", etc. The pronunciation of the long *o* diphthong is described in §27 of the Dissertation.

The rhyme *geäte/liate*:"Jenny's ribbons"; *geät/a-beät* is in "Ridèn hwome at night" in the second collection.

Spellings with *âight* for standard English *eight*:"Easter time", "Eclogue: Two farms in oone","Farmers' sons", etc.

Rhymes of *go* or *ago* with the vowel sound in *too*: "Dock leaves" (*do*), "Bringèn oon gwâin o' Zundays" (*you* and *two*), "Hope in Spring" (*through*), "Jenny's ribbons" (*yew*), "Uncle an' ànt" (*shoe*), "Rivers don't gi'e out" (*true*), etc.

Spellings of *half* as *hafe* or *hâfe*: "The milk-mâid o' the farm", "Easter time","Eclogue: A bit o' sly coortèn", etc.

The rhyme *(a)woy/buoy*:"The girt woak tree that's in the dell", "Eclogue: Viairies","Grammer's shoes", etc.

Rhymes indicating the *ar* pronunciation of words spelled with *or* in standard English: *starm/harm*: "A zong ov harvest huome", "The shep'erd buoy", "The huomestead a-vell into han'"; *carn/barn* "A zong ov harvest huome"; *shart/heart* "Readèn ov a headstuone", "The beam in Grenley Church"; *snart/heart* "Hây-carrèn".

The rhyme *hoss/across*:"I got two viel's", "Eclogue: Two farms in oone", "Eclogue: A ghost", etc. *Do'set* does not occur in the 1844 edition, but is well known from "Praïse o' Do'set" and "The Do'set militia"; it occurs also in "Wheat", "Dobbin dead", "A Do'set sale", and "John Bloom in Lon'on", in the second and third collections.

Spellings with short *o* for short *a* or vice versa: *zot* for *sat*:"Jeän's weddèn dae in marnen", "Thatchèn o' the rick", "Harvest huome: The vust piart: the supper", etc.; *drap* for *drop*: "Hây-carrèn", "Wher we did kip our flagon", " Woak wer good enough oonce", etc.

See the following paragraphs in the Dissertation for Barnes's comments on consonant sounds discussed in this item: metathesis of *r*+vowel, §34; voicing of initial *f*- and *s*-, §31 and §36; the use of italics to indicate voicing of *-th-*, §38; *dr-* for initial *thr-*, §29; simplification of final *-nd* to *-n'*, §30; *-èn* for present participle *-ing*, §42; loss of *-v-* in *give* and other words, §40; insertion of a syllable in the consonant cluster *lm*, §32.

POLICY, POLITICIANS, AND THE POLICE
For Brook's comments on the word *politician* see his *A History of the English Language*, p. 188.

PRECISION RULES, OK?
Alan Maley's tribute to Lionel Billows appeared (with another from Andrew Wright) in *IATEFL Issues* 179 (June–July 2004), p. 18. I am grateful to my wife, Jill, for showing me these pieces.

PREPOSITIONS AT THE END OF A SENTENCE
Gowers's comment is from Sir Ernest Gowers, *The Complete Plain Words* (1954; 3rd edn, rev. Sidney Greenbaum and Janet Whitcut, London, Penguin, 1987), p. 106.

The various Fowlers quoted in this item are as follows: H.W. and F.G. Fowler, *The King's English* (1906; 3rd edn, London, Oxford University Press, 1931); H.W. Fowler, *A Dictionary of Modern English Usage* (1926; 2nd edn, rev. Sir Ernest Gowers, Oxford, Clarendon Press, 1968); *The New Fowler's Modern English Usage*, 3rd edn, ed. R.W. Burchfield (Oxford, Clarendon Press, 1996).

PROVERBS (2)
A fuller collection of proverbial phrases in *Sidrak*, together with a more detailed discussion of what constitutes proverbial language, may be found in my "Proverbs, Sentences, and Proverbial Phrases from the English *Sidrak*", *Mediaeval Studies* 51 (1989), 329–54.

SAD

"With longing I am lad" is quoted from *Middle English Lyrics*, ed. Luria and Hoffman, p. 28.

Browning's *Confessions* are quoted from *Browning: Poetical Works 1833–1864*, ed. Ian Jack (London, Oxford University Press, 1970).

Benjamin Franklin's comment on death and taxes is found in a letter to Jean-Baptiste Le Roy, 13 November 1789.

SEETHING AND SODDEN

The recipe for blancmange is quoted from *Pleyn Delit: Medieval Cookery for Modern Cooks*, ed. Constance B. Hieatt and Sharon Butler (Toronto, University of Toronto Press, 1978), p. 89.

Jack Strapper's comment is in Tom Ronan's *Vision Splendid* (1954; repr. Hawthorn, Vic., Lloyd O'Neil, 1972), p. 42.

SILLY

For this definition of *playing silly buggers* see Eric Partridge, *A Dictionary of Slang and Unconventional English . . . in Two Volumes. 1: The Dictionary. 2: The Supplement*, 5th edn (London, Routledge & Kegan Paul, 1961), vol. 2, p. 1404.

For a discussion of Chaucer's use of the word *sely* in the Miller's tale see Geoffrey Cooper, "'Sely John' in the 'legende' of the Miller's Tale", *Journal of English and Germanic Philology* 79 (1980), 1–12.

For the full text of "New Prince, new pompe" see *The Cambridge Hymnal*, Vocal edn, ed. David Holbrook and Elizabeth Poston (Cambridge, Cambridge University Press, 1976), hymn 143, and *The Oxford Book of Carols*, by Percy Dearmer, R. Vaughan Williams, and Martin Shaw (London, Oxford University Press, 1928), carol 170.

Shakespeare's variable spellings of *silly* may be checked in *William Shakespeare: The Complete Works: Original-Spelling Edition*, General eds. Stanley Wells and Gary Taylor (Oxford, Clarendon Press, 1986).

SLEDGING

Ian Chappell's comments are from his book, *Chappelli: The Cutting Edge* (Nedlands, Swan Publishing, 1992), pp. 153–5.

SOTSHIP
The annal for the year 1127 in the *Peterborough Chronicle* may be found in *Early Middle English Verse and Prose*, pp. 202–4.

SPEED
Ohthere's words to King Alfred are quoted from *Bright's Old English Grammar & Reader*, p. 188/35.

SPELLS AND SPELLING
Ohthere's account of the Karelians is quoted from *Bright's Old English Grammar & Reader*, p. 187/24–5.

SPILLS
The Battle of Maldon is quoted from *Bright's Old English Grammar & Reader*, p. 362/34; Dame Sirith from *Early Middle English Verse and Prose*, p. 88/233–4.

SUBJUNCTIVES
Johnson's comment on Pope, from "Alexander Pope" in his *Lives of the Poets*, is quoted from *Johnson: Prose and Poetry*, selected by Mona Wilson, p. 928.

SURPRISE, SURPRISE
"Surprised by joy" is quoted from *The Poetical Works of William Wordsworth*, ed. E. de Selincourt and Helen Darbishire, [vol. 3], 2nd edn (Oxford, Clarendon Press, 1954).

TERMS OF ASSOCIATION (1)
A comprehensive discussion of these terms was first provided long ago by John Hodgkin in "Proper Terms: An Attempt at a Rational Explanation of the Meanings of the Collection of Phrases in 'The Book of St. Albans,' 1486, Entitled 'Companys of Beestys and Fowlys,' and Similar Lists", *Transactions of the Philological Society. Supplement*, 1907–10. Unless otherwise stated I have adopted Hodgkin's explanations of the various terms. A "Complete List of Proper Terms" appears as part 4 of Hodgkin's article, pp. 79–175. An excellent new analysis of all known lists, and of the associated material that appears with them in medieval manuscripts,

is now available in David Scott-MacNab's *A Sporting Lexicon of the Fifteenth Century: The J. B. Treatise*, Medium Ævum Monographs, New Series 23 (Oxford, Society for the Study of Medieval Languages and Literature, 2003).

In the table below and in that in the next note the item number in column 2 is from the "Complete List of Proper Terms" in Hodgkin's article, that in column 3 is from Appendix 1 of Scott-MacNab's *A Sporting Lexicon*.

Term	Hodgkin	MacNab
a covey of partridges	75	148
a brood of chickens	73	32
an eye of pheasants	76	152
a team of horses	11	100
a team of oxen	11	144
a gaggle of geese	111	77
a sloth or a slowness of bears	55	8
a skulk of foxes	54	75
a labour of moles	48	135
a pride of lions	52	122

The surprising speed of an aged bear features in chapter 1 of John Irving's *The Hotel New Hampshire* (1981; repr. London, Corgi, 1982), p. 28.

TERMS OF ASSOCIATION (2)

Term	Hodgkin	MacNab
an abominable sight of monks	168	136
a superfluity of nuns	167	141
a skulk of friars	165	76
a lying of pardoners	158	147
an untruth of summoners	177	196
a sentence of judges	175	109
a damning of jurors	169	111
an execution of officers	171	143
a gaggle of women	136	221
a gaggling of gossips	137	85

Term	Hodgkin	MacNab
a nonpatience of wives	138	219
a multiplying of husbands	139	106
a rage of maidens	145	124
a rage of colts	36	38
an uncredibility of cuckolds	140	50
a venture of shipmen		180
a temperance of cooks	187	41
a promise of tapsters	204	203

A *venture of shipmen* occurs in only one list, which was not available to Hodgkin; see my "Late Fifteenth-Century 'Terms of Association' in MS. Pepys 1047", *Notes and Queries* 223 (1978), 7–12, and (for a different view) Scott-Macnab, p. 298, item 180.

THRILLS

The Old English Riddle is quoted from Bright's *Old English Grammar & Reader*, p. 342, no. 44); the passage from *Ancrene Wisse* is from *Ancrene Wisse*, ed. from MS. Corpus Christi College Cambridge 402 by J.R.R. Tolkien, EETS 249 (London, Oxford University Press, 1962 (for 1960)), p. 199/21–7.

VISIBLE

This word and other lexicographical problems are discussed in my "Drudgery, Bludgery, and Fudgery: Lexicography for Editors of Middle English Texts", *Lexicographical and Linguistic Studies: Essays in Honour of G.W. Turner*, ed. T.L. Burton and Jill Burton (Cambridge, Brewer, 1988), pp. 19–30.

WAR WORDS (1)

The comments on *diggers* are derived from Baker, *The Australian Language*, pp. 164–7. For the use of *dugout* in South Australia see Ian Auhl, *The Story of the 'Monster Mine': The Burra Burra Mine and its Townships 1845–1877* (Hawthorndene, SA, Investigator Press, 1986), pp. 128–9, a reference I owe to Deborah Welch.

For a discussion of the term *bikini* see Brian Foster, *The Changing English Language* (1968; repr. Harmondsworth, Penguin, 1970), pp. 127–8.

WAR WORDS (2)

For the explanation of *gone for a burton* given at the end of this item see *Brewer's Dictionary of Phrase and Fable* (1870; Centenary Edition, rev. Ivor H. Evans, London, Cassell, 1970, 4th impression (corrected) 1975), s.v. *Burton*.

WASSAIL

For the Christmas carol "Now joy be to the Trynyte" see *A Selection of English Carols*, ed. Richard Leighton Greene (Oxford, Clarendon Press, 1962), p. 66, no. 13.

WORKS CITED FREQUENTLY

The Australian Concise Oxford Dictionary of Current English, ed. George W. Turner, 1987, 3rd edn, ed. Bruce Moore, Melbourne, Oxford University Press, 1997.

The Australian National Dictionary: A Dictionary of Australianisms on Historical Principles, ed. W.S. Ramson, Melbourne, Oxford University Press, 1988.

The Australian Pocket Oxford Dictionary, ed. Grahame Johnston, Melbourne, Oxford University Press, 1976, 2nd edn, ed. George W. Turner, Melbourne, Oxford University Press, 1984.

Baker, Sidney J. *The Australian Language*, 1945, 3rd edn, Milson's Point, NSW, Currawong Press, 1978.

Beowulf, ed. C.L. Wrenn, 1953, 3rd edn, rev. W.F. Bolton, London, Harrap, 1973.

Bright's Old English Grammar & Reader, ed. Frederic G. Cassidy and Richard N. Ringler, 3rd edn, New York, Holt, Rinehart and Winston, 1971.

Brook, G.L. *A History of the English Language*, London, André Deutsch, 1958.

The Cambridge Encyclopedia, ed. David Crystal, Cambridge, Cambridge University Press, 1990.

Chaucer, Geoffrey. *Canterbury Tales*, ed. A.C. Cawley, London, J.M. Dent, 1958.

Chaucer, Geoffrey. *The Riverside Chaucer*, 3rd edn, General Ed. Larry D. Benson, Boston, Houghton Mifflin, 1987.

A Chaucer Glossary, compiled by Norman Davis, Douglas Gray, Patricia Ingham, and Anne Wallace-Hadrill, Oxford, Clarendon Press, 1979.

The Collins Concise Dictionary of the English Language, 2nd edn, Australian edn, ed. G.A. Wilkes and W.A. Krebs, London, Collins, 1988.

Collins English Dictionary, 3rd [Australian] edn, Special Australian Consultants G.A. Wilkes and W.A. Krebs, Sydney, HarperCollins, 1991.

A Dictionary of Australian Colloquialisms, by G.A. Wilkes, 1978, 4th edn, Melbourne, Oxford University Press, 1996.

Early Middle English Verse and Prose, ed. J.A.W. Bennett and G.V. Smithers, 2nd edn, Oxford, Clarendon Press, 1968.

The English Dialect Dictionary, ed. Joseph Wright, 6 vols, London, Henry Frowde, 1898–1905.

[Isidore's *Etymologiae*.] Isidore de Séville. *Étymologies. Livre XII: Des Animaux*, ed. and trans. Jacques André, Paris, Belles Lettres, 1986.

The Macquarie Dictionary. Editor-in-Chief A. Delbridge, 1981, 3rd edn, Macquarie University, NSW, The Macquarie Library, 1997.

Middle English Dictionary, ed. Hans Kurath et al, Ann Arbor, University of Michigan Press, 1954–2001.

The Middle English Physiologus, ed. Hanneke Wirtjes, EETS 299, Oxford, Oxford University Press, 1991.

Milton, John. *Complete Poems and Major Prose*, ed. Merritt Y. Hughes, Indianapolis, Odyssey Press, 1957.

The New Oxford Dictionary of English, ed. Judy Pearsall, Oxford, Clarendon Press, 1998.

The New Shorter Oxford English Dictionary, ed. Lesley Brown, Oxford, Clarendon Press, 1993.

The Owl and the Nightingale, ed. Eric Gerald Stanley, 1960, Manchester, Manchester University Press, 1972.

The Oxford English Dictionary, ed. James A.H. Murray et al, 1933, 2nd edn, prepared by J.A. Simpson and E.S.C. Weiner, Oxford, Clarendon Press, 1989, Online edn, ed. J.A. Simpson, <http://dictionary.oed.com/>, 2000–.

A Shakespeare Glossary, by C.T. Onions, 1911, 3rd edn, rev. Robert D. Eagleson, Oxford, Clarendon Press, 1986.

Shakespeare, William. *William Shakespeare: The Complete Works*, General eds. Stanley Wells and Gary Taylor, Oxford, Clarendon Press, 1986.

Sidrak and Bokkus: A Parallel-Text Edition, ed. T.L. Burton, 2 vols, EETS 311, 312, Oxford, Oxford University Press, 1998–9.

Sir Gawain and the Green Knight, Pearl, Cleanness, Patience, ed. J.J. Anderson. London, J.M. Dent, 1996.

Thomas, Dylan. *Under Milk Wood: A Play for Voices*, 1954, ed. Walford Davies, London, Penguin, 2000.

Turner, G.W. *The English Language in Australia and New Zealand*, 1966, 2nd edn, London, Longman, 1972.

Webster's Third New International Dictionary of the English Language. Editor-in-Chief Philip Babcock Gove, Springfield, Mass., Merriam, 1966.

White, T.H. *The Book of Beasts: Being a Translation from a Latin Bestiary of the Twelfth Century*, London, Jonathan Cape, 1954.

Whiting, Bartlett Jere, with the collaboration of Helen Wescott Whiting. *Proverbs, Sentences, and Proverbial Phrases from English Writings Mainly Before 1500*, Cambridge, Mass., Belknap Press, 1968.

GLOSSARY OF
TECHNICAL TERMS

amelioration a kind of specialization in which a word acquires pleasanter or more favourable senses than it originally had: the opposite of pejoration.

analogy the process by which a word develops a new form or forms in imitation of other (usually commoner) forms (e.g., the plurals *words* and *cows*, in imitation of plurals in -*s*, in place of the earlier plurals *word* and *cy*; the past tense *laughed*, in imitation of past tenses in -*ed*, in place of earlier forms like *hloh* and *lough*).

aphetic form a form of a word in which an initial unstressed vowel has been lost (e.g., *squire* from *esquire*).

back formation the process by which a word is formed from one that looks like its derivative (e.g., *to grovel* from the adverb *grovelling*, which was taken to be its present participle; *to reminisce* from the noun *reminiscence*).

back slang a kind of slang in which words are pronounced as if spelled backwards.

clang association the influence of the sound of a word upon its sense: see *buxom*.

cognate belonging to the same linguistic family; representing the same original root.

commonization a kind of semantic transfer in which a proper name is taken over by a concept or object associated with it: the name (now spelled with a lower case initial) becomes the general term for this concept.

concatenation literally 'chain-linking': semantic development in which each new sense can be seen to be linked to and derived from the preceding one in a logical progression. (Contrast **radiation**.)

degeneration a synonym for **pejoration**.

deterioration another synonym for **pejoration**.

euphemism literally 'speaking fairly': a figure of speech in which a term intended to be inoffensive is substituted for one thought to be offensive.

folk etymology the (mistaken) assumption that words are related because of some perceived similarity in spelling or pronunciation.

functional shift the process by which one part of speech functions as another (a noun for a verb, an adjective for a noun, etc.)

gain of intensity an increase in the emotive power of a word.

generalization the process by which a word with a narrow and specific sense acquires a broader range of meanings.

hapax legomenon (plural **legomena**) a word or form of which only one recorded instance is known.

indicative mood the normal form of the verb, used to express statements of fact.

lateralization a synonymn for **semantic transfer**.

loss of intensity a decrease in the emotive power of a word.

metathesis the process by which adjacent sounds in a word change places and the spelling is altered to reflect the new pronunciation.

metonomy a figure of speech in which a thing is named after something associated with it, as when a *language* is called a *tongue*.

Middle English the name given to the English language between about 1100 or 1150 and 1500.

narrowing a synonym for **specialization**.

Old English the name given to the language spoken by the Anglo-Saxons before the Norman Conquest.

pejoration a kind of specialization in which a word acquires unpleasanter or less favourable senses than it originally had: the opposite of **amelioration**.

popular etymology another term for **folk etymology**.

purr-word a word carrying a strong overtone of approval (Brook p. 168).

radiation semantic development in which each new sense is derived independently from the root sense, rather than developing from some intermediate sense. (Contrast **concatenation**.)

RP the "Received Pronunciation" of standard British English, as formerly used by all BBC announcers and used as a model in elocution lessons.

semantic transfer the development of a new sense by transferring the sense of a word to some unrelated object or concept.

snarl-word a word carrying a strong overtone of disapproval (Brook p. 168).

specialization the process by which a word with a fairly broad range of meanings acquires a narrower, more specific sense: the opposite of **generalization**.

strong verb a verb that forms the past tense and past participle by changing the vowel (e.g., *speak/spoke/spoken*) as opposed to adding *-d* or *-t*.

subjunctive mood a form of the verb used to express hypotheses: formerly expressed by a specific inflection ("If she *go* tomorrow" as opposed to "if she *goes*"); in MnE normally expressed by an auxiliary verb ("If she *should go*").

synecdoche (pronounced "sin-EK-da-kee") a figure of speech in which the name of a part of a thing is used for the whole of it or vice versa, as in "thirty *head* of cattle".

weak verb a verb that forms the past tense and past participle by adding *-d* or *-t* (e.g., *talk/talked*) as opposed to changing the vowel.

widening a synonym for **generalization**.

INDEX